MIG Crew

Mig Down

Mig Down

Tommy Robinson

Pennant Books

First published in hardback in Great Britain 2005
By Pennant Books
A division of Pennant Publishing Ltd

Text copyright © Tommy Robinson 2005

The moral right of the author has been asserted.

All rights reserved. No part of this publication may be reproduced, stored in a retrieval system, or transmitted, in any form or by any means, electronic, mechanical, photocopying, recording or otherwise, without the prior permission in writing of the publisher, except by a reviewer who wishes to quote brief passages in connection with a review written for insertion in a newspaper, magazine or broadcast.

British Library Cataloguing-in-Publication Data:
A catalogue record for this book is available from
The British Library

ISBN 0-9550394-0-1

Typeset by John Saunders

Printed and bound in Great Britain by
Creative Print and Design, Ebbw Vale, Wales

While every effort has been made to trace the relevant copyright-holders, this has proved impossible in some cases and copyright-owners are invited to contact the publishers.

Pennant Books Ltd
A division of Pennant Publishing Ltd
PO Box 5071
Hove, BN52 9BB

Photograph acknowledgements: The Author thanks the lads who gave permission to use the private photographs supplied for the picture section. The Author also expresses his thanks for pictures produced by kind permission of Massimo Tessitori, Camera Press (London), Nickie Divine www.nickiphoto.com and Lorne Brown www.acasuallook.co.uk.

Backcover quotes from *The Naughty Nineties* by Martin King and Martin Knight, published by Mainstream Sport. *Naughty* by Mark Chester, published by Milo Books. *Top Boys* by Cass Pennant and *Bovver* by Chris Brown both published by John Blake Publishing Ltd.

Dedicated in the memory and respect of four top boys Daryl, Tony Prosper, Warren Heath and Paddy.

God bless

Contents

Acknowledgements ix
Foreword xi

Introduction 13

1 Trust Me 19
  Man City, Reading, Pompey

2 Welcome to the First Division 36
  Man Utd, Spurs, 6.57 Crew, Sheff W, Ipswich, Cardiff, ICF, Forest

3 I Am What I Am 58
  Leicester Baby Squad, Stoke

4 You Can't Come Down Here! 74
  Oxford, WBA, Zulus, Villa, Chelsea, Oldham, Norwich

5 You Won't Get Better Than This 95
  Chelsea, Newcastle, Bradford City, QPR

6 Catching the Shady Express 119
  Central Element, EBF, Hull, Swansea, Mansfield, Coventry

7 Someone Slap That Baby 138
  Baby Squad, Coventry City

8 They Soon Knew They'd Met the Luton Blacks *ICF, Under-Fives, QPR, Tottenham*	159
9 Herding the Herd (Another Bloody Replay) *Everton, Palace, Gooners*	175
10 They Bit His Ear Off *Millwall, Gooners, Leeds*	197
11 Old Enough to Know Better *Watford, Peterborough, Forest*	215
12 When in Rome *Bristol City Service Crew, Gas Hit Squad, QPR, Baby Squad*	232
13 Mig Down, Over and Out *Palace*	246
Glossary	251

Acknowledgements

The author would like to specially thank Cass Pennant and Tuse, without whose help and enthusiasm this book would not have been possible.

Foreword By Charles Bronson

When I heard Tommy Robinson was doing a book on Luton Town FC, I said to myself, 'Fucking brilliant, awesome. About time somebody did it and who better than Tommy.'

It was 1963 when my old man took me to see them play; I was eleven years old…

All I can say is, 'Kick some arse, Tommy. Keep on punching till the lights go out.'

After three decades, I'm still in a cage but I still follow the 'Hatters', Promotion Champions 2005. We are coming for glory. We won't stop till we hit the three cherries. Yahoooo… Yippeeee…

Well done, Tommy… Max Respect!

Charles Bronson
C.S.C. Unit, HMP Wakefield
2005

Introduction

I am 39 so my experience from running around at Luton (and away) was from '80 to '87. I was a very long way from being a main boy, but I was there more often than not and put myself through it for the cause. There was no hiding at the back with the Migs – there usually wasn't the numbers! You knew you would get hit, you knew you would have to fight your way out of trouble and you knew you would get nicked. I liked to pose around and all that, but you couldn't really just style it at Luton, you had to do the other stuff too.

After getting nicked three times during the first year of my law degree (and sitting in Birmingham Magistrates' Court being put through all the Police and Criminal Evidence Act stuff I had been studying at university the day before!), I realised there might be a problem! Although I was innocent every time (obviously), it was clear that 'lawyer' and 'hooligan' were mutually exclusive occupations and so I had to look into other ways of spending my Saturdays!

And I did. But running with Luton at that time was special and it has stuck with me ever since.

I will stick to the top bods from my own time, so the characters and events are quite 'old school' and long before the mobile-phone crews:

Tommy Robinson

He's a year or two younger than me, but Tommy was in the thick of things from when he was about 14 or so. I can remember him 'wind-milling' in the away end even then. He had one side of his head completely shaved for a while, in like a half wedge! A man of many hairstyles. I remember him leading the way in his pink moonboots when we got on the pitch at Southampton in '85 or so. A badman in pink moonboots! Fantastic. We loved a wind-up (see Paddy below). Even the name 'Mig Crew' started as a joke.

It was two kids from Tommy's school that came up with the name and idea. I always hear that 'Men In Gear' stuff, but I swear all that came after the original meaning, which was actually based on the Russian fighter plane. Migs = Fighters. And a plane needs a crew! Anyway, it was a snappy name and covered two sides of the thing – the clothes as well as the street choreography!

Back then, there were a few different little crews and cliques at Luton, but on match days even the older guys in the firm would shout 'Migs, Migs, Migs!' They were the dominant force at the time and the umbrella under which Luton operated. Tommy was one of the leaders (maybe *the* leader) in my day and, over the years when I have been along to big games, he has usually been there and is still simultaneously very intelligent, charismatic and bonkers.

There were times in that era when Luton's crew was mainly black, whereas Tommy was a white face among the top boys – which is kind of the other way round from many of the football crews I remember where they would be majority white, but often had black top boys. Anyway, I'm no sociologist and that was a particular moment in time, but there was an interesting mix at Luton, as anyone who visited will tell you.

Thinking of Tommy Robinson always brings a smile to my face. He was one of those 'anything is possible' kind of guys.

Paddy

Despite the name and being in a town with a lot of Irish folks, Paddy was from a Jamaican family. He was the face of the crew. The leader at Luton in most ways, except the fighting department.

A total character, style don and comedian, Paddy was a DJ but also ran the coaches and took care of business. He would be spinning a tune, chatting on the mic and selling tickets, all at the same time. I just wonder how he managed to juggle so many big characters and always stay smiling.

It was Paddy that got us singing 'Doctor Beat' and doing funky dances in the seats and making monkey noises at Luton's black players to pre-empt and confuse the Geordies etc. Any away fans who came to Luton in those days know what I'm talking about because we were sat right next to them.

He was also a promoter and one day, not long after the Migs had quietened down, I heard the legendary Steve Walsh complaining on the radio that he'd had a business dispute at some gig in Luton and then reading that they were looking for someone known only as 'Paddy'! I don't know if it was him, but he was just as wide as his smile, so you never know. Sadly, Paddy followed Steve Walsh's method of departure and died in a car crash a few years ago.

An all-singing, all-dancing street superstar, Paddy set the tone for the Migs' kind of rude bwoy (but Casual) style in the early 80s. The walk was important, the talk was important, but there were always jokes too. He helped it to be so much more of a kind of cause rather than just kicking lumps out of people.

DP

When I was about 16, I had the good fortune to be with DP when me and a couple of mates had been in the seats at a night match in Leicester. Anyway, we were young Casual kids and D and his four pals were probably 10 years older. We were the only Luton in the seats and we won, so the Leicester crew sat in front of us knew exactly who we were. But DP and our elders didn't care and after the first goal they took us under their wing and told us to just relax and enjoy it.

Afterwards, we got jumped by a big crowd of Leicester outside. Moments before, DP had come and put his arms round us, telling us that we were going to be jumped any second and 'Whatever happens, don't run!' I didn't run! And in the end what was left of us ended up chasing them down the road. Which was obviously a major triumph for a kid.

And DP kindly bigged me up afterwards, because only me, him and a legendary Luton boxing instructor had been left standing our ground. I never bothered pointing out that I had nowhere to run, unless I fancied jumping in the canal. So I had no choice but to get stuck in.

DP was part of the older West Indian crew that the younger Migs looked up to and which were kind of assimilated as part of the Mig Crew for football purposes. I wouldn't ever have described D as a hooligan (I wouldn't dare!) because he and his peers were football fans, but also protectors of the local community. They led by example.

I believe that he is still a top man and well-respected figure about town in Luton.

Aubrey B

Aubrey was another larger-than-life character. A bit of a Luton style guru. I remember he had great Buggles/Junior Giscombe-type glasses (dodgy bins!) and very fine cashmere scarves. And a lisp. He spoke more like a city gent than a geezer. I saw him put the dreadlock top boy from the Baby Squad (this guy was no softie – I lived in Leicester for a while and he was the man at the time) flat on his back with one punch. And more.

Although he was one of the guys who helped to turn 'the Luton Blacks' into such a force at football, he also used to run with Arsenal (as many Luton did at the time). When he was with the Migs, though, Aubrey kind of slipped in front of Tommy and Paddy, because he was 'the Tactician'.

Like DP, I think Aubrey got involved because from the end of the 70s so many big clubs would wreak havoc at Luton. The only way to stop it was to stand up and teach people to have more respect. Nowadays, the policing of football keeps things under control, but in those days the sheer number of visiting fans meant things were way out of control and maybe self-defence was the only way to stop the rampages. The beginning of the 80s was a different time to now and, if football fans wanted to walk around seig-heiling like it was fashionable, then a trip to Luton soon taught them this was not the place to do it.

I was with all four of the above characters in our seats before the Luton v Millwall match in 1985, when the police brought loads of Millwall round and stuck them in with us. In some of the famous TV footage, both Aubrey and DP can be seen holding back the Millwall who were trying to climb up into the Main Stand. The police were completely swamped and they should have got medals because they were practically the only people between Millwall and the directors. Actually, come to think of it, David Evans was our chairman then, so maybe they should have let them through!

I've heard so many tales about that night. Well, I was a few yards from Aubs and was there from hours before until a couple after, and everyone goes on about how they did this and they did that. So what! They should have tried being one of the 500 Luton facing the great wave. I mean, we were their main target and it was going off from the afternoon till midnight. Now that's what I call a challenge! We were there too!

In the book *Congratulations*, Butch Stuttard, the producer of Thames Television documentary *Hooligan*, said Luton had no hardcore firm to oppose Millwall. I have to disagree, old chap. But I would defy anyone to have done very much other than be swamped when up against 8,000 all-time all-star Millwall, plus a couple of thousand from the rest of London's crews. All on a mission! This was not a 'minority' crew. Everyone I saw with Millwall that night was a thug.

We were insane to even step in the ground after the wars that had been going on for hours beforehand. It was going off everywhere outside and I saw a stretcher crew get knocked over as people fought round their ambulance. Things were out of control that night and all the rules were out of the window. We did our best! Looking back, we put ourselves through quite a lot just to represent and support our team in those days. Kept me fit though!

Then, after the assault course getting to the ground, the police brought Millwall over and put them in with us. It was utter chaos and I ended up in the middle of them. I was stuck there for about 20 minutes trying not to look terrified and doing my best impersonation of a lamppost. There were a couple of other Luton who had got cut off as well, but we just looked at each other like: 'How are we going to get out of this one' and 'Don't get too close or they'll notice we're the only ones who don't know the songs!' I mean, I don't even sound like a Luton geezer let alone a Sarf Londoner, so I couldn't open my mouth. And there's only so much acting you can do.

With everyone round me going crazy, I knew I couldn't style it out for much longer and, when they started going on about 'killing the northern bastards', I knew it was time to make a break for the border. We were 25 miles up the M1 and they thought we were northerners!

I went to the top of the steps at the back of the Maple and, with all the Millwall below checking me out, I told the police that I was Luton and asked them to let me up to the Main Stand. They weren't having it and pushed me backwards, but one glance down at the Millwall looking up at me and I just bundled through all of them like I was on PCP. They could nick me if they wanted to, but there was no way I was going back down there with that lot.

After the game, 15 of us climbed into the directors' box and watched Millwall pour across the pitch like a tornado. Everyone's seen those images on TV, but we had the best view in Kenilworth Road. We were on the edge of our seats and stunned to silence. Then, when we finally left the ground, they were still everywhere. There was no way you could get home. I ended up hiding in a garden with some big Reggae man. And he was as scared as I was!

When we finally got back to the car, we were about to jump in and vacate the area when my mate poked his head out from underneath. He'd been hiding down there for more than an hour! As Millwall had gradually left the scene, more local vigilantes seeking revenge had appeared and he'd decided the best way to avoid any crossfire was to lie under a Ford Capri parked behind the West Side Shopping Centre in his nice leather jacket!

I even made a couple of little appearances in the match footage used at the beginning of the *Hooligan* documentary. I was forcing my girlfriend to watch the DVD recently and told her, 'I was in the middle of all that, you know,' and she said, 'I know, I can see you!' I looked and there I was, stood like a lamppost with my pink scarf on, trying desperately not to look terrified in the middle of Millwall going mental and looking for 'northerners' to kill!

Anyway, basically, Aubrey was a dude and again big in the charisma and character department and a reference for the Migs style/approach (see also Paddy). I am not sure there was anyone at football quite like him.

He moved to London and he's still a face around the West End. I think he was involved in clubs and all that and he had a very famous girlfriend for a while – although I think she knew that *she* was actually the one going out with the celebrity! He was and still is a raconteur, so maybe he should tell you all about it himself!

There were others too of course, but I don't think that anyone would deny that the above characters were some of the top boys at Luton in the 80s and, personally, I learned from most of them. As an entertainment lawyer, manager and now a filmmaker, I've worked with a lot of pop stars and 'personalities' and, believe me, these chaps would run them all off the stage and then put on a better show afterwards!

They're all books! But, in terms of providing a frontline account about the Migs and their antics from the Casual days till now, Tommy is your man because he stuck with it and never quite seemed to kick the habit!

Tuse, 2005

1 Trust Me

Watching the rain hitting the windscreen of Windy's company car, I felt a mixture of excitement and pain, as it started to sink in that this would be another benchmark day in my life. I was on my way to Luton Crown Court to be sentenced for my part in the violent scenes that blackened another Watford away day for the Town, with televised pitch invasions and chaos outside the ground before the match had even started.

I glanced across at Windy in the driver's seat. In some kind of fucked-up way, he was responsible for me being in this position in the first place. He'd nagged at me to go to the game all through the week leading up to it: 'Let this be your last one. Come on, Tommy, you know it makes sense, mate.' He was like a stuck record...

I'd already decided weeks before that I didn't want to be involved any more. But he had a point, it would be the right way to say goodbye to the one thing I could count on to give my week a lift and make me feel alive. For longer than I cared to remember, I'd been getting up on a Saturday with a spring in my step just from knowing it was a football day and that violence was possible. Not meaningless or mindless violence as the media like to portray it either, but orchestrated and deep-rooted violence.

Windy was hunched over the wheel, frowning and concentrating on the road, which was a relief as he wasn't the best of drivers and it was pissing down. He was singing to himself as usual and I had to laugh, as anyone who has heard him sing would understand.

'What's so funny?' He knew what was up, but asked anyway.

'You can't sing.'

So he sang a bit louder now, hoping to get a bite out of me. But I just shook my head and looked out at the nobodies making their way through life in lovely Luton town. 'Bunch of mugs,' I thought, in my usual arrogant way.

Windy stopped singing as we approached our destination. 'Where are we going to park, Tom?'

'Get as close to the court as you can… I don't want to ruin my new Armani suit in the rain, do I?' Little did I know that the suit was only going to be on my back for the next three days and then it would be chucked in a bin liner like rubbish.

The rain was slowing to a drizzle now. As I stared out of the car window, we passed The Sports Bar. This place could tell a few tales, although it was Man City that immediately sprang to mind. I hadn't been there that day, but the stories made me wish I had been. Unfortunately, I was otherwise engaged serving my country in the Royal Navy and couldn't wangle time off.

I'd been in the mess deck when one of my shipmates rushed in and made straight for me with a big smile on his face. 'The Migs got bashed by City on Saturday and Nick's fucking ear is missing!' He looked smug about it too, but then he always looked pleased with himself when delivering bad news, especially when it was to me.

From the first day we met, I knew Gaz was a fake. He talked a lot, but had never actually done too much, if you know what I mean. And from early on he was always talking about the way I dressed and asking if I was into the football scene. He was from Brighton and knew a few lads who'd run with their mob at one time or another and it seemed to ask questions of his own involvement. At first, I kept my mouth shut and swerved his interrogations, but always gave him a sly smile to suggest that one day I might just let him into my secret life.

One run ashore in Pompey, fate took its course when I bumped into a local football face who'd met in Holland some years previously. We got chatting about how things were going with the 6.57 Crew and how things had changed in the Portsmouth firm – even Docker Hughes got a mention. That was enough for Gaz to corner me with sufficient ammo to get me to open up and admit to my darker side.

But, from then on, he had to doubt me – because his own experiences were all second hand, he just couldn't believe that I was involved in it all. 'It can't really be as bad as that, though, can it? I think you make half of it up in your head, mate!'

I decided to teach this prick a lesson. It was time to show him just how it was in the real world of a football thug. All I needed was the right game and a good excuse and I'd give him the best day out he'd had for years.

The opportunity arose when Gaz asked me to set him up on a blind date, with the help of my missus back in Luton. So I arranged for him to come and stay round our house one weekend and we'd all go out together to get everything off to an easy start for him and the lucky lady. It just so happened that the Town were at Reading that same weekend and a decent mob would be making its way over there for a bit of fun. Gaz didn't know it yet, but he'd be coming too and wouldn't have a choice in the matter either!

'What's she like then? She better not be a pig. I'm from Brighton and we've got high standards down there, mate.'

'Beggars can't be choosers, Gaz,' I said, chuckling.

'I don't trust you. I shouldn't have come, should I?'

He was so right, but it was too late to turn back and he was going to see exactly how much I'd 'made up in my head'.

Now, to most people football violence is totally unacceptable and something to be avoided. But I've always noticed just how much it intrigues people from all walks of life and I have often wanted to give them a taste of the buzz you get when you're standing in some unknown town with just a handful of mates and you see a mob two or three times your size come bouncing down the road towards you, their faces all contorted, shouting and screaming and calling you on to do battle.

You don't know if this is all of them or if there's more on the way – maybe coming up behind to bushwhack you. Are your mates going to perform today or are they going to scatter like the Watford mugs always do? You just have to believe in each other and draw on the togetherness and spirit that all the battles in the past have created over time and hope that it's stronger than the firm in front of you now. But whatever books you read or reissued sportswear you buy, you can never really understand the rush that hits you unless you've been there. Today Gaz was going to become one of those fortunate enough to have felt it first hand.

'Come on, Gaz, let's go for breakfast down the café and then we'll find something useful to do with our day.'

He'd stayed at mine on Friday night and now it was about 7am on Saturday. He looked half-asleep and had a sore head from all those lagers the night before, but he was up and scrubbed in no time. Twenty minutes later, we were in the café stuffing our faces.

'All right, Yeti?' It was JR, or Shit Hair to those who know him a bit better. We've both been a bit 'experimental' with our barnets over the years and have suffered for it with dodgy nicknames ever since.

'Gaz, meet Shit Hair.'

'All right, mate,' he offered, nodding and sticking out his hand.

Shit Hair sneered back in response, 'You ain't one of these Navy poofs, too, are ya?'

Gaz looked a bit taken aback, but he was on his own now and I wouldn't be able to protect him from the lads' banter all day, so I thought it was probably best to leave him to find his feet early on. He looked at me questioningly, but I just put a blank expression on my face to let him know the score. Fair play to him though, he held it together and fired back quickly, 'Yeah and I love your long hair too! What hairspray do you use, darling?'

We all pissed ourselves laughing and the ice was broken.

Gaz spent the next 10 minutes asking some searching questions about the day ahead, until finally I broke it to him that we were going to a football match – to see the mighty Luton Town no less. He shook his head at this and didn't seem too happy about the prospect of watching a Second Division game at all. But I wasn't going to give him the chance to back out now.

'Let's go. It's time to move.'

It was only just after eight when we arrived at Luton Station, but there was already a fair mob gathering around the ticket windows. I checked Gaz and wondered if he knew what I had planned for the day. But he hadn't even realised that there was a football crew stood in front of him yet. That's one of the problems for Joe Public – most of them wouldn't know a football thug if he was stood right next to them at the bus stop.

'All right, Yeti.'

'All right, Windy.' I looked around the station. 'How many then?'

'About 50, I reckon.'

'And the Babies?' ('The Babies' are our younger lads and essential to any good day out at football, as you will discover.)

'They've gone already, Tom. About 30-handed.'

At last, I could see Gaz starting to look uncomfortable – he was scanning the lads in the station and had finally clocked the dress code. Now he could see the nods and winks and the hand shaking between all these chaps with big smiles on their faces. It was like a load of old school friends meeting up for the first time in years. And to a point that's exactly what it was – except these former school mates met up every few weeks to watch Luton and fight the enemy.

'OK, Robinson, what's going on then?'

'I've told you already, Gaz, we're going to football.'

'Yeah, I know that, but what is it you're *not* telling me, mate?'

I knew he'd realised what was in the pipeline, but I still refused to give him the confirmation he wanted. It was part of the payback for doubting me. He couldn't really walk away without losing face now, and he knew it. All he could do was hope that things wouldn't be as bad as my tales and that he might find a way of slipping away if it got too hot for him to handle.

As we boarded the train, I felt the buzz of anticipation as once again we set off on an adventure into the unknown. Would it go off? Would I get nicked? Would I get a slap? These thoughts trigger the familiar rush that keeps football hooligans coming back to the firms year after year. For me personally, it's the ultimate drug and I'm still trying to kick the habit.

The journey south west was pretty uneventful and the lads behaved impeccably. Sometimes high spirits can get the better of the younger lads and they need to be reminded to behave or they'll fuck the whole day up. But this crew was an older and more experienced gathering and had no such problems. We arrived in Reading at about 11am, 50-handed and quietly confident.

'So when's it going to go off then?' It was Gaz and he'd been drinking quite heavily with the lads at Paddington and on the train afterwards as well.

'Oh… in about two minutes by my calculations.'

'What?!' Panic spread across his face and he slowed down, dropping towards the back of the mob. The old fight or flight mechanism had started to fuck with him, but, for me, controlling and channelling this mind trick helped to build the buzz.

I knew that just outside the doors of the station there was quite possibly a firm of Reading lads waiting for us. They might be tooled up, they might be 200-strong and they might well be confident of their chances. I pushed through the doors and led the way out of the station.

'Keep it tight now! Let's give it to these cunts!'

The truth was I didn't even know if there was any Reading waiting, but I had to get the chaps' blood pumping and their adrenaline flowing so that we were ready for anything.

We turned the corner and headed straight towards their boozer. I spotted the Old Bill running across the road to our left, but they were too few and too late. There were some Reading lads outside, although not enough to have it with. So, instead of kicking off, we just walked straight past them and into the pub, hoping that there was more inside. There was, but only 20 or so.

'Let's have it!'

The Reading lads scattered and headed for the exits. Some got a slap, but most escaped unharmed.

It was a disappointment for us because we'd expected a big reception party, but Reading hadn't got their act together yet. Hopefully, they'd be back later. We'd fucked up though, because the OB knew where we were and would soon bring in the Robocops and dogs. So now it would be even harder to get some action.

Still, we were here and, according to the calls we'd received, the next group of Migs was about to arrive and double our numbers, which would make it even harder for the filth to keep us under wraps for the day. And, of course, the Babies were still out there somewhere and they were just plain unpredictable.

'This is mental!' Gaz was starting to get the buzz and, once the other lads bowled into the pub taking our numbers close to 100, he really started to let go: 'Was that the best they could do? They were fuck all, the mugs!' Now he was game and felt the confidence that being part of a mob gives to the individual. 'Is that it or are they coming back for more punishment?'

I explained to Gaz that we'd be on the move soon and he should keep his eyes open because Reading could well turn the tables on us at some point in the day. But I don't think he took it on board and, fuelled by more beer, he disappeared into the crowd of newfound friends from Luton.

Not long afterwards, the Babies arrived under police escort and were shoved into our watering hole as the OB tried to keep all the Luton hooligan element together in one place and so easier to control.

Baby B came straight over. He'd spotted Reading regrouping after our earlier clash. 'They're at the top of the road opposite the Newt & Cucumber.' He reckoned they didn't have much more than 40 and that most of them were youngsters. 'We tried to get them to come out of the pub, but they didn't want to know.'

This was another letdown because, if they didn't fancy going toe-to-toe with our kids, then they weren't likely to have a pop at the older and more experienced Mig Crew.

'Black K is talking to some of them now,' added Baby B.

As I followed him into the bright sunshine, the scene outside was comical. About 70 of the lads were throwing chairs and shouting at the 25 OB lined up in front of them. Dogs were barking and baring their teeth, police horses were arriving on the scene and, in the middle of the chaos, who was right at the front of the baying mob with his arms outstretched? You've guessed it. Gaz!

He'd totally lost it and was calling the OB on: 'Get a real job, you cunts!'

I went straight over, pulled him to one side and told him to get a grip. He seemed to listen and I sent him inside to get a round in. Then I headed over to speak with the Reading lads that were chatting to Black K.

But, as I approached, the conversation that was in full swing suddenly stopped. In my time attached to the Migs, I've earned a good standing on the national grapevine of thugs and this can bring a certain amount of respect, but also jealousy and unwanted attention. This time it was respect. Football lads know the real 'faces' at any club aren't hard to spot and they're usually treated in a certain manner to reflect their status in the alternative society of football hooliganism. It was this that had stopped the chat, because now the small group of lads wanted to hear me talk and maybe learn how a real face wanted things to run.

'All right, chaps?'

'All right, Yeti.'

'So when are you lot going to get it together then?'

'Yeah. Er… Sorry about earlier. We didn't know you were coming so early.' He was making excuses for Reading's poor welcoming committee and any football lad has been there before. It's not easy facing one of the enemy in a controlled or peaceful environment and having to explain why your mob hasn't done the business. You feel as though he's really got one over on you and just want to wipe the smug look off his face, because you both understand that every single match and every single clash makes a difference to your reputation. And reputation is what it's all about. Now his own crew's rep was under threat.

Only weeks before, a couple of Reading lads had appeared on BBC's *McIntyre Reports* giving it the big one about how good their mob was these days, which was one of the reasons we'd chosen to travel over to this game. But, so far, they weren't living up to the hype.

'Don't worry about it, mate.' I was being smug now. 'Just try to sort yourselves out. We'll be in town all day and we won't be going home till late, so just swap numbers with one of these lads.' I nodded towards Baby B. 'Tell us where you want us and we'll get there – trust me.' My favourite line!

He agreed and I headed back to the boozer.

Gaz was waiting in the doorway and was grinning ear to ear. 'All right, top boy! I didn't know you actually organised this stuff, mate…'

'Shut the fuck up, Gaz. You don't know what you're talking about,' I snapped back. I explained that the Migs don't have a top boy – we function as a group and natural people-management skills are what decides who makes the decisions at certain times and in certain situations. I also politely suggested that he shouldn't go round saying things like that anyway, because you never know who might be listening. He never said it again.

At about two o'clock, our Luton police liaison officer came over and enquired how we planned to get to the stadium, which was some distance away. I informed him that we might not actually go to the game and were considering staying in town to enjoy the local hospitality instead. But he quickly made it clear this wasn't an option today and that the local OB were prepared to lay on free transport to the ground as long as the lads went quietly and there were no problems en route.

The fact that they will negotiate to keep the peace when it suits them is an aspect of the football hooligan situation which the police never admit to. The public might think the OB hold all the cards, but I can assure you that they don't. The problem they were facing at this particular moment was that they had over 100 known football thugs facing them and some of these were drunk as well. If the OB got too heavy and started to upset them, they were going to be stretched when things turned ugly. The mob would have fragmented and split and then they'd have had small groups of 10 or 15 spread out all over Reading town centre on a busy shopping day and in contact by mobile phone too. These splinter groups could then re-form into a bigger mob to clash with any local hoolies at five minutes' notice. It's a nightmare scenario for the OB, as these skirmishes are harder to control and more demanding on their resources. They are also more likely to occur in close proximity to the general public, which doesn't make them look too good either.

The lads all climbed aboard the double-decker buses brought in for us and then we were off to the Madejski to watch the game. A quick glance to check Gaz hadn't gone missing and I got down to business with Baby B. I explained that the only way we were going to get any action today was to split up as we came out after the match. Meanwhile, we should sit apart from each other inside the ground and behave ourselves. I didn't want to see 100 Migs all seated in the same section because we had to give the impression that we weren't a threat and had given up trying to cause any problems. Then, as we left the ground, we would send a large group of our lads to try to push past the OB. The rest were to act calm and attempt to stroll out of the police cordon at a weak point. If all went to plan, I was pretty sure I could escape the attentions of the OB and slip away into the crowds of normal fans leaving the match.

Once inside the ground, I grew even more confident of evading the OB afterwards because the travelling support was huge. As many as 3,000 had made the journey from Bedfordshire and this would give me a better chance of doing the off. Everyone did as they were asked. Or rather everyone except about 20 of the lads who, being the worse for wear after their pre-match drink, chose to move across towards the Reading lads sat on our right, shouting threats and abuse.

'Yeti, you want to have a word with your mate.' It was Flower, one of my closest friends and definitely one of the main lads – someone you always wanted to have with you in a scrape. Flower was one of the Juveniles – the original baby crew at Luton, although they would never have let themselves be known as that! This lot really grew up fast and originally intended to take out the early Migs so they could prove their position as Luton's best football mob.

I looked across at Gaz and sure enough there he was, right at the front of the small mob congregated next to the Reading support. He was standing on his seat with his hands out in front of him, beckoning the home fans to come over for a fight. I replied, 'He's the wanker from the Navy who slags me off when my back's turned. Fuck him – I hope he gets lifted!'

We watched the game and we watched Gaz too. I'm not sure which was more entertaining! He seemed to calm down as time passed, though, and at one point he slumped in his seat as if he was about to fall asleep. But then one of the lads threw an empty paper cup at his fat head and he was up again, abusing the fans opposite. He'd become a different person in the space of a few hours. Now he was a football hooligan just like me and he seemed to be enjoying it! This would soon change though.

The game finished and the lads began drifting towards the exits with clear instructions on what to do once outside. One difference between a good firm and a bad one is that, when it comes to outwitting the OB, you have to have the confidence to act as an individual, even when you're part of a larger body. So many of the mobs I've encountered over the years act like total sheep and just aren't flexible enough. The big northern mobs especially had a tendency to act like a clueless herd. That always allowed the police to round them up easily and keep them safe – which is sometimes the goal of most of these lads anyway. I know that they'll spit feathers if they read this, but it happens too often for my liking.

As our chaps started to split up and mingle with the good folk making their way home, the OB gathered in the road outside scanning the bustling crowd. It's like a game of cat and mouse with the OB looking to gather all the 'thugs' together in one place. Meanwhile, the lads are looking to splinter into smaller groups, evade detection and then put some space between themselves and the OB.

While the police used their spotters and cameras to try to pick out the boys, I managed to slip through. It was quite easy, as the OB had seen a few of the chaps and, acting like sheep, they'd all rushed over there, leaving holes in their net, so to speak.

'What about the others?' Gaz had stuck with me, but was already missing the security of the firm.

'Shut up and just keep walking.'

We were through the cordon now and mingling with the Reading fans heading home. I spotted a couple of buses heading for the town centre and in no time we were climbing the stairs to the upper deck.

'They'll never find us now,' I told Gaz.

'They stopped most of the others, but I think a few got through.' It was Mixer – a good bloke to have by your side. 'Jimmy is getting on now too,' he shouted across to me.

I told him to keep it down and took my seat.

The bus set off towards the town centre, away from the ground, the OB and, of course, the rest of the crew. For me, this was the perfect scenario, but to poor Gaz it wasn't exactly ideal, as here we were on a double-decker surrounded by the enemy, with only four of us to put up a fight. He went very quiet and started to stare out of the window, no doubt wishing for the second time that he hadn't come up to Luton this weekend. And no sign of his blind date yet either!

I could read his body language – in the ground, he'd been spouting his big mouth off as the alcohol pumped through his veins and the atmosphere got to him. He liked the safety in numbers and the fact that 20 coppers had placed themselves in a human shield between him and the Reading boys sitting near by.

But now he was faced with the reality that, if someone actually knew he was with Luton and fancied breaking his nose, then they could do it very easily. The booze was wearing off and so was his bottle. I wondered if he was worrying about all those hundreds of Reading fans that could pick him out after his clownlike behaviour inside the ground. Maybe one of them was on the bus right now and lining up Gaz's jaw for a big dig.

'Relax, Gaz!'

'What do you mean?'

He knew exactly what I meant. As it happens, the Reading supporters knew we were Luton, but they were mostly scarfers and weren't likely to want to have a pop. Although Gaz, being new to all this, continued to feel threatened.

We arrived close to town and stopped outside the train station. I noticed a few plod huddled around a van, but they weren't positioned in any sort of cordon, so they weren't looking for any potential football thugs right now. We left the bus confident that we'd soon be sinking a few beers in a pub down the road and, more importantly, that the OB wouldn't have a clue where we were.

As we strolled past them, a quick glance was about all we got, but then I heard the tell-tale crackle of a police radio reporting that the Luton supporters were about to arrive at the station and should be escorted straight on to the train for Paddington.

'Did you hear that? The rest of the lads will be arriving any minute.' Little Jimmy had heard it too – he doesn't miss much. 'Let's wait over there,' he suggested, pointing towards a shop doorway about 100 metres from the station.

It looked a good spot as it had a view of the station front and also provided cover from the OB parked on the main road. We plotted up there, and then, checking in the direction of the town centre, I remembered there were a couple of pubs just round the corner.

'Stay here, Jim. I'm going to find a boozer for the boys. Try to call them out when the escort comes through.'

I told Gaz to stay with Jimmy and Mixer and set off towards the high street. I looked back to check no one was following and spotted my pal from the Navy strolling along a few feet behind. He said that, as he didn't really know the other two, he would prefer to stick with me. After all, we were heading back to Luton shortly, weren't we?

'Maybe, Gaz… maybe.'

'What do you mean "maybe"? Didn't we tell the girls we'd be taking them out tonight?'

'Listen, Gaz, I know we said we'd take them out later, but this is football and right now all I care about is getting the lads together for a beer and seeing what Reading are made of. Let's give it an hour and see what happens.'

Gaz just nodded and we continued our recce.

Reading is quite a big place and a lot nicer than Luton. It's not one of those towns that have decided to try to cram all its shops under one roof and it still has a couple of wide pedestrianised shopping streets. This means that you still have boozers mixed with high-street shops, which in turn also means that the approaches to these alehouses are filled with people just going about their daily business – brilliant cover for moving a football mob about unnoticed.

I soon found the perfect boozer; it was small and faced a larger pub with a garden to one side. It only had one way in and the door led directly on to the street. I popped inside and it looked dated and was just about empty, apart from a couple of old geezers at the bar. I guessed that we could fit most of the lads in with a squeeze so the enemy would have to work hard to take it by force.

We headed back to Jimmy and Mixer, and by now Gaz was showing all the signs of a man uncomfortable with his surroundings, constantly checking his watch and asking stupid questions about what would happen later, as if I had a crystal ball or something. He felt impending doom and didn't like it. This is where the best football boys thrive, but Gaz's hands shook and he kept on smiling nervously as if to reassure all around that he was OK. Now all those horror stories I'd told him in the past were adding up and he wanted to go home.

I asked Mixer if he'd seen any of the chaps.

'They just got off that bus… look at the state of it,' he said, laughing.

Across the road, I could see a large police presence gathered round a double-decker bus with most of its upstairs windows put through. More importantly, the main body of the Migs was also surrounded, although I noticed a few 'strays' had managed to slip through the net, but were staying in touch with the mob. I spotted Shit Hair lurking behind a bus shelter trying to look like a normal member of the public, which is laughable when you look at his haircut. He'd have more chance of blending in at a Bon Jovi concert!

Not far from him was Small, or Big Cliff as some like to call him. As you would expect, Cliff is a lump of a lad. We'd spent most of our childhood at the same school and were good friends. He was always very opinionated – maybe a bit too much for some people's liking, but this was just part of his character and it never really bothered me. I'd had my fallouts with him – both of which ended up in blood being spilled, but it was only to be expected, as I can be just as opinionated as him. Still, what really mattered now was that Cliff was a good lad to have close by if things kicked off, because he wasn't going anywhere in a hurry.

I managed to attract his attention and beckoned him over. That was one more and soon we'd have enough to move back to the little boozer in the town centre. Over the following minutes, one after another of the firm drifted away from the police and joined us. Once we had 10, we started to move back into the centre of Reading, leaving Jimmy to direct any others up to our meeting point.

As we were heading to the pub, we spotted a couple of football lads. Because we didn't recognise them, one of our boys put a trot on to have a chat, but they took off as soon as they saw him. This confirmed that they were Reading and suggested they might have a mob gathering near by.

I mentioned this to Gaz and, along with the general excitement, it started to push his fear over the edge. 'How many more of the crew will be coming to join us?'

'None at the minute, but that's cool. It'll just mean we've gained more of a result if we hold our ground,' I replied.

'How many do you think Reading will have?'

'Loads, I reckon. After all, they're at home, and after earlier they'll want to even the score and save face. But don't worry, we'll be too tight for them.' I was trying to reassure him and breathe some confidence into anyone within earshot. I don't think it was working for Gaz though.

The next few minutes passed quickly as we focused on what might happen shortly. Would Reading turn up? How many would they have? Would they be game? The adrenaline was really flowing now.

We entered the pub calmly and positioned ourselves at the bar. The landlady seemed relaxed enough and smiled as she exchanged banter with the lads. I guessed she wasn't used to seeing a group of men our age in her place at this time of day. The truth was that the pub had seen better days, so hopefully our money would help to relax her even more and she wouldn't realise that she had a potential powder keg on her tired old hands.

'Tom, look at this.' Shit Hair called me over to the window on to the street.

Peering out, I immediately saw what had caught his interest. Straight across the road was the bigger pub and standing in the garden to one side of it was a fairly large group of football lads. They had to be Reading and there was obviously more inside the boozer. 'That's them,' I announced.

Gaz was over to the window in a shot and almost put his head through it in his haste to see what was going on. When he realised that they had more than twice as many as us, he looked worried. But, when Mixer pointed out that they had even more inside, that was it – he was going home. 'When are the rest of them going to get here?'

'Here they come now,' said Shit Hair. 'Oh! It's only Jimmy and Scottish Brian.'

For a moment there, Gaz thought the cavalry had arrived and in a way they had, not that he'd have realised it. Maybe if he'd known that Jimmy and Scottish Brian were as game as they come, he might have felt a little better. Brian in particular looks the part; he's a big lump and resembles your stereotypical football Neanderthal – bald head, pasty looking and scarred features. To cap it all, he's a Jock and hard to make sense of at the best of times. I've seen thugs from other mobs lose their bottle within seconds of meeting him.

He came to be part of the Mig Crew in the mid-90s when he left Scotland and came south looking for work. He'd been running around with Motherwell and Celtic Casuals for a few years and had a good grounding in how things are done. When deciding to head south of the border, he'd looked at a map of England and come across Luton. 'They've got a wee bit of a mob,' he thought to himself and that was it.

Once he touched down, Brian wasted no time finding us and working his way in. He has been a face at Luton ever since and we were happy to have him with us today.

So now we had a dozen good lads, plus Gaz of course, just a few metres from Reading's mob and they didn't even realise it. The OB didn't have a clue either so everything was in place for a good tear-up.

For the next few minutes, we tried to gauge the quality of the competition. Each one of their boys that came into view was judged: 'I'll knock that fat cunt out' and 'Look at the state of that geezer – he'll be on his toes as soon as it goes off.' These are the usual compliments paid to other firms at times like this and we decided that, even with the weight of numbers in their favour, we could hold our own and maybe even take the battle to them. Mixer, in particular, was in favour of our small team bowling across the road and straight into their pub. Taking them on like that was always tempting because, win or lose, it gets an immediate result.

'Er… Tom,' Gaz said, 'I'm just nipping to the paper shop to get some gum.'

'What?! You want some chewing gum?'

'Yeah, I've run out, mate,' he insisted.

Gaz left the pub and passed the window we were all huddled around. I guessed he'd lost his bottle and was heading home, so I followed to satisfy my curiosity. I stayed about 20 feet behind him, darting in and out of doorways and bus stops like I was in some detective movie. He headed away from the town centre and, as I watched, our brave Gaz, who'd spent most of the day taunting Reading supporters and the OB, made his way quickly into the station. He'd let his fear get the better of him.

I guess the final straw had been Mixer's intention to launch an attack on Reading's pub with only a dozen Migs. I'm not saying that I don't understand why Gaz bottled it, because I do. It takes that little bit of extra nerve to be a football lad and he didn't have it. I know that most people will say that it's just stupidity to even think like we do, but that's life – everyone does things that others don't understand or don't agree with.

But in our defence I have to say we have a good reason for behaving like this and that's to chase the buzz. I am sure that most people have tried drugs of some sort in their life. Well, you only do that to get the buzz and there isn't a better drug than adrenaline when it's racing through your heart, and football violence is the best way to get that. It's the best drug available and guess what – it's free! The only problem, of course, is that it's very hard to shake out of your system.

Now Gaz had done the off, I marched back to join the lads and prepare for the action that was sure to follow. But, as I approached the boozer, I noticed a certain Bedfordshire Police football intelligence officer heading in the same direction. It turned out that, while I'd been following Gaz to the train station, a couple of the lads had fronted some of the Reading group. Our boys had told them we were staying the course and weren't going home till closing time, but the OB had spotted the confrontation, probably on CCTV, and sent spotters down to check things out.

The cat was out of the bag now and the OB quickly called in back-up to swamp the place. We decided to leave and head deeper into town, but they put a police horse in the doorway of the pub. To cut a long story short, they escorted us to the station and sent us packing.

So we headed back to sunny Luton and met up with the rest of the lads later that evening. Gaz was a bit sheepish at first, but he had his excuse ready: 'I was grabbed by a copper and he searched me only to find my train ticket… blah, blah, blah.'

I looked him in the eyes as he droned on and registered his lying face for future reference – next time I'd know for sure when he was talking shit.

Back on the mess deck again, Gaz was stood in front of me telling me how my mates had been turned over by Man City in our own pub. I was checking for signs that he was lying. But he wasn't giving me the right signals. In fact, his eyes looked like they were looking for signs of worry in me instead. He didn't find any though.

'Run that by me again. There's no way the lads got done on their own patch, Gaz,' I stated firmly.

Gaz could see that I didn't want to believe him. He looked uncomfortable now and maybe wished he hadn't said anything to me at all. 'Look, I saw Fat Dave on Sunday and he told me it had gone off big time. Nick was in a bad way, mate,' he continued in a strained voice.

It soon became obvious that something serious had indeed occurred between Man City's lads and the Migs, but I didn't want to believe that it had gone down the way Gaz was telling it. I had to know more and legged it across the mess deck and up the stairs to the phone. I called a couple of the lads and got the full story.

Apparently, the Mancs had turned up in a couple of vans and spent most of the day walking around Luton mob-handed and drinking in various watering holes. They'd gone in The Brewery Tap, in the heart of the town and bumped into three of the Migs including Flower and Trigger. Now these two are game, but they had 30-odd Mancs breathing down their necks, giving them loads of shit about the Migs being fuck all and not even showing their faces. Flower and the other two kept their cool and played dumb, even when some of the abuse turned racial and personal. They just strolled calmly out of the Tap and kept their heads down. Once outside, though, they got straight on the blower to the rest of the lads, drinking only five minutes away, and reported in.

As often happens in these situations, by the time a mob of 50 Migs arrived, the Mancs had already left and plotted up in The Sports Bar – one of the main boozers used by the Mig Crew. They'd gained a result of sorts by even getting in the place and now they were in a defendable position. It was going to take a big effort to take it back and save face. But, by now, they probably thought that the Migs weren't even out that day and started to relax – mission accomplished.

However, they couldn't have been more wrong and the clock was ticking on their day's liberty-taking. The Mancs' first mistake was not to hold the door. What were they thinking? The Migs just walked straight in 50-handed. The place went quiet as the tension rose.

Dibble approached the City lads, giving them the option to take it outside, but they declined and instead sent the few young lads they had with them out for their own safety. The Luton lads let them leave untouched, after which Dennis walked over to the doors of the boozer and locked the bolts. The silence was deafening as the two mobs sized each other up across the newly decorated establishment. Then it went off.

The Mancs rose from their corner as one and launched every glass, bottle and ashtray they could. As Luton steamed into them, the City lads fought back, but couldn't hold their ground and some of their numbers broke off and forced a fire exit to escape the battle.

The trouble was over, but one City lump stood up trying to get his comrades to rally for another go: 'Come on, get up – don't let them think they've done yer,' he bellowed.

But it was too late. City were done and, as the OB entered the pub from the forced fire exit, the Migs unlocked the main doors and slipped out and into the darkening streets. But Gaz had been right – somewhere in all this Nick did have his ear half torn off and ended up in Luton and Dunstable Hospital with three of the City lads.

I hadn't been there, of course, but I wished that I had been. What I really wished now, though, was that I hadn't been at Watford on that fateful September day in 2002. But now it was nearly time for me to face the music and I could only hope that things didn't go as badly in Luton Crown Court as they had done for Man City's lads in The Sports Bar!

Welcome to the First Division

It was 11 December and, as the rain started to clear, the sun appeared for the first time that morning, giving me a lift. 'Maybe, just maybe, I'll make it home to my own bed tonight,' I thought, in a bid to reassure myself.

Since I'd woken from a surprisingly deep sleep, it had rained steadily and the thick grey clouds had hidden any hint of sunlight. To be honest, I hadn't wanted the night to pass so quickly, as all my waking moments over the past few months had been full of the thought of prison. I knew that I'd probably end up behind bars and had tried to prepare myself for it mentally, but I was still scared and didn't want to face the music.

I'd thought about getting on my toes and doing the off to some hot country or other, but I would have to come back eventually. And did I seriously expect the Old Bill to forget all about me and what I'd been a part of? It was messing with my mind and had been for a while now. I wasn't the only one, though, and some of the lads involved in the clashes that day in Watford had already gone missing, including Baby B.

A few weeks earlier, the two of us had travelled down to Peloponnese in Greece to have a break and prepare for the months of bang-up ahead. We'd flown to Athens and jumped on a train down to Kalamata. It had been a five-hour journey through some fantastic countryside with incredible views of the Corinth canal. 'Why hadn't I done this earlier?' I wondered.

We spent the week visiting Sparta and Pylos, before catching the overnight ferry from Gythio back up to Athens. The conversation had been about anything but the impending court case and we tried to block out the whole thing as if it wasn't happening. At one point, I wondered if this was a sign of change and that perhaps we were showing some remorse for our actions. Maybe we could actually put football hooliganism behind us now.

Then, one evening, as we were sitting in a taverna enjoying a laidback Mediterranean sunset, a Greek guy sitting near by started chatting to Baby B. He'd noticed the Mig Crew tattoo on B's leg and wanted to know if we were 'Ultras', as he put it. Well, the little chat soon turned into a whole evening planning how the Migs could meet up with Kalamata's Bulldogs the following season and make our way to Athens to help smash Olympiakos' famous 'Gate 7' Ultras. We explained that the Athens crew wouldn't expect it and the shock of 20 to 30 English lads dressed accordingly, hoods up and shouting, 'Come on, you cunts, let's have it!' would throw them completely – allowing Kalamata's lads to pile in and scatter them.

We wanted him to think of the result and imagine how legendary his firm of Ultras would become. He wasn't too sure though and explained that the difference between Greek football boys and the English was that they only acted in the interest of their club, whereas we only really cared about the violence. In some ways, I agreed. How could I disagree? But we decided to trade e-mail addresses anyway, in case he changed his mind.

When I woke up the next morning, my head banging with an ouzo-fuelled hangover, it dawned on me that I hadn't really learned anything at all. If the thought of prison wasn't enough to change me or make me see the error of my ways, what would be?

Baby B had already had enough of the mind-fuck and secretly decided to go missing. He hadn't told me, but only a week after getting back from Greece he booked a flight straight back out with Sol, another of the MI2s. Now Sol is a bit of an unpredictable character at the best of times and has been bouncing back and forth from Kenya for a while. He was a submariner until he was called a 'black bastard' by a senior rate while on board. Sol handed out a few swift digs to the surprised petty officer and was duly arrested by the Navy Provost. He served some time in Colchester Glass House and left the RN shortly afterwards.

Being over six feet tall, he's quite a lump and well game too – one of Luton's better 'babies'. He's struggled to settle in life and is always up for a new adventure, so, knowing how B felt about facing up to prison life, he had a chat and suggested that they go abroad. With the memories of Greece still fresh in young Baby B's head, he decided to go for it and the first I knew about it was a phone call from Heathrow. They went on the run and headed back to Kalamata before moving on to Bulgaria, Turkey and eventually Egypt, where B ended up training as a scuba diving instructor in the Red Sea.

However, back in Luton, I was making a different kind of journey today and the views were far from fantastic. In fact, sitting alongside Windy as we ploughed our way through the drizzle to the Crown Court, I felt as bad as I ever had in my life. It was certainly much worse than the first time I went to prison. Back then, I was only 16 and had been sentenced to two months for non-payment of fines. But in those days I didn't have a care in the world and wasn't afraid of anything, the law included. I was the product of a tough upbringing, so I found the best way to get through life was to not think too much – just get the fuck on and do it.

I'd been through some bullying at school, as I was a bit different to most of the kids and I think this was crucial to me becoming a thug. One day, the wrong lads picked on me and, even though there were three of them, I just went for it – screwing up my eyes and wind-milling my way along the school corridor, connecting with all three of them.

On reaching the doors at the far end, I turned and opened my eyes to see one of the bullies on the floor and the other two looking shocked and backing off. At this, I felt a surge of invincibility and started the return journey back down the corridor, this time with my eyes well and truly open and looking to connect with the cunts. The two remaining boys looked at each other in disbelief as I closed on them for a second time, arms flailing about me. I did indeed connect and very nicely too, but unfortunately not with either of the two lads. It was the head of year, who'd just stepped out of his room to see what all the commotion was about!

Obviously, he was none too pleased and dragged me into his office by my ear for a serious bollocking. I didn't care, though, because something happened to me that day and there wasn't going to be any more one-way violence – it was coming back at whoever I decided deserved it. Including my mother.

One Saturday, I came downstairs to face this drunken woman who liked to lay into me as and when she pleased. This particular morning, though, it finally stopped, as I pushed her over and told her that I'd kill her if she ever dared touch me or my younger brothers again. She looked in my eyes and saw the anger there. Without a word, she got up and just walked out into the kitchen. I wanted to follow, but knew that I might well hurt her if I did.

Welcome to the First Division

Two weeks later, my mother walked out of the front door and out of my life for good. I've never looked back since.

Soon after this, I found myself sitting next to a lad called Demus at school. I'd hardly spoken to him during my early years at Stockwood, but noticed that he had the same interest in all things football. Eventually, I struck up a conversation about our mutual passion and soon we were like old mates catching up on lost time. We talked for hours about this and that cup final, before the chat inevitably came round to Manchester United. It turned out that, like most kids at the time, we both had a soft spot for them and shared a common dream to go and watch the Reds for real instead of just on the box.

That lunchtime, we sat in the playground and, in a sign of what was to come over the following years, planned every detail of the trip, from our departure time to what we would wear and even where we would go to eat. As we chatted, a couple of other lads from our year came over and decided that they wanted to come on our day out to watch the mighty Reds too. We soon found ourselves making allowances for these intruders and our meet time moved back to allow one chap to get dropped at Luton Station by his parents. Soon, all was sorted for our mission to see Man United play Tottenham at the famous White Hart Lane the following month.

The day in question finally arrived and Demus and I met up as planned, but after all the talk none of the others bothered. We felt a bit let down, as it would have been good to have a few more of us heading off into the 'Big Smoke', but we decided to push on and see the day through on our own.

As the train for St Pancras pulled slowly out of Luton, I felt some trepidation, as I was heading into the unknown with only my newfound best mate for company. Maybe he felt the same, but he certainly seemed that bit more sure of himself than me. Over the next few years, I was to discover that he was indeed more confident than I was and often had a lot more bottle than I did too.

We arrived in London at around 9am with our supposedly detailed planning already in tatters, as we were forced to ask one of the platform staff the best way to get to Tottenham! He kindly suggested that we follow a Spurs fan in front who was heading the same way, so we stuck close to his tail, making sure we kept him in sight at all times.

We were doing fine until we got down to the Underground and came into the King's Cross ticket office where we'd never seen so many people going in so many directions in one place before. Everyone seemed to be crossing each other's paths, bumping and shoving to get to their escalator or gate and move on with their journey as quickly as possible. We found ourselves in a state of shock and froze for a moment in the midst of the chaos, and then our guide was gone, disappearing into the busy throng of shoppers and tourists. What now?

We ambled over to a tube map that Demus had spotted by the ticket barriers and, trying not to look too much like tourists ourselves, we spent ages looking for Tottenham.

Demus found the colour of the Underground line we needed to take. 'Victoria Line to Seven Sisters,' he stated confidently and we headed over to the ticket office, bought our Underground tickets and set off for the platforms below.

As we were riding down the escalator we heard it: 'We love U-nited, we do! We love U-nited, we do!' It echoed around the tunnels of the Underground and seemed to be sung by a thousand voices.

'Come on, Tom, let's go see what's happening.'

But I wasn't so sure. In fact, I was scared and Demus almost begged me to come with him.

'We hate Scousers and we hate Scousers – we hate Scousers and we hate Scousers!'

The noise was deafening. I spent the next few seconds wrestling with the fight or flight trigger inside my head – my heart was racing and my legs had turned to jelly. I cursed myself for being there and wished that I'd swerved the meet at Luton Station in the morning, like the others.

'Well I'm going to see anyway,' announced Demus and he was off.

Now I had to go too and hurried after him trying to close the gap between us in case I lost him in the crowd. I broke into a sprint and jostled my way through the throng, trying to catch up. 'I'm with you, Demus,' I choked through my drying throat.

We emerged on to the northbound platform to find it packed solid with men aged from 16 to what I guessed was about 35. They looked intimidating and were bundling each other about and singing as one: 'We fu-ckin' hate City, we fu-ckin' hate City!'

Demus pushed forward and I followed. To my surprise, they didn't even bat an eyelid as we approached them, so, with the smell of alcohol all about us, we eased our way through the group. There must have been a couple of hundred of them altogether and they were mostly pretty pissed so I was jostled a few times by the crowd, but I didn't feel threatened any more.

Eventually, we passed right through the mob, found some space and leaned up against the platform wall trying to look relaxed. We didn't say anything to each other, but we both knew the score – we wanted to be part of this gang. We sensed danger and excitement with these United fans and wanted to stay with them for the ride.

The tube pulled in and I spotted one or two Tottenham supporters through the windows. They were wearing their club's shirts and had scarves too. With their colours on display like that, I thought they were going to get a kicking when the doors opened. However, to my surprise, the United lads didn't touch them at all – sure they gave the Spurs boys some stick, but no actual violence occurred. In fact, everything was quite light-hearted and humour was the order of the day as we headed north under London's streets.

'Hey, Cockney, I hear there's a major fault with that new stand your lot have built.'

'What's that then?'

'It's built the wrong way round… it faces the pitch!'

We tagged along with the Mancs all the way but, once overground, they went into a nearby pub on the Seven Sisters Road and, seeing all the police outside, we decided not to follow, as we looked far too young. Instead, we would make our way down to the ground on our own – after all, it couldn't be too far, could it? We asked a copper which direction to take and he happily pointed us on our way. 'Enjoy the walk, lads!'

Well, I don't know if you have ever walked from Seven Sisters Station to White Hart Lane, but let me tell you now – you don't want to! It's fucking miles and, being my first time and as young as I was, it seemed even further than that. We marched on and on, taking in all the sights and sounds as we went.

There was a mixture of supporters from both clubs on the streets, but no signs of any trouble at all. That is, until we got near the ground, where we stumbled across two big lads knocking the stuffing out of each other. They were really going at it too and I became transfixed as these two heavyweights clashed.

One had a bloodied nose, but seemed to have the upper hand: 'Cam on, you Chelsea cunt,' screamed the bleeding fighter. 'You want it, do ya?'

What? Chelsea?! It was Tottenham and Man United today, but this fella was talking about Chelsea! What was that all about?

They went into each other again, but this time the bigger Chelsea boy knocked the Yid to the floor and proceeded to kick him in the head. I was mesmerised by the fighting and didn't want it to stop, but all good things come to an end and soon two of the Met's finest came flying across the road, crashing straight into the Chelsea fan. Red-faced and helmets wobbling, the bobbies pushed him to the pavement to join the Yid lying in the lane and then handcuffed and dragged him, still struggling, into the waiting police van.

Meanwhile, the poor old Yid got up slowly, dusted himself down and then glared over at me and Demus. I wondered if he'd seen us watching the fight and was annoyed that we hadn't helped him. But, on looking around, I became aware of all the others taking in the spectacle just like us and I felt reassured by this because I didn't fancy getting the blame for the beating he'd just taken. He wiped his nose on his sleeve, checked the results and then smiled and spat blood on to the concrete. He looked over at us again, but this time flashed us a sly grin and winked.

I still wonder why he chose to pick us out of everyone there, but I like to think it was because he saw a little of himself in us. Maybe he wanted to avoid frightening us away from football violence by showing us that he could take a beating, but still retain his senses and his cool, or maybe not. Whatever the reason, we smiled back and I almost waved at him, I was so happy to be acknowledged.

This was the first time I'd seen football thugs in action and the feelings I had reminded me of when I wind-milled my way down that school corridor. I was gradually becoming accustomed to violence and maybe even starting to find a purpose to it all now. In fact, I wanted to emulate this battered Yid – not by getting a kicking, of course, but by entering the world of football violence. So the die was cast. Whatever will be will be and all that.

With an extra little spring in our steps, Demus and I went and queued outside the away fans turnstiles. But, being so early, we had a while to wait, so we sat our arses down on the pavement and just watched the world go by. I soon noticed a few lads gathering across the road at a pub called The Corner Pin. They were walking in and out of the bar, chit-chatting with each other and warmly greeting new arrivals.

The Spurs boys looked a bit different to the Manchester lads we'd travelled with earlier, though, and they weren't draped in their team's colours, or maybe only a few of them were. But, for some other reason that I couldn't quite put my finger on, they stood out from the rest of the football fans we'd seen on our trip. The Cockneys were all in their late teens and early twenties and weren't bellowing out songs every few minutes like the Mancs. In fact, they were quite low-key.

We'd both clocked them and watched keenly as their numbers grew steadily. I realise now that it was the self-confidence these Spurs lads exuded that I couldn't quite place at the time, but I was picking up on everything that was going on around me and it was all having an effect.

The turnstiles opened and the pair of us jumped up and paid to get into the ground. Once inside, we ran straight on to the terrace and down behind the goal, then scaled the tall blue fence and stuck our heads over the top. 'United are here, United are here, hello, hello!' we sang, copying one of the songs we'd heard on the tube earlier.

'Get down, you little cunts,' a deep voice boomed in reply. It was OB and he meant it, so we climbed down a little sheepishly and retreated to the back of the stand to find some Wagon Wheels or whatever.

Once there, we discovered that, by climbing a tall staircase, you could see out on to the road below. So we hurried to the top, both keen to see what the mob of Tottenham outside The Corner Pin were up to, but were disappointed to find that they'd gone. I wondered if they'd entered the ground yet.

We watched the game along with nearly 50,000 others and it was like nothing I'd ever experienced before. The noise, the excitement and the sense of belonging – I loved it all. I'd found my passion in life and it was better than I could ever have imagined. Here I was at a huge stadium in the capital city of England, watching household names display their special skills only yards away from me. I was in there and part of the whole event as my voice joined the 5,000 Mancs roaring United on to victory and I felt honoured.

About 20 minutes into the game, though, there was a sudden surge from behind us and within seconds I was pinned up against the same perimeter fence that we'd been ordered down from earlier. I was helpless as the weight of hundreds of United supporters crushed me against the metal caging and was starting to panic, when suddenly I found room to free my arms and force some space between me and the surrounding folk. Then it was over and everyone returned to pretty much the same positions on the terrace where they'd been standing only seconds previously.

Once I was upright and back alongside Demus, I checked to find out what had caused the surge and saw a large group of Mancs moving through the crowd in the direction of the Tottenham fans over to our right. I scanned the faces in this mob and realised that I'd seen them before. It was the gang that we'd travelled with from King's Cross to Seven Sisters, but they didn't look quite so happy now.

Intrigued, we tagged along and soon found ourselves up close to the blue barrier separating the two sets of fans.

Demus pointed to a tier higher up in the stand facing us. 'That's the Shelf,' he claimed knowingly. 'It's where the top Tottenham chaps go.'

It was packed with young men all seemingly eager to fight and they were beckoning the Manchester lads to 'Come join us, come join us, come join us over here!'

The Manchester mob replied with a dramatic, but not entirely convincing rush at the fence. Tottenham responded similarly and so it continued throughout the rest of the match without either side actually climbing over, which was a little surprising as Demus and I had had no trouble in scaling a similar fence earlier. Maybe they didn't actually want to do it!

We listened to the banter between the two sets of rival supporters and soon found out where the mob of Yids gathered outside The Corner Pin had gone. Apparently, a gang of United lads had been heading down the Seven Sisters Road, when they were ambushed by a larger firm of Spurs fans at the entrance to Lordship Lane. The United boys had turned and run back up the Seven Sisters Road with a couple of them taking a serious hiding. It seemed Tottenham had drawn first blood and were now crowing about it in the ground.

As the match progressed, the atmosphere became uglier, with both sets of supporters throwing missiles and some being taken out injured. More police were turning up all the time as well and I began to get nervous again. So, with about 15 minutes to go, I decided that it was time to leave White Hart Lane and head for home. My only problem was Demus, because he was in his element and loving every moment of the drama. He wanted to hang around and catch the inevitable battle outside, but I wasn't so keen. It took some chat, but eventually I managed to persuade him to leave early and we pushed our way through the legions of United supporters packed into the away end and out of the ground.

As Demus and I walked across the road towards The Corner Pin, we noticed a broken window being boarded up. There had obviously been some trouble here after we'd entered the ground, which only heightened

Welcome to the First Division

my concerns about what might happen when the two groups of warring fans left White Hart Lane and met on the highways of N15. I knew that in about 10 minutes it was likely that the two mobs of hooligans would be walking the same streets as us and I didn't find too much comfort in the idea.

In fact, I wanted to get as far away from here as quickly as possible. I pointed towards a double-decker a short distance ahead of us on the Seven Sisters Road. 'Let's get that bus.'

We both scrambled on board and were off and heading back to Luton after our first football adventure.

I learned a number of things that day, but the most important lesson was that I wasn't as tough or brave as I thought I was. I certainly couldn't have taken a beating and then get up and laugh about it, like the Yid before the match. And I clearly wasn't as game as my new friend who'd been so keen to stay and witness the trouble afterwards. But I hoped that one day I would be.

As I got to know Demus better over the following weeks, the violence became as much a part of our conversations as the actual football itself. And now we began to talk about Luton Town as much as any of the big teams. Demus eagerly showed me the press cuttings which he'd collected from the *Luton News* and a few national papers too. Apparently, Luton had a significant hooligan element who'd been involved in a lot of trouble at home games recently. This coincided with the team on the pitch enjoying a rising reputation too, under the management of David Pleat. So we decided to go and see for ourselves exactly what made Luton tick on a Saturday.

Around midday on September 1981, Demus and I met up at the Luton Town Hall ready for the visit of Sheffield Wednesday and a big Second Division game that was set to be televised on BBC's *Match of the Day*. Earlier in the week, we'd spoken to a couple of older lads at school, Ging and Les, who had a wealth of information about football violence. In fact, they claimed to have been directly involved in some trouble at Luton already. Most importantly for now, though, they told us about The Castle Bar – the place where all the Luton football thugs congregated before and after a home match. It sounded easy enough to find because it was in a prominent position in the town centre, beneath the Strathmore Hotel.

After meeting up, the two of us set straight off to find this legendary hooligan HQ. It stood facing the green in the town centre and seemed to have only one entrance. Although it wasn't quite a drawbridge, it was no less intimidating, as the heavy panelled door had no glass. In fact, there were no windows in this pub at all. The only way we were going to find out what was happening in there was to walk right in and that didn't appeal too much to these two 14-year-olds in leather box jackets and skin-tight Levi's.

Nevertheless, we strolled over to the door as calmly as we could and were just about to enter when a big lump of a skinhead walked out and almost bowled us both over in the process. He stopped and stared down at us for a few moments, sizing us up. 'You fucking Wednesday then?'

I shit myself as he stepped towards us with a look of hate in his eyes, but we both quickly muttered something about being Luton and he smiled.

The next thing, though, he looked daggers at Demus. 'What about you? You look like a fuckin' Duggan…' The Duggans were a family of 'plastic Paddies' who had a bit of a reputation for violence in the area.

'No way, mate, I'm from Park Town.'

The big monster then turned back to me and held me in his intimidating stare for what seemed like a minute or more. 'How old are you two anyway?' he snarled through gritted teeth.

I froze, but Demus responded quickly again, 'Seventeen, mate.' He stopped short of adding the usual moody 'Why?'

But the big fella remained unconvinced and shook his head at us. 'Fuck off back to school, you horrible little fuckers!'

We didn't hang about to argue.

Sheffield Wednesday's fans had been banned from travelling to away games and this was the first game after the lifting of the ban, so they were expected to travel in significant numbers. Nearly 4,000 made the journey south and filled their two sections in the Kenilworth Road End of our ground. It was a big day out for them and as the teams ran out they made a right racket, throwing scores of toilet rolls on to the pitch and sending hundreds of blue and white balloons floating around the ground.

However, at the same time, a small pocket of the Sheffield support had found its way into the Main Stand and, within seconds of the teams emerging from the tunnel, fighting broke out. This was my first sight of trouble inside a football ground, but it was all over in a flash as Bedfordshire Police swamped the area, forming a human wall between the rival fans.

As it was going off, I also noticed a large gathering of Luton lads packed tightly into the narrow terrace area immediately below the stand in which the clashes had just taken place. They'd become agitated when the fighting was in full swing and reminded me of the supporters close to the segregated areas at White Hart Lane. They had that same menace about them, if not quite the same numbers.

Over time, I was to discover that this was Luton's Maple Road End or as the local OB knew it 'the Triangle' – so-called because of the shape of the terrace, which was wide at one end, but came to a narrow point near the away fans. This was the main place within the Kenilworth Road ground where Luton's hooligans congregated. There were other spots like the central section of Oak Road terrace, where I was standing with Demus, but as far as I could see the Maple were the main boys. At least it seemed to be where the majority of The Castle Bar gathered to cheer on the Hatters and abuse the visiting fans.

The game was played at a frantic pace and, as their large support cheered them on, Sheffield Wednesday took the game to Luton. By the time Megson had knocked in their second in the 73rd minute, it was all but over for the Town. This had a sudden and surprising result, as all around me people began heading for the exits. I couldn't understand it, as there was still 20 minutes left to play. Listening in, we learned that those leaving were heading around to the Maple to join up with the rest of the Luton thugs and attack Wednesday as they left the ground.

The thought of this had Demus literally bounding for the exit. I hurried after him and we joined about 50 others who left the Oak Road and re-entered the ground round the corner on Maple Road. This lot was a right mixed bunch of older skinheads, pissed-up builders and youngsters not much older than us. Everyone was jumping up and down excitedly and pushing each other around at the prospect of confronting the Sheffield hordes.

We bundled back into the ground, headed to our right under the Main Stand and entered the Maple Road End at the Triangle. As we pushed our way on to the already packed terrace, we caused a surge in the crowd, which increased our sense of anticipation even more. Wednesday came pouring down to confront the Maple, throwing coins and gesturing towards the home support, goading us to come forward. It was a direct challenge and Luton quickly sent coins and concrete lumps from the crumbly terrace flying into the dense body of Yorkshiremen.

The police now ran the full length of the pitch to put themselves between the two sets of angry supporters and, for a while, it looked as though the menace had faded. However, as the Wednesday fans celebrated noisily at the final whistle, Luton were gathering behind the Triangle with one intent – to attack them on the way out.

As the away supporters left the ground, they had to walk to their right up Kenilworth Road and then through an opening into the coach park. Meanwhile, the home fans leaving the Maple had to head to the left and down the same road in the opposite direction. This meant that, if we left at the same time as the away fans, our paths would inevitably cross. The OB knew this too, though, and had positioned dog handlers and regular officers in front of the large exit gates, which were the only obvious way out.

Without any command, the 200 Luton fans who'd grouped behind the Triangle, charged as one towards the police lines in an attempt to confront the Wednesday leaving the ground. A handful looked as though they would make it through, but even more OB were waiting outside in the road. The away support that had emerged split in two – the majority ran back into the ground, but a number of them headed through the opening into the coach park. It was on this group that the Castle Bar lads now focused their attentions.

Even if we'd outnumbered the police four to one, it would have been impossible to break through them and get out of the ground on to the surrounding streets. So, instead, some of the main characters in our angry mob headed back into the ground and climbed up the fence at the rear of the Maple. It was over 12 feet tall but, undaunted by this, over 100 of us, including me and Demus, followed them.

As we scrambled up the fence, it became difficult not to fall off because too many of us were trying to do the same thing at once. But I managed to stay the distance and soon found myself perched on the top looking down into the dingy coach park. This put me in an even more precarious position, as I was becoming an obstruction to the rest of the mass of angry Luton thugs trying to get over. I glanced down again and didn't like what I saw. Not only was there a longer fall on the other side, but also a straight drop on to concrete with nothing to break your fall.

I watched as lad after lad leaped down and landed with heavy thumps. Some got straight to their feet, but others struggled, clutching at sprained ankles and twisted knees. I just couldn't find the courage to make the jump myself. Then I saw Demus go over and, after a bit of rolling around, he was up and running towards the coaches parked in neat rows a few yards away.

He didn't look back for me, though, and, as soon as I was sure he wouldn't see, I climbed back down the fence and into the ground. I'd bottled it, but so had plenty of the others, it seemed to me. The police, meanwhile, had followed the commotion to the coach park, so now we could make our way out of the ground unhindered.

There was still about 100 of us left in this mob, including the big lump from The Castle Bar who we'd met in the morning. He was in control now and everyone followed his orders to head down Kenilworth Road. I marched along with the rest, looking as menacing as possible, when suddenly a roar went up and we charged as one down the hill.

I slipped to the side of the herd preparing to fight and, although I wasn't right at the front, I was near enough to see exactly what happened next. The group of about 20 youths, who'd been strolling down the road ahead, now looked back at us steaming towards them and panicked. Most of them ran as fast as their legs could carry them, but a couple just stood rooted to the spot with their jaws on the floor. In a matter of seconds, these two lads were on the deck and receiving a thorough kicking.

It was sickening, so I just watched it happen. But I wasn't too sure I liked what I saw this time. It wasn't like the fighting I had seen in the ground – this was just bullying. The way these lads had frozen like rabbits in a headlight and offered no resistance, I wasn't even convinced that they were here for trouble. In fact, I wasn't even sure they were from fucking Sheffield!

As the mob moved on, I glanced back at the bodies sprawled on the corner of Hazelbury Crescent and Kenilworth Road – they weren't moving and I guessed they were probably unconscious. I watched as some of our group celebrated and re-enacted the punches and kicks they'd delivered. I felt a bit sick myself, but then another roar went up and we were off again and stampeding down Hazelbury Crescent towards our next target.

We'd spotted a group as big as our own further down the hill but, as we closed on them, it became apparent that it was the Luton lads who'd scaled the fence into the coach park earlier. Stories were swapped and we discovered that they'd wrecked most of the coaches, battered a group of Wednesday thugs and then chased the rest of them back into the ground. Our own story seemed insignificant in comparison and, when I linked up with Demus, I was in awe. He told me he'd punched two of the Sheffield boys during the rucking and I knew he wasn't lying either. I was well jealous of his exploits that day and had some serious catching up to do now.

The rest of the season went well for Luton and, after thrashing Shrewsbury 4–1 in front of nearly 15,000 at Kenilworth Road, we were promoted to the top flight and hundreds invaded the pitch to celebrate in style.

Between the Sheffield Wednesday match and this promotion party, Demus and I hardly missed a game home or away and had been caught up in more minor incidents of football violence.

We'd been chased around Newcastle city centre in April and I punched my first northerner when the Geordies infiltrated our section of St James' Park at the match later that day. We lost that one, as Imre Varadi smashed the ball into the net in the dying seconds of an exciting game. I actually shed a tear that night and cursed the half-Hungarian, half-Italian Luton reject who won the game for them in front of a typically huge and passionate crowd of Geordie loons.

I also got on my toes when Ipswich came to town in the FA Cup fourth round. It was a big occasion for us, as they were top of the First Division and could count on big names like Eric Gates, Alan Brazil and Paul Mariner. Off the pitch, they brought nearly 7,000 supporters with them from Suffolk and their fair share of thugs too. We'd bashed them before the game, but afterwards it was to be a different story.

As was customary in those days, we marched from the Oak Road End and down Dunstable Road through Bury Park. We were over 200-strong and hungry for Ipswich, as they'd put three past Luton in the second half to knock us right out of the Cup. We waited at the West Side Shopping Centre, as this was the way they would have to come to get back to the train station. There, we were soon joined by some of the Maple Road lads, although most of the Castle Bar were noticeably absent that day. Still, we had a big force gathered, ready for action and all looked well.

A handful of lads headed up Hazelbury Crescent to see if there was any sign of the Tractor Boys and guess what – they found them! The Luton that had set off so boldly on the recce came sprinting straight back around the bend and down the Crescent towards us.

'Stand, Luton!' came the cry.

I'd heard this before – it meant we were about to face a large mob of opposing fans and be seriously tested. But the West Side was packed with our lads and I didn't think it would be a question of standing or holding our ground. I reckoned we should be going on the offensive and smashing straight into the Ipswich boys. But then I saw them…

Welcome to the First Division

The Suffolk lads filled Hazelbury Crescent as far as the fucking eye could see and still they came – hundreds upon hundreds of them. They weren't all thugs, but they had the same intent as us – they wanted a row. Luton charged forward in a half-hearted attempt to bluff them into running and it nearly worked as some of them began to flee back up the hill. But it was short-lived and they came pouring across Dunstable Road with a deafening noise.

The cry came again, 'Stand, Luton. Stand!' Luton ran.

I panicked and tried desperately not to fall or trip in the chaos that followed. The images of those Sheffield Wednesday lads getting kicked unconscious earlier in the season filled my mind, but I looked down at my feet and concentrated on not colliding with all the other lads running and pushing each other to escape. I just couldn't believe that we'd got run so easily, but we did.

Our last game that season was against Cardiff City at Ninian Park in May. It was a midweek game and we should have been at school, but the buzz was getting to us now, so Demus and I bunked off and travelled to the match with the supporters club. That night, we sent an unhappy Cardiff down to the Third Division and, on the final whistle, hundreds of the Welsh boyos came straight over the fences on to the pitch and pelted us with missiles. Then they broke a fence down separating our end from theirs to attack the hundred or so Luton who had made the long journey west. There were some scuffles, but the police kept us out of harm and, to be honest, I didn't feel too threatened. Even when we came out of the ground, I got myself to the front of the escort, ready to stand my ground if it came on top.

The Cardiff boys had been chased away by the OB and there was no more trouble that evening, but there was one important development on the way home. As I sat staring out of the coach window at the moonlit Welsh countryside, I cast my mind back over the past season and realised that I was finding my feet as a football hooligan. However, I also knew by now that Luton's mob, although enthusiastic, was actually not that good at the job. Maybe I could help to change things. I was becoming more ambitious and I couldn't help but get excited about the prospect of our first season back in the First Division.

The summer dragged by and I spent the days talking about football violence with Demus and a few other chaps, including Ging and Les – the two older lads who knew everything there was to know about it all. I just couldn't get enough of their stories. Then one day they told me about the Inter City Firm.

They explained how West Ham's lads were really organised and totally different to Luton's and most other clubs' hooligans as well. For a start, they didn't wear any colours and also met at pre-arranged times, travelling to matches by train. I knew some clubs put on 'Specials' to away games, but Les explained that this was different. Apparently, the ICF mingled with regular folk and always travelled in first class, because they didn't want to be noticed as they moved. That way the OB wouldn't be waiting for them when they arrived in the opposition's town. And for the same reasons they didn't get pissed and start smashing up everything in their path either. This intrigued me, especially when he described a TV documentary showing them in all their glory.

Then he said something that changed a part of me forever: 'They wear Pringles.'

'What the fuck is a Pringle when it's at home?' I didn't have a clue what he was on about.

Ging patiently explained that they were jumpers that cost loads of money and could only be bought from Scotch House in Marble Arch.

So, with the summer holidays still in full swing, I travelled to London with Demus, Ging, Les and a few others and we all returned to Luton proudly sporting our pure lambswool diamond Pringle jumpers. We'd paid out between £120 and £140 each for our new knitwear and without even knowing it had become football Casuals in the process.

We spent the rest of the summer discussing the coming season and even came up with a name – the 'Stockwood Pringle Boys' after our school. We were deadly serious about it all by now, as the new season was nearly upon us and we wanted to be ready for action in the top flight. Standing in the dinner queue at the beginning of a new school year, Demus passed me the fixture list. 'Take a fucking look at that.'

I paused as it dawned on me exactly who it was that we would be entertaining for our first home game of the 82/83 season. After an away trip to Spurs, which I couldn't get to, we were due to face an invasion from East London – West Ham and the famous ICF were coming to town! We were going straight in at the deep end.

Ging had knowingly informed us that Luton and the Castle Bar boys in particular were going to put on a real show for the Cockneys, in the hope of sending a message to the rest of the First Division that little Luton were no pushovers. So, on the evening of 31 August, I donned my new Pringle jumper and best jeans to face the top firm in England.

I met Demus on Market Hill and he turned up looking sharp in his Pringle and faded jeans. Alongside him were a couple of lads from Park Town who'd accompanied us on our shopping trip to London in the summer. Admiring each other's garms, the four of us headed down towards the Town Hall, up the ramp into the lovely Arndale Shopping Centre and made for the Strathmore Hotel.

We arrived on the walkway above The Castle Bar and looked expectantly down on to the green in front of the library, but there was only a few lads drinking pints and milling around in the doorway. We hung around for a while, but didn't see much in the way of a mob gathering, so we made our way over to Bury Park to see if anything was happening there.

As we bowled through the West Side, we stumbled across hundreds of West Ham supporters gathered outside The Dutchman pub. They were a frightening-looking bunch and quite vocal too, so the four of us gave them a wide berth and quickly headed on up to the ground. We went in the Oak Road as usual, although really I wanted to go in the Triangle with the Maple boys.

But, once inside, we soon heard how West Ham had run Luton back into The Castle Bar earlier on in the day. Apparently, Luton hadn't done too well and the ICF's reputation as England's most fearsome mob had been easily upheld.

During the match, they then tried to take the Oak Road as well, but they just made a lot of noise and scared a few youngsters, before shrinking back behind police lines and getting escorted around the pitch to the away end.

The Hammers went on to win, but after the game the dark streets surrounding Kenilworth Road were full of threat with broad Cockney accents all about us in the night air. I was apprehensive as our small band of Pringle Boys made its way through Bury Park and expected to hear the roar of the ICF at any moment. But the wail of police sirens was the only soundtrack to our journey, as we tiptoed our way back to the town centre. We made our way back up to the walkway above The Castle Bar, from where we hoped to spot any trouble if it went off.

After we'd been perched up there for a while, we suddenly became aware of a large body of people moving quietly, but purposefully, up the ramp from the direction of the Town Hall. They were scanning the green below searching for something or someone and they looked serious too. But what made this group of 30 or so particularly menacing was the fact they were all black.

They didn't take too much interest in us youngsters, but something had certainly caught their attention. They ran past the Strathmore Hotel to another vantage point providing a clearer view of the street below.

'That's them cunts from earlier,' one of them hissed to his mate. 'That's the fucking ICF.'

I sneaked up next to the black crew to see what they were looking at, but they were already heading off in the direction of the West Ham firm.

And then I saw the famous ICF for the first time – they were moving towards a multi-storey car park, about 40-handed and all in their mid-twenties. They walked in a tight group formation and to a man were scanning the shadows for Luton's mob. They looked confident, though, both in their group strength and in each other. It would take something special to smash this lot and I doubted that Luton had it. I certainly wasn't sure that I fancied taking them on. But the firm of Luton black boys thought otherwise and headed down through the car park and straight towards them.

Within seconds, the shouting started. We hadn't followed at first, but without a word all four of us ran towards the sound of the fighting and saw that the black mob had backed off into the car park, while the ICF stood in Guildford Street, defiantly holding their ground. As we joined up with the black chaps, other Luton boys were drawn by the noise and soon our numbers were up to about 60. Once we'd got it together, we stormed back towards the Cockneys.

The first couple of Luton went straight into them and traded punches, but, as it was developing into something serious, the OB appeared from behind the West Ham, bringing a swift end to the proceedings, with honours even. In truth, I was quite happy for the fight to stop when it did, as I might actually have been called upon to get my hands dirty. Although now I could definitely say I'd seen the best firm in the country in action. In fact, I'd been within a few yards of their swinging fists and all of us had passed our first serious football hooligan test because we hadn't run.

A couple of months later, it was Nottingham Forest's turn to be entertained. They came to Luton with no real reputation that I knew of, but I was soon to discover that this didn't mean they had no firm. Once again, we headed to the town centre with the aim of tailing the Castle Bar boys and once again we were late for the action. This time we had an excuse though – Forest arrived early.

One of my mate's older brothers who ran with the Castle Bar mob called me over to explain. Thirty Forest lads had walked into the place just after opening time and chased the handful of Luton that were in there straight over the bar. By all accounts, they were big lads – all baldies and in their thirties. They'd caught Luton on the hop by coming down early and totally unexpected. His pride had been seriously dented and he wanted to do something about it. The opportunity soon arrived.

Sometime after midday, about 100 Luton mobbed up and headed off to confront the Forest thugs. Despite our superior numbers, as we approached The Duke of Clarence where they were holed up, I could sense the apprehension among us. We knew we were about to take on a right rough old mob of seasoned football thugs. And we were right to be worried too, because Forest came charging straight out of the pub with bottles and glasses flying and, after a brief struggle, we scattered everywhere. It was Ipswich all over again, as we fled tripping over each other and scrambling through the shoppers on George Street.

Some headed back towards The Castle Bar, but I ran towards the Arndale Centre, glancing back to see if anyone was close to catching me. Instead of someone snarling over my shoulder, though, I saw a fat Nottingham lad laughing and waving at us as he bellowed, 'Welcome to the First Division, Luton!'

By now, I was starting to feel down about being part of Luton's firm, as we were getting run far too often for my liking. It seemed as though our older boys weren't as good as some of the faces at other clubs and having so many youngsters wasn't helpful either. But Christmas was to change that as we faced Watford in the traditional Boxing Day derby fixture. Both clubs had been promoted the previous season and, having been to a couple of derby games already, I knew feelings ran high among Luton fans and had heard rumours that Luton were going to try to take Watford's end.

There were 21,000 packed into Kenilworth Road that day, with around 3,000 Watford fans all squashed into the section closest to the Maple. The Triangle was heaving, as hundreds of drunken lads bayed at the visitors and a constant barrage of coins was directed at them, with just as many coming back. I stood up close to the yellow parasites and spent most of the game lapping up the hostile atmosphere and gesturing towards them.

As the teams came out to warm up, it happened – a huge gap opened in the Watford section as a battle broke out at the back of their end. Luton were wind-milling into them and Elton's choirboys backed off. They regrouped below and tried to rally more lads to regain the lost ground and some did actually come forward, but again Luton forced them back and the chasm between the two sets of fans widened further. At this point, Watford stayed put and decided not to force the issue. Back in the Triangle we were in a state of frenzy by now and surged forward, trying to get on the pitch. But the police grabbed the first couple of Luton that leaped up from the Maple terrace and threw them straight back into the mass of bodies below.

Slowly, the police regained control of the Kenilworth Road End and led the Luton contingent down to the front of the terrace and towards the exit gate closest to the pitch. Once they reached the bottom, though, Watford's boys decided to steam in. Fighting started to spread back up the terrace, but once again Bedfordshire Police did their job and soon quietened things down. The Luton lads were then marched round the pitch to a riotous round of applause and choruses of 'We're proud of you…' They were our heroes for the day, along with Clive Goodyear who scored the only goal in a famous victory for us.

Later that season, I reached another landmark on my journey into hooliganism, when I was arrested at Watford in the return fixture. We lost 5–2 at Vicarage Road and I almost lost my mind too when Luther Blissett celebrated right in front of us after knocking one in. I was later released without charge, as I hadn't really done anything more than allow myself to be pushed into the police lines which came on to the terrace to curb the missile throwing during the second half. It was my first encounter with the police at football and at Watford, but not my last.

This defeat by our local rivals put Luton in a precarious position at the bottom of the league. We were staring relegation in the face and by May faced a tough challenge to stay in the top flight. On the last game of the season, Luton had to travel to Manchester City's Maine Road and win to stay in the First Division. A draw would not be good enough, but what gave the encounter even more of an edge was that we were actually competing with Man City themselves for the last remaining survival spot. If we won, it would be them going down instead of us, so it was all or nothing for both teams.

I travelled on a supporters' coach from Luton, joining more than 5,000 others on the journey up the M1 and M6. What happened that day was a miracle. We had the lion's share of possession, but couldn't get the all-important goal, until a certain Raddy Antic found himself in the right position to meet an Alex Williams punch on the volley and banged it in the net five minutes from time.

Many will no doubt recall David Pleat's brown suit and merry jig across the Maine Road pitch, but what I will always remember is the less amusing sight of an enormous crowd of raging Mancs waiting outside to kill us. Normally, I wouldn't have wanted to be locked inside a ground after full-time, but I was more than happy to be kept in as long as it took to clear this lot. There were still some scuffles in the streets, although on the whole Manchester OB did a great job of keeping things in check. I was just pleased that we'd stayed up and lived to fight another day, so to speak…

I wished now that I had stayed up last night too and maybe then the time wouldn't have passed so quickly. But here I was on the way to Luton Crown Court and so fucking nervous that I thought I was going to chuck up. Looking back to the old days helped me feel a little better – at least it showed how quickly time passed. I could only pray that it passed as quickly if I had to do porridge.

Windy was looking for somewhere to park and I insisted that we get as near to the court as possible. I didn't want my suit ruined, did I? We found a space in Staples car park, but, as soon as I opened the door, the heavens did likewise and it started to piss down again.

'Doesn't look like your day, does it?' offered Windy.

'Yeah, cheers for that, mate.' He was right, though, the omens weren't looking too good.

Then, as we turned the corner heading in the direction of the court, I saw one of the few things that could make my day even worse – a fucking camera crew. I paused. Could I afford to have my face on TV? Nope.

'Cameras – get back to the car,' I whispered.

We turned and started to jog back through the pouring rain towards the car park. I was on my toes again – all that was missing now was some fat cunt from Nottingham laughing after me and shouting, 'Welcome to the First Division, Luton!'

3 I Am What I Am

As we climbed back into Windy's motor, it dawned on me that I had to find a way of getting past that camera crew and into court without being captured on film. For years now, I had grown accustomed to avoiding the police cameras filming at most of the matches I went to. It's a bit of a mystery why the OB still takes photo after photo and film upon film of suspected football thugs. I guess it's part of their so-called 'intelligence gathering' and any evidence, however small, adds up and helps them to secure a conviction or banning order.

But I also reckon that half the football liaison teams actually get off on looking at photos of football firms going at it in their best clobber. I often wonder how Joe Public would feel if they knew that some of the police who watch over the football hooligan gangs enjoy their jobs so much because they're fascinated by the whole football scene – particularly the clothing and the violence. Some even like to tout their local club's thugs as tougher or better organised than other firms – higher in the 'League of Hooligans', as it were. Perhaps police chiefs should take a look at the numbers of officers applying for jobs on the football intelligence teams and ask why.

Usually, you get one of two possible reactions from football lads being filmed. Some play up and pull faces or give hand gestures, while the smarter ones just tuck their chins into their chests and pull their collars up instead. There is, of course, a darker side to this intelligence gathering. For many years now, the British authorities have tried to stop 'known hooligans' from travelling abroad to watch England. Until recently, the trouble they've had is that many 'known hooligans' haven't actually got any previous football-related convictions, or any convictions at all for that matter. This meant the OB didn't have the legal right to control their movements.

That's all changed now, though. The government have given the courts the power to stop any convicted football thugs from travelling abroad whenever England are playing, whether it be a competitive or a friendly match. This I can understand because, if you've been caught in the act of football violence, then in their eyes it's likely to happen again so you shouldn't be allowed to travel.

But there's another example of how the courts can stop you travelling at the time of an England game and that's where the potential problems lie. If the police suspect you are a football hooligan, they can get a court order to prevent you travelling simply by presenting 'sufficient evidence' to a judge. What amounts to sufficient evidence could be as little as a few handy snaps of you keeping company with known football hooligans.

Again, you might think this is fine. However, what if you aren't a football boy and have no previous convictions, but occasionally drink with some headcase that runs with a football firm. Let's say that one time, when you had a pint with said nutter, you were photographed by the OB and they put two and three together and decide you must be a yob as well. What if you have booked the time off work, spending good money on your flight, hotel and match ticket? You get to Heathrow Airport and Mr Plod apprehends you for being a 'known hooligan' and you miss your flight. You're also forced to go through the embarrassment and inconvenience of being towed away by the law and spending time in a cell. Then the judge looks at these photos of you socialising in the same 'notorious' public house as a known hoolie and decides that a) you're a thug and issues a banning order on you; or b) you probably aren't a football hooligan after all and refuses the OB's request for a ban, sending you on your way.

Whatever the decision, you've had to forfeit your holiday and wasted both time and money. I don't think either of these outcomes is acceptable, because 'innocent until proven guilty' is a cornerstone of our country's legal system and these new tactics ignore any decent notions of fair play.

However, any such theories were of little use to me now as I approached Luton Crown Court in the rain. Windy walked in front like a human shield, because we'd discussed in the car that, if they filmed only him, they would be less likely to show it on the evening news. We walked together with me crouched behind, trying not to look like Laurel and Hardy and keeping as close as possible to the walls of the buildings that we passed en route.

I peeped over his shoulder as we approached the camera crew, but they seemed oblivious to us and more concerned with protecting their expensive equipment from the downpour. They looked pissed off and ready to go home, as if they wanted to be there even less than me. 'Mugs,' I thought, chuckling quietly.

As we passed behind the press boys and their cameras, I broke cover to flash a smile at the nearest hack while Windy glared menacingly in an attempt to intimidate him. The sodden journalist realised he had missed me and maybe a little treat for his cameras too.

As we moved through the foyer and into the court building, though, I felt a chill pass through me. I greeted the court ushers and handed over the small kit bag of essentials that I would take with me if sent down. I dropped my wallet and a few coins into the plastic tray, then searched my other pocket and found my front-door key – I wondered when I would need that again. As I was about to place it in the tray, I hesitated, noticing the key fob made of white plastic with black print, which read 'Luton Mig Crew'. It was hardly a 'Not Guilty' plea. The usher looked at it, then at me. I smiled as I remembered the day we said goodbye to the name Stockwood Pringle Boys and merged into 'the Migs'.

Back in 1983, I was entering the final stages of my secondary education. I hadn't really been putting much effort into lessons for a while now and only really enjoyed English literature, because I got to sit next to my pal Demus. Together, we based as much of our written work as possible on football violence. I wrote about being a copper – trying to escort 30 Oldham Casuals safely to Hillsborough from Sheffield Station, foreshadowing a trip I would make a few years later. I gave a detailed account of the day's events and my attempts to keep the two sets of fans apart – I was quite successful too and managed to only make the one arrest!

Demus, meanwhile, was a local reporter who witnessed scenes of mass violence as Luton supporters invaded sections of Vicarage Road. He used a collection of clippings from the local rag about a fight between punk rockers and skinheads at the local carnival, putting them to great effect as illustrations for his essay. I was impressed, although I couldn't help but giggle at the idea of a football firm looking like those spiky-haired freaks!

I had recently returned from a trip to Brittany in France and couldn't wait for the football season to get into full swing and our mid-August away trip to Leicester City. I'd gone with only one thought in mind – to purchase a Fila tracksuit at any cost. I wasn't alone on this mission, as Big Cliff (or Small, as he was sometimes known) was also keen to get some decent clobber for the coming season. He was in our year at school, but it was only recently that he'd shown any signs of wanting to get involved in the hooligan scene. Cliff was a big lump for his age – well over six feet tall and built to match. He had been to a fair number of Luton Town games before, but stood alongside his sister at most of them! Now he was showing more interest in becoming part of the Stockwood Pringle Boys and was the owner of some fine designer jumpers, including a rather nice stone-coloured Lyle & Scott roll-neck.

On the first day of our week-long trip, we found our way to a small sports shop and spent every penny we had. I bought a white Fila tracksuit top with navy blue trim, while Small got a full Sergio Tacchini tracksuit – sky blue with red trim. I was made up with my purchase because every Fila item I had seen until then had a Bjorn Borg 'Bj' logo next to the Fila badge. Mine didn't have the tennis player's initials, so I felt I had something special to make me stand out.

For what would be the last time in their history, the Stockwood Pringle Boys set off to watch Luton Town – at Leicester for a night match. It was 13 August 1983 and things were about to change forever. On a cool summer evening and after an uneventful promenade prior to the game, we strutted into Filbert Street as happy as can be. We weren't the same as all the other Luton football lads, we were Casuals and fucking proud of it too. We looked the dog's bollocks in our Fila, Tacchini, Pringle and Lyle & Scott garms and nothing could knock the grins from our faces as the dozen of us walked on to the terrace.

But then two things happened when our little crew appeared among the 1,500 or so Hatters fans. First, most of our fellow Lutonians chose to stare and quite a few openly giggled at us. In a way, though, this was just the reaction we wanted because our dress code made a statement – 'we aren't like you and we don't want to be'. After the initial interest, though, they left us to it and went back to their singing. But then, to our right, a whole block of lads in the home supporters' seats stood up and applauded us. It was the Leicester Baby Squad.

Before then, I hadn't even heard of them, but there must have been 200 seated together and nearly every one of them had the 'gear' on. It was like a tennis players' convention! Ellesse, Fila and Sergio Tacchini as far as the eye could see. They even had a couple of girls dressed in Fila tennis skirts with them. I was gobsmacked.

The Baby Squad boys were mainly in their early twenties with the classic wedge haircut and beckoned us over to the fence for a chat. They immediately asked me about my tracksuit top and where I'd found it. It felt good having these older lads paying me some respect for my dress sense. They also complimented us on our little crew, as they hadn't expected Luton to have any Casuals at all. Then, just as we were feeling all chuffed with ourselves, one of them asked, 'So what's your mob called then, lads?'

We all went blank, silenced by the question. I thought to myself, 'Stockwood Pringle Boys?! How the fuck am I going to tell them we're named after our fucking school?'

It was clear that we'd outgrown our name, especially as Pringles were old hat now that the tennis labels were taking over as the gear to be seen in. Then Ging came over to join our huddle and reminded us of a row his own little crew had been involved in during an FA Youth Cup match against Norwich. His desire to create a good young football mob was infectious and we were soon singing from the same hymn sheet as him and his mate Les. They had already made the transition that Luton needed and no longer was the firm going to act like a predictable bunch of drunken brawlers. Now they were going to think about their every move and do so under a new name as well. We knew we had to get on board.

During the previous 18 months at Stockwood High School, the pair of them had been etching a certain name – 'Mig Crew' – into the desks and by now it was scratched practically everywhere. It started to appear around the time that everyone picked up on the first West Ham ICF documentary *A Knocker's Tale*. Ging and Les told us that it was a piss-take of the ICF and Leeds Service Crew names. They'd heard about Mig fighter planes in the news reports from the Falklands War – the Argies had a couple – and taken the word 'Mig' to mean 'fighter' in Russian. A Mig is a combat plane and an aircraft needs a crew – hence the Mig Crew. I guess that old documentary on the ICF has a lot to answer for.

So what had started as a bit of a laugh as we mimicked the West Ham lads in the film was now about to be taken a step further. We strolled back over to the Baby Squad standing closest to the fence. 'By the way... we're the Migs.'

We all smiled – it sounded good. We weren't just kids any more and were finally being accepted by the older lads. We had become part of the new football scene happening not only at Luton, but also right across the country. Now we were a proper football firm – the Luton Mig Crew. Leicester's lads nodded and returned to their seats, their curiosity satisfied.

I spent more time watching the Baby Squad than the match. I was checking the array of garms on display and wondering if our mob would ever match them for size and appearance. At half-time, we got chatting with them again. The conversation was friendly and mostly about clothes, until the OB came over to move us away from the fence separating our sections.

They came in shoving and spewing out insults, which made one of our lads, Cube, lose his rag. He grabbed the fence and wouldn't let go when the OB tried to pull him away. It became farcical as four policemen grappled with a 16-year-old school kid, but just couldn't dislodge him. We shouted encouragement and to our surprise some of the Baby Squad joined in too. The noise levels rose higher still as everybody started to jeer the police. Soon we were all laughing together.

Eventually, they grew tired of trying to move him by peaceful means and an officer on the opposite side of the fence began hitting the back of Cube's hands with his government-issue baton. He managed not to show any signs of pain, but finally had to let go and was led away to spend the rest of the evening in the nick, although fortunately he wasn't charged.

The game was great for Town fans as we strolled to a comfortable 3–0 victory. Leicester had just been promoted and the step up looked too much for them at times – you'd never have guessed that they would finish above us come the end of the season. So, the Stockwood Pringle Boys were absorbed into the newly formed Mig Crew and as we left Filbert Street I felt a new wave of optimism run through me – things were going to get better now, for sure.

For the remainder of the 83/84 season, we had little action worthy of comment until Stoke came in early May. They were struggling against relegation, but could boast Ian Painter who had a good performance against Luton earlier in the season, although he was on the wrong side of a 4–2 scoreline that day.

Prior to their visit, all the talk had been about the chances of trouble. They had a reputation as a mob not shy of a proper row – unlike some of the northern mobs who only came to Luton to smash shop windows and abuse any black player on show. We were expecting them to travel in huge numbers, as they needed to lift their team in the fight to avoid the dreaded drop. On the day, they only brought around 2,500, much less than expected, but gave wonderful vocal support to their side anyway.

At the final whistle, some of Stoke's jubilant fans invaded the Kenilworth Road pitch to celebrate their win, but, as was traditional at the last home game of the season, Luton supporters also ran on to applaud their heroes. I climbed the heavy fencing to join the mass of people gathering on the turf and, within seconds, it kicked off. The Stoke boys were positioned in front of the away terrace at the Kenilworth Road End of the stadium, which put them in close proximity to the Maple Road. As they stood clapping their fellow supporters back on the terrace, Luton fans rushed over the wall and started to wade into them. They fought back, but the ruck died down momentarily, as the OB led them off the pitch.

However, rather unwisely, the police chose to escort this small band of 50 Stokies through the Triangle. From there, Luton launched a series of assaults at the police lines. Luckily for Stoke and the OB, though, many of the Maple lads were already on the pitch and couldn't get back to the action.

As we stood watching these scuffles break out, one of the Luton lads on the pitch started to call everyone together. Once there were enough of us listening, he ordered us all to run across the pitch and out of the emergency gates in the Bobbers Stand opposite. Around 150 of us moved as one out into the cramped alley that runs the full length of one side of the ground. There we turned right and headed towards the junction of Kenilworth Road and Hazelbury Crescent.

When you come to the top of the alley, it opens out into a wider space where fans access a corner section of the ground. We filtered out into this area to mob up and, without anyone explaining what the plan was, we instinctively set up a bushwhack.

We knew that the battles in the Maple Road would soon end and the Stoke fans in the away section would then be allowed to leave and link up with the rest of their compatriots who'd been fighting on the pitch. Once outside the ground, the Stoke fans who came by coach would make their way to the car park, but there would be another crowd that travelled by train and would want to continue fighting on the streets. These were the targets of our surprise attack. We hoped that, by charging them when they didn't expect it, we would create enough panic to run them, giving us the result of the day – especially as they had no way of knowing exactly how many of us might be hiding round the corner.

But, as we waited, we grew nervous. Some of the lads discussed the fighting that had gone on before the game, when Stoke had impressed everyone with both their willingness to trade punches and the sheer size of their mob. The firm gathered for the ambush was growing impatient now and plenty had already drifted away from the pack. We still had close to 100 huddled in the alley, but I knew the row had to start soon or we'd just melt away altogether. So I left the safety of the mob and started towards the top of Kenilworth Road to see where Stoke were. It proved to be a mistake.

As I was about to turn the corner into Kenilworth Road, I almost bumped straight into 30 lads whose accents told me they weren't from round these parts. I turned sharply and walked back towards the ambush point. The Stoke boys stopped and beckoned the rest of their crew down the busy road to join them. Around me, lads from either side started to square up, while the normal fans in the street began to evacuate the area, not wanting to get caught up in the violence about to break out.

As I approached the waiting Luton firm, a big roar went up as the lads caught sight of the Stokies and charged forward, sending them fleeing back up Kenilworth Road towards the rest of their number. It seemed like we had them on the run as planned, but I was wrong – we had sprung our trap too soon. Stoke came steaming back down towards us and they looked game as fuck, bouncing up and down in a solid pack, maybe 100-strong. They had no fear at all and began trading heavy punches with some of our older lads. It was too much for most of us. We turned and ran towards the relative safety of the dark alley from which we had emerged only minutes earlier.

The narrow path became a mass of bodies clambering over each other in an attempt to escape the Stoke lads behind and panic spread as the bottleneck quickly became a dead end. We shoved and pushed in total disorder as fear took hold. Then, when we couldn't all get into the alley, things actually started to change for the better because we were forced to turn and face them. And it wasn't as bad as I first thought. Sure, we'd run, but a few Luton lads were still putting up a fight and, even though they were obviously coming second, we responded to their calls for back-up.

I am sure if Stoke had wanted to they could have carried the battle right into the alleyway, but their hesitation gave us a chance to get our act together. I felt a rush of pure adrenaline and, along with a dozen or so others, charged back at them. They backed off just enough for other Luton lads to believe in the cause and join our rearguard action. We soon closed the space that had opened up between the two groups to engage the enemy.

The fighting became particularly intense and vicious, as both sides tried to outmanoeuvre the other in the street. Some lads were swinging wildly at each other, while others backed away, fearful of becoming isolated from their group. I threw myself forward as a gap opened in front of me. Immediately, I was punched twice in the head by this stocky Stoke lad in a red sweater and tried to throw one back, but didn't quite connect properly.

Then, as I searched the line of Stokies for my next target, a lad not much older than myself burst out of the crowd and launched half a brick at me from close range. I swear he had horns sticking out of his head! Instinctively, I turned away from the missile flying towards me and... bang! It hit me just above my right ear, knocking me straight on my arse. It was more of a shock than anything else and actually hurt less than you might think.

In a split second, Cube pulled me to my feet. Then everything was a blur, but I was still aware of the OB getting involved in the fights raging all around and my mate screaming at them that I'd been hit by a brick. The next thing I remember is the police forcing me back towards the Luton crowd. I was shepherded along by Cube who was fuming and swore revenge on the bloke who'd nearly knocked my head off. I couldn't see the wound myself, but knew I had been hurt because blood was flowing down the side of my head into the neck of my Patrick cagoule.

I was worried about the injury, but didn't want to show it because a few of the older lads were starting to take an interest in me now. I received words of encouragement from total strangers and pats on the back from faces I recognised. My head hurt, but the feeling of pride eased the pain. In fact, the wound was worth the good vibes I felt as I strolled proudly along Dunstable Road among Luton's boys. I had stood my ground and many of them hadn't.

Within the hour, I left the mob and made my way to my girlfriend's house. As the attention I received from my fellow thugs subsided, though, the thumping in my head increased. I knocked on her door and she was glad to see me until she caught sight of my war wound and screeched, 'You've got a hole in your bloody head!'

Shortly afterwards I was on my way to Luton and Dunstable Hospital to get stitched up.

As I sat in the waiting room, I thought over what had happened earlier.

The Stoke lads were so game in the face of our badly timed ambush. Why were they better than us? Numbers hadn't played a part in proceedings, as they were pretty equal. And it wasn't as if they had caught us on the hop either – we were the ones who laid the trap and had the element of surprise in our favour.

I decided it was their mental strength that had made the difference. They had greater self-belief and were so much more confident than us. As they had stormed down Kenilworth Road, they had smiles on their faces and a togetherness that we just didn't possess. I wanted us to be as confident and tight as them and for other crews to doubt themselves when they faced us. I soon found myself getting frustrated. Not only was the day over and we had missed a chance to claim a pretty big scalp in the hooligan world, but it was also the end of the season and there wasn't any more football for months. No football and no football violence – what was I going to do?

I spent the summer of '84 telling and retelling the story of our piss-poor attempt at an ambush and how I'd stood my ground against blokes twice my size. I showed my little battle-scar to anyone who cared to look, but usually ended up embarrassed, as most people asked 'is that it?' disappointed after all my big talk. In July, my father went on holiday with my two brothers, but I stayed at my next-door neighbour's house with 'the Jew'. He was two years older than me and I had known him for most of my young life. He wasn't actually Jewish, but had earned the nickname for being so fucking tight and having a huge nose – although, come to think of it, my nose is even bigger than his!

It was while I was staying with his family that the following season's fixtures came out. I had already bored him with my stories of football violence and retold the tale of the Stoke clash almost every night, as we smoked joints listening to Lionel Ritchie's *All Night Long* album. He'd had his ears bent out of shape with stories about the designer labels we wore, who was game and who wasn't so game.

Up until then, the Jew hadn't really taken that much interest in football or the violence that surrounded it, but as time passed he seemed to be asking more questions. He became particularly interested when I swore revenge on Stoke and wanted to know how I planned to do it, as their firm sounded far superior to ours.

I'd decided that I would seek revenge by whatever means possible. I already had ambitions to be one of Luton's main faces and wanted to earn a reputation for bravery. The rewards were there to be taken. I had discovered this after the clash at the end of the previous season and enjoyed the feeling of pride when people I didn't know praised my actions. Now I wanted more. I wanted Luton to have a mob to be proud of and I was prepared to risk my own safety to help achieve it.

The fixtures for the 84/85 season had a real surprise in store. As I opened the Jew's newspaper, searching eagerly for the Town's opening fixture, I saw it – 25 August, Luton v Stoke City! I leaped around the Jew's bedroom in ecstasy. He snatched the paper to see it with his own eyes and within moments was sporting a huge smile as well.

Once we'd calmed down, we started to talk more seriously about what might happen. It seemed logical that Stoke would travel in force again because it was the first game of the season, when every team's supporters travelled in greater numbers. They've been starved of football through the long summer and expectations are high. This temporary growth in travelling support also increased the potential size of any hooligan element. So it was almost guaranteed that Stoke's mob would be in Luton town centre again come the 25th and we would have to be prepared.

Some of Luton's young mob had decided to meet in a pub known as The Studio. This was an alternative boozer which local lads congregated in on some match days, popular with skinheads during the late 70s and early 80s. It was in a great spot for defending the town centre against invading away supporters, because if they came by train and wanted a few jars they had to pass its big windows, from where they would be spotted immediately.

Many of Luton's lads would no doubt meet at The Castle Bar or one of many other pubs in the town centre, but I decided to go to The Studio and join the many younger faces now evolving into Luton's next generation of football hooligans. The Jew was also talking like he was going to join the lads that day as well, which was surprising as he hadn't been to more than a couple of matches in his whole life and wasn't really the type to get involved in football violence. Nevertheless, I wasn't going to discourage him. In fact, I did the opposite and tied him into a pact.

Within just an hour of reading the opening day's fixtures, I had a rough plan of action. I knew Stoke would be coming and figured they'd be too strong for Luton again, so something had to be done to raise our confidence. I decided to confront their crew – on my own if necessary – and, if they hesitated long enough, I would make the first move just as I had with the bullies at school. I knew I'd probably get hurt, but it didn't matter. If that's what it took to inspire Luton's firm to take the initiative, then so be it. The worst that could happen is I would collect another scar to show the girls!

Now I brought the Jew in by explaining that Luton would almost certainly be pushed back by Stoke's lads and may even end up getting run around town in complete panic. Before long, he had promised to stand by my side and swore not to let me take a kicking on my own. I'm not sure why, but the thought of someone sharing my fate gave me confidence. So it was set – the Jew and I would face the Stoke hordes, alone if need be.

The next few weeks dragged by. I split from my girlfriend, which didn't bother me much at the time, but I also grew more distant from my father. He was a good man and wouldn't have approved of what I was getting involved in and I didn't want him to know, as I could do without more arguments. To him, loutish behaviour was unacceptable and I'm sure he would have confronted me to try to show me the error of my ways. It wasn't his fists I was scared of, though – I just didn't want to disappoint him.

When I opened my eyes on the morning of the Stoke game, I was back at home. My family were still talking about their holiday, but I couldn't have cared less. All I was interested in was drying my Fila tracksuit top and cleaning my Diadora trainers in time. Once dressed appropriately, I knocked the Jew up and was pleasantly surprised to find him dressed like a proper chap rather than one of the Castle Bar throwbacks.

We bounded down Hightown Road and on to The Studio, but were disappointed to find ourselves some of the first to enter the place. We'd hoped to find the pub heaving with hundreds of lads keen to confront the visiting hordes and I felt a flash of anger pass through me – was I the only one who cared about our reputation?

The Jew surprised me again by getting the drinks in and, as we sat close to the pub doors, I kept on telling myself that I would steam straight into the Stokies as soon as I saw them. I was hyper and the Jew soon tired of listening, so, when a few more of the lads entered the bar, he soon joined them. I sat alone, mulling over what I was preparing to do – it was going to take real bottle and I was apprehensive.

I rubbed the scar over my ear and, thinking back to just a couple of months earlier, pictured the face of the Stoke lad who had dropped me with that lump of masonry. I wanted him to be there, I wanted revenge.

Then, the doors of the pub burst open and Norfs, a Runfold lad, hurried in. 'Stoke are here! They're at The Clarence!'

Norfs was one of the earlier Migs and had a strange sense of humour, which usually involved belittling members of the public. You either liked Norfs or hated him but, one thing was for sure, he was a real character. He'd just got off the bus into town, spotted Stoke's mob arriving and run straight to The Studio to report the news. Apparently, they were about 50-strong and big lads.

I rose from my stool and walked out of the pub without a word. As I marched in the direction of The Clarence at some pace, I went into my shell and felt a little light-headed. But then I became aware of lads all around me – Luton's mob was on the move and, although we were young, it had more quality on board than usual. I was determined to complete the task that I set myself. I think, if I had turned back at this point, I would have probably retired from the football scene forever.

As we neared the Town Hall, we heard shouting and the sound of breaking glass. We sped up the march to a slow jog until we arrived at a scene that gave me hope for the future of Luton's firm. Stoke's crew of around 50 had left The Clarence and were faced by a similar-sized mob of local lads. At the front of the Luton mob was Gypsy John, a really game lad who had a reputation for knocking people out and was said to be a veteran of bare-knuckle fights. Now he was offering one to the Stokies.

Behind him, the rest of the Luton lads were jostling with each other and shouting at the opposition. They weren't Casuals, but mainly beer monsters that'd got caught up in the fighting and were sticking around to give it a go. The pavement around the Town Hall was littered with broken glass and it looked as though the Stoke lads had come out of The Duke of Clarence with everything they could get their hands on. The local boys were more than happy to have their numbers doubled by the arrival of our smartly dressed crew.

Now was to be my moment. I walked calmly around the edge of the Luton contingent at the Town Hall and straight into the 10-foot gap between the two rival firms. I glanced across at John as I turned to the northern mob and knew he would back me.

'Come on, you cunts,' I screamed, flying towards the centre of their line.

Punches rained down on my head as I steamed in, but I kept windmilling and things seemed to be going well as a roar warmed my eardrums. Luton were joining the battle and Stoke were definitely backing off. The adrenaline was pumping through my veins like never before and I loved it. I got whacked in the face, but didn't feel a thing – I was high as a kite and thought nothing could stop me ploughing into them. I was wrong.

A punch from nowhere caught me clean in the nose and I halted, struggling to make out who had hit me. My eyes were watering, but I could make out the colour of his clothing – he was dressed in black and wore a tall black hat. I squinted again and gritted my teeth as he closed on me, anticipating his next blow. But then came a shock of a different kind: 'You're nicked!'

The copper grabbed me and dragged me towards the waiting van parked just yards from the scene of the battle. I looked back and lads were fighting everywhere, but more OB were on the scene now and it would all be over soon. I was shoved into the back of the meat wagon and handcuffed roughly. Then I noticed someone else already sitting in the van. We both laughed, it was the Jew.

'You ain't going to believe this,' I choked and turned to the copper, 'we're next-door neighbours!'

He had stood by me after all and got nicked for running into the Stokies with me for the privilege. I couldn't stop laughing all the way to the cells and the coppers in the van with us saw the funny side too. In fact, somewhat surprisingly, they were very impressed with our efforts against the Stoke mob and congratulated us on our bravery, explaining that they'd expected Luton to run away.

For the Jew and me, the day was over – we spent the rest of it in the cells. Outside, though, the violence carried on with Luton continuing to take the battle to them before the game. But, afterwards, things didn't go so well when Stoke gathered a huge crew on Dunstable Road and ran our boys back in the direction of Beech Hill School.

In September, we appeared before the magistrates at Luton. We used the duty solicitor and offered no credible excuse for our actions. But the briefs did their bit, explaining that we were only 16 years old and had been led on by older lads. My solicitor plucked on the magistrate's heartstrings and pointed out that I'd had an unhappy childhood. The Jew was less fortunate, because he was from a solid family background and couldn't play the part of social victim, especially with his whole family viewing the proceedings from in the public gallery.

We were both warned about our conduct and told we were a disgrace to normal football fans and indeed football itself. I was fined £250 and he got

£350. I left the court smiling alongside my mate Nigel P, but the Jew looked sheepish as he was hustled away by his family into one of the waiting areas used by solicitors to chat with their clients. I didn't envy him at all.

I ended up drinking with half a dozen Stoke lads who'd been arrested at the game. We chatted as if we were long-lost mates, swapping stories of violent encounters and our thoughts on the events of the month before. They were at least 10 years older than me, but one thing was for sure – Luton had earned their respect. They knew they'd been in a row and invited us to make the trip up to Stoke later in the year. Of course, we accepted and swore blind that we would bring a big firm up to the Potteries for the return game, although deep down I think we knew that wasn't very likely.

'When the Migs get older, they'll be a decent mob, mate,' declared one of the larger Stokies, but I wondered if he was taking the piss.

'Well, if you're a decent mob, we ain't that far off now,' said Nigel P, fixing his glare on the big northerner.

I wondered if he was thinking what I was thinking. But the Stoke lads decided to leave. They shook our hands and one even patted me on the back before saying his goodbyes.

Staring at my key fob, I wondered what those Stoke lads thought of the Mig Crew now. Had we lived up to their expectations and become a 'decent mob' – or were they still taking the piss? As I was about to appear before a Crown Court judge and possibly pay a heavy price for football violence, I hoped they remembered that day and recognised that the Migs had become the sort of football firm they'd envisaged all those years ago.

It was strange. Here I was facing a prison sentence and all the consequences that go with it, but I was still wondering whether we had made the right impression on some group of lads from another part of the country 20 years ago. I placed my key in the tray already containing the other items removed from my pocket, making sure I placed the writing face down. I didn't want the court staff to notice the words. But, just as the smiling security man reached for the tray, I grabbed it back and turned it over again. 'I am a Mig,' I thought. 'I'm a football thug and that's that. I am what I am and nothing can change that now.'

I passed the tray to the guard and he stared down at the contents before passing it through the scanner.

I looked him in the eye. 'He knows… he fucking knows.'

If he did, he never said anything, passing back my belongings and wishing me good luck, which threw me a little. Then I turned to head up the stairs towards my fate.

 **You Can't Come Down Here!**

There are times in a man's life when he questions his own actions and maybe even his own sanity. I have certainly had do to this quite regularly. At the top of the Crown Court stairs, I paused and wondered whether it had all been worth it – and I wasn't just thinking about the recent 'off' on Watford High Street that had put me here today. I asked myself – not for the first time and probably not for the last – if being involved in football violence for over 20 years had been a waste of time. What else could I have done with my life if I hadn't joined the mob that fought with Stoke's lads that day? What if I had just stayed on the terrace until the end of the match and headed home with the 'normal' fans?

If I'd just strolled towards Hightown and my family home all those years ago, maybe I would have lived a 'normal' life. You know, two-point-four children and all that. I could have been an IT manager and walked the dog every morning, before climbing into my hatchback and ploughing down the motorway to my recently refurbished office building near the M25. I thought about it for a total of three seconds and then, 'Fuck that!' I got my senses back.

What could be better than standing outside The Bell in the centre of Norwich, knowing that you've just run the local firm twice, despite being outnumbered three or four to one? What could beat the buzz of laying into some mouthy idiot who's just charged 100 metres up a busy shopping street, shouting and screaming for your blood? Then you bash him into submission, watching him curl up in fear when his mates fail to back him. What could be better than watching hundreds of Norwich lads who'd just been put on their toes realise they were only running from a small band of

Luton, suddenly regain their bottle and launch a counter-charge back up the High Street towards us? And, finally, what could be better than running the gauntlet of masses of East Anglian thugs seeking revenge for the embarrassment of being run by a mob so small it hurt their pride? So that was my sanity sorted – no problem there!

My real problem was the impending hearing in front of Judge Cripps and the sentences he was likely to hand out. I'd been to court on many occasions before, so I felt more or less at ease in these surroundings. The last time had been in Scotland a couple of years earlier, when after a two-hour trial I was rightly found 'Not Guilty' by the magistrate.

I'd been nicked near Jamaica Bridge for threatening behaviour prior to the Scotland v England playoff. The OB claimed that I had provoked a fight with other English supporters, but in fact I'd been hassled by a group of Oxford United fans who thought I was from Reading, after spotting me drinking in the same pub as some of their rivals. Initially, they had come up close behind me, kicked at my heels and challenged me through tight lips: 'Come on, Reading.'

I stopped – mainly because they were crowded right round me – but I also had to process exactly what had just been said. I was on my own at the time, but knowing there was about 30 Migs just round the corner, I took the bait. 'Migs ya dealing with,' I replied.

They looked a bit taken back at this, as they were probably expecting me to shy away from the confrontation. Their main player was an older West Indian lad. He took his chance for a lead role in the scene being acted out, approaching me as menacingly as he could. But, when I looked in his eyes, there was no real aggression and I knew he wasn't really that keen on having it now.

I made a quick decision to control what happened next. 'Let's take it round the corner then, you muppet, the OB are too close here.'

He was quick to pick up the gauntlet, but some of his little crew weren't so keen.

Just as we turned the corner away from the prying eyes of the OB, two Migs, Baby B and Buzz, came to my aid. When it comes to football violence, Buzz had all but given up on the club scene, although he still enjoyed watching England away, especially in the Eastern Bloc. So now there were three of us and we were more than game, despite being heavily outnumbered by these Oxford chaps in their best Stone Island gear.

Their leader stepped up first and I went forward to meet him. He was stocky but looked well past his sell-by date. I quite fancied my chances of knocking him out in one and formed my right hand into a fist, lining up his jaw ready to strike as soon as he stepped into range. He hesitated for a moment and glanced around – obviously wary of OB and also any lads that could strike him from the side or behind. Every football boy runs these things through his mind when it's about to kick off, otherwise the consequences can be terrible. He glared at a couple of his troops and nodded to encourage them to come closer – but they didn't respond. I thought they'd bottled it, but soon clocked why they didn't fancy it… police.

The OB came straight over and started to push and pull people apart. Of course, the Oxford boy chose this moment to step forward and stuck his nose right in my face. He gave it the usual bullshit – 'come on, Luton' and all that crap, even though he knew full well that it couldn't happen now. I shoved him back to get his ugly mug as far away from me as possible and the OB pounced immediately. They didn't stop to ask any questions, dragging me away from the scene back on to the main road and ordering me to move on or I would be arrested.

I started to walk, but became aware of lads closing around me – more Oxford. 'You fucking mugs, who the fuck do you think you are?' I was fuming, they were nothing and I wanted to get stuck in and prove it. Spotting Baby B nearby, I told him to run ahead and get a handful of our lads together so we could smash them. Then I was pushed firmly in the back. It was the same copper who had ordered me away from the scene earlier. 'Move, or I'll nick you!' he bellowed in a thick Jock accent.

I did so, but in my anger headed across the busy road towards the 20 or so Oxford lads opposite. I wanted to have a word so we could sort out a meet as soon as possible, but the OB were having none of it and ordered me back on to the pavement. The Oxford crew moved quickly along their side of the street, hurrying through the hundreds of supporters making their way to Hampden Park.

I wanted to keep pace and stay in contact, but the crowds on my side of the road were moving too slowly, so I stepped out into the street separating us. This time I managed to shout across at the Oxford lads within earshot: 'You're nothing – what have you ever done?' I asked. 'You're going to get it, you stupid cunts!'

None chose to reply; they just kept on walking through the crowds.

I was grabbed by the OB again, called an 'English bastard' and ordered back on to the pavement to join Buzz. He read my mind. 'They're fuck all, Tom.'

I started to calm down a little. 'OK. Let's keep them in sight until we can get close again.'

The two crowds were shoved together again further down the road at a busy junction. I could either join the crowd being corralled behind a crash barrier close to the junction of the two main roads and risk losing sight of the Oxford lads, or walk around it on to on the road and upset any OB who spotted me. I chose the second option.

As I edged around the fencing, I kept my head down and stayed as close to the kerb as possible so as not to attract more attention. But two Jock coppers pointed at me from across the street. 'Stop right there, son!' It was an older constable. I explained that I knew how to cross the road and didn't need him as my lollipop lady, to which he replied, 'That's enough from you today – I'm arresting you for breach of the peace.'

I thought he was joking and started to laugh, but soon realised he was all too serious when I found myself bundled into the back of a meat wagon and heading off to spend a weekend in the cells.

As I was locked up, of course, England won 2–0 and took a giant step towards qualifying for the European Championships. My cell, meanwhile, was beyond disgusting and certainly hadn't been cleaned in the last decade or so. I was greeted there by a young, shaven-headed northerner who seemed happy to hear another English voice.

His name was Martin, from Oldham, and he ran with their firm, the 'Fine Young Casuals'. Martin wasn't the healthiest-looking thug I had seen, although drinking lager for 12 solid hours prior to his arrest probably didn't help. But he'd kept his sense of humour and remained in high spirits for a while. After a couple of hours, though, he started to feel thirsty and became desperate for a drink. We tried the 'call' buzzer, but either they didn't care or more likely it just didn't work. He was getting really dehydrated now and started to bang on the cell door for help. Still no one came. In Martin's view, there was only one thing to do now… drink from the toilet!

He approached the pan in the corner of the cell and looked down at the water. It was filthy – the bowl was green from corrosion and dried shit stains covered the side of the pan. There were piss splashes all over the filthy cesspit and most had turned crusty with time. It was horrendous, like the bog scene in *Trainspotting*, but at least Renton hadn't intended to drink from the fucking thing!

'You can't, mate! Don't do it!' I wanted to throw up just looking at the stinking toilet, but this poor bastard was seriously contemplating parching his thirst with a cool, refreshing glass of bog water! I couldn't believe it and watched with a mixture of horror and concern as Martin bent down to drink. Suddenly, though, his face became a picture, as he realised the full horror of what he was about to do. And then it happened – he let out a gagging sound and reeled back trying not to chuck up his insides. He looked as though he was crying and clamped his hand over his mouth. 'No fucking way,' he dribbled.

I rolled about on the dusty cell floor, pissing myself with laughter at the ridiculousness of the situation. I was locked up in a semi-disused Glasgow Police Station, inside a grubby dungeon with no lights and a buzzer that didn't fucking work. I was dehydrating fast and getting hungry too, with no real hope of solving either problem in the near future. What's more, I was sharing my cell with a nutty northerner, who was so desperate that he was almost prepared to permanently risk his health by drinking from a toilet crapped in by the filthiest junkies in Scotland. It was getting medieval in here.

I pictured my mates pissing it up in Glasgow Cross, probably toasting my health throughout the night and celebrating England's fine victory over the 'Old Enemy' – although, I actually found out later, that they were laughing their heads off and chasing ginger women around all the pubs in the city.

Martin managed to hold on to the contents of his stomach, but he didn't look too good at all. Eventually, he slumped down next to me, rolled sideways on to the dirty cell floor and started snoring. I paced around the fast-darkening cell and, after giving the malfunctioning buzzer a few hopeful prods, followed the Lancashire lad's example, stretching out in the corner to sleep.

I could have slept for a good while too, but suddenly a strange sound caught my attention. It was only quiet, but it was enough to wake me. At first, my sleepy senses couldn't make head or tail of what was happening on the other side of the dingy room – the noises were somehow familiar, but unnatural in this place. I thought I could hear gulping sounds.

I forced open my eyes and saw a shape moving around over in the far corner of the box-shaped room. Confused, I looked back to where Martin had bedded down and saw his horrible purple shirt draped over his overweight torso as he snoozed away. So who else was in with us and what in

God's name was going on over there in the dark? I looked again in horror. Whoever it was that had joined our happy band was going further than even Martin had dared and was bent over drinking the rank toilet water!

Our new cellmate stood upright, licked his lips and wiped his face with the front panels of his shirt. He was a skinhead in his mid-thirties, towering well over six foot and introduced himself as Marcus. Apparently, he was a 'Headhunter'.

The Chelsea Headhunters were a big name in football and a force to be reckoned with right from the 70s through to the early 90s. They left their mark on the map by rampaging all over the country in huge numbers. I had seen them infiltrate the Oak Road End at Luton on two occasions in the early 80s and watched in disbelief as they rioted through Bury Park like a terrace tornado, causing maximum damage to anything in their path.

Now here was somebody claiming to be a proper Headhunter. I had my doubts, but, as the sun rose and the light in the cell improved, Marcus became more visible. I was impressed by the dense scars littering his head and face – he was clearly a man of action and not just words. Certainly, his encounter with the bog had shown he wasn't scared to get stuck in and as we spoke it soon became apparent that he'd been involved in numerous incidents of football violence with Chelsea, receiving a string of convictions for his trouble.

Any lingering doubts regarding his Headhunter claims were removed when the cell door suddenly swung open and two plain-clothes OB stuck their heads in, enquiring in a childish tone, 'Which one's our Headhunter then?'

'Who's asking?' Marcus replied and stepped towards the coppers standing shoulder to shoulder in the doorway. They stood their ground, smiling as he approached them. 'Any chance of a cup of tea, chaps?'

The two rozzers looked at each other and then back at Marcus before agreeing to his demand, wearing smarmy grins. You had to admire the bloke, he was at home in this environment and wasn't at all rattled or upset, even with his ample stomach containing the contents of our now horribly visible toilet. We all got some tea, though, so no more trips to the improvised drinking fountain were required.

The following morning, we made our way to the court in a windowless minibus along with 20 or so 'usual suspects'. Everyone was handcuffed to the guy next to them and I got Mad Marcus. With us were various faces who I'd met prior to my arrest, including a short Asian lad from West

Brom. I'd seen their mob in the city early doors and they were pretty fortunate because 10 minutes after they left a huge crew of Birmingham arrived, asking if we'd seen any West Brom or Villa lads about. I don't think they were looking to have a quiet drink with them either! We heard later that they found Villa Youth in a pub just round the corner and smashed them in a ferocious attack.

Once contained in the holding cells beneath the court building, we were fed a Scottish fish supper. It was the first thing we had eaten in 36 hours and we ate ravenously, swapping stories about our arrests. Each tiny cell housed eight inmates inside three solid brick walls and a metal grille, like the ones you see in old Western films. Directly opposite was a large caged area, which was empty at first, but within an hour was stuffed with 60 noisy Jocks.

So, as we sat crammed in our tiny boxes, just six or seven feet away stood a whole herd of sweaty Scottish crims. And they knew that we were English. I suspected that most of them had never been to England and never wanted to. I respected this more than I did those plastic Jocks who live down south and rant and rave so much about 'Bonnie Scotland', but still choose to stay and make a life in our 'Jerusalem'. However, I didn't respect them much for the scummy behaviour that followed.

As the Englishmen relaxed, kicked back and traded war stories, these cunts took turns to run up from one side of their cage and spit through the bars in our direction. It was quite possibly the most childish behaviour I have ever witnessed from so-called football lads. They were pathetic and I had to tell them, so I stood up to a chorus of catcalls and screaming Jocks. 'That's why you cunts will never be taken serious as a mob,' I bellowed at the Sweaties in their animal pen and awaited their response.

But all I got was more obscenities in rough Glaswegian accents and, of course, about a dozen more gobs of Scottish spit aimed in my direction. Then the direct threats started, with one in particular mentioning a certain government establishment: 'Yooz will dee' in Barlinnie tay-night!'

I couldn't believe what I was hearing. These cunts were really trying to intimidate us, and to a point it was working, as I noticed many of our boys letting their heads drop. I wasn't prepared to let it happen though and had to do something to stop the rot. Again, I spoke directly to the wankers in the cage opposite. 'Listen, you Jock cunts, do you really think we're going to start worrying about you lot after chasing you all around Glasgow this morning?' I was on a roll now. 'We've been taking liberties all day long –

bowling round your manor and smashing any of you who actually dared show your fucking faces. You just wait till we get to Barlinnie tonight – we're gonna have a right tear-up!'

I got the predictable reaction, but knew the point had been made and at least I'd pissed on a few Scottish fires.

Throughout most of the commotion, Martin had kept quiet, but suddenly he leaped to his feet and abused the sweaty clan opposite. Then the others joined in too. The noise levels rose as Scots and English voices screamed across at each other through the gaps. Now I saw the temper that had got Martin arrested – he was hanging off the bars and pointing at one Jock in particular. He really wanted to get at him and I would have loved to see him in action.

The taunts and spitting eventually died down, until this Protestant contingent of Scots decided to start rowing with their Catholic counterparts instead. It turned out that the Glaswegian plod kept them apart in separate pens, with the Catholic cage out of sight to us. This was a new one to me, but gave me a small glimpse of the sectarian problems in Scotland. If the Protestants hated us this much, then fuck knows what abuse we'd have got from the Catholics.

As the day wore on, I was moved from one cell to another and Marcus was moved with me, but we didn't see Martin again. The following season a small band of Oldham's firm came to Luton and put on a pre-match show. They even sent a couple of their number into one of our watering holes with a greeting from Martin. He didn't appear himself, though, as apparently he'd decided to knock it all on the head. Good luck to him.

Meanwhile, Marcus and I settled into our new surroundings and were pleased to find ourselves banged up with some of Birmingham's notorious Zulus, who'd been nicked after the attack on Villa. They laughed as they described the look on Villa's main boy's face as they stormed the pub. During the tale, I looked over one of the Blue Nose's shoulders and spotted another familiar face sat in a cell that ran at an angle to ours.

He didn't look too happy and his head hung low, but, even though I could only see part of him, I instantly recognised who it was – the Oxford main man! I couldn't believe it. The bloke who had rattled my cage earlier in the day and started me on a course that ended up with me watching mad Marcus drink from a dodgy toilet was only a few feet away from me. I wanted revenge and wanted it badly, but what could I do?

It certainly wouldn't be simple to get at him. The security staff were taking people from the cells to face the judges one by one and none was returning, so if he left before me he might escape my retribution. If released, he would disappear into the streets of Glasgow and, if remanded, he would probably be placed on a different wing in Barlinnie Prison. I doubted that I could get at him and decided my best chance was to find out his name and hunt him down in Oxford at a later date. Standing close to the steel bars of the cell, I waited patiently for a guard.

Eventually, one appeared and I asked for our neighbours' names, but the old-timer just blanked me, so I would have to wait a little longer and hope my man was called to face the music before me. Alternatively, if my presence was requested by the sheriff first, I would hang around outside the court building until his case was heard and have it one-on-one afterwards.

As it turned out, he was called before me. I heard the court security call out three names to his cell and watched as they filed out. Two white geezers, one black. I called out the names looking for a response. The first got no reaction from the target, but as soon as I called out 'Lewis' he spun round. 'Got you!' I smiled. 'Lewis it is then.'

He said nothing and returned his chin to his chest, but now he knew. The guards led Lewis along the corridor and out to the courtrooms, passing my cell en route. I whispered to him to wait for me outside afterwards, but he didn't reply.

Eventually, when my own time came, I appeared before a stern-looking sheriff who seemed to hate the idea of me even visiting Scotland, let alone being an English football thug. He looked even more pissed off when his staff got my name and the details of my offence wrong. After sheepish looks all round, they pressed on with the hearing and asked me how I pleaded.

'To which offence?' I responded smugly.

They shuffled their bundles of paper and, following much whispering between educated types, charged me with a public order offence.

I pleaded 'Not Guilty' and was bailed to reappear at a later date.

But as I marched out of the courtroom there was only one thing on my mind – revenge. The sky had darkened again and it occurred to me just how long I'd been held by the OB. It was Monday evening and I'd been lifted Saturday lunchtime. A long weekend – but far from a pleasant one.

Glasgow isn't exactly beautiful on the best of days and, at night in the rain, it's grim to say the least. I walked up and down the soggy road like a schoolboy waiting for a fight outside the school gates, but there was no sign of Lewis at all. On the long journey home, I consoled myself with the comfort of having his name and my knowledge of Oxford watering holes.

A year later, we played Oxford in the LDV trophy on a Tuesday night. I travelled over with a tight crew and looked for Lewis, but he wasn't about. We visited one of his favourite pubs, finding only an old skinhead dressed in his regimental Stone Island jumper, desperately trying not to look like a football lad. Having failed to find our target, we didn't bother to watch the game, and instead stuck our heads into a friend's pub in the city centre before heading back to Luton.

My case eventually came to trial nine months later. This delay was down to a little 'jolly' around the Arabian Gulf with the Navy. Then I ended up in Sierra Leone helping put a stop to the 'West Side Boys' attempt to seize control of the country's lucrative diamond-mining business. After those missions, the trip to court up in Scotland seemed like a simple one.

The prosecution called two police officers, who both claimed that I was a 'known Casual' and had been arrested in the process of confronting another group of English hooligans. The only problem with their evidence was the contradictory accounts of the events in question, which the sheriff couldn't fail to notice.

Then it was time for me to face cross-examination and, prior to taking the stand, my solicitor had a quick word of advice for me: 'Don't drop your guard or be complacent just because the prosecutor is a woman – she'll be no pussy cat when she gets her teeth into you.'

Within minutes, I knew what he meant. She tore into me for not wearing colours, not being interested in the football and only coming for the fighting. I beat this back as best I could, explaining that in the military we were encouraged not to wear football shirts or scarves and followed up with proof of a match ticket. She just changed her tack and started on my drinking, enquiring how much I had consumed before my arrest. Barely had I replied, 'About 10 Beck's,' when she had twisted this into me being pissed-up and out of control.

I argued the point and in the end she gave it to me straight. 'I put it to you that you were drunk and also that you are a leader of a known hooligan gang who came to Glasgow looking for a fight.' She hadn't finished yet either. 'And I put it to you that you are a liar and have told untruth after untruth to this court in your attempts to escape the punishment of the law. Isn't that so?'

I paused and took a deep breath, trying to control the anger she had provoked in me. 'No, Ma'am, you're mistaken. Sure, I'd been drinking, but I was in control of my senses and decisions – I mean I wouldn't have driven a car at the time, but I knew what I was doing. I was provoked by others and certainly didn't come to Glasgow looking for a fight.'

The sheriff ordered that proceedings stop for lunch. When he'd left, I asked my brief how it looked and he said it had gone really well, but that perhaps we could have done without the '10 pints'. I laughed and explained that I'd said '10 Beck's' and that it came in a bottle, so it was nowhere near the same thing.

I spent the lunch hour with Shit Hair who'd come to Scotland to be a witness on my behalf. He giggled at the '10 pints of lager' mistake, which soon became 20 as he took the piss. Next, he decided that he didn't really fancy standing in the dock because his hair gel had dried up and he looked a mess. I could see that he wasn't taking this too seriously and stressed to him how important it was to get the point across to the sheriff that there had been a minor cultural misunderstanding – Beck's is sold in bottles, which contain about half a pint. He agreed and confirmed that he would say he had consumed the same amount and was still in good control of his actions and decision-making on the day.

But, within seconds of the fiery female solicitor starting her cross-examination, he was playing with his hair and matting his blond locks together with trembling fingers. His nerve went and, the more she dug into him, the more he began to tremble and resemble a cheap imitation of Carlos Valderama, the Colombian footballer, as his hair lumped into a frizzy mass. Next, he totally forgot to clear up the bottle versus pint misunderstanding. In fact, he claimed to have only drunk three pints all day and was dismissed from the dock having done me no favours at all. I was fuming, but he just winked across at me as if he'd sorted me right out.

Surprisingly, though, my brief then rose, putting it to the sheriff that the prosecution had no case to answer and that I should be acquitted. The Glaswegian sheriff paused for a moment before asking me to stand, announcing that it would be unsafe to find me 'Guilty' of any offence. I was free to go.

So in Luton Crown Court, although I hadn't been 'up' for a few years, I was hardly a stranger to the surroundings or that feeling of facing your destiny. I wouldn't say I wasn't worried, though, because that would be a lie; I was still nervous at the prospect of getting sent down and clung to the faint hope that Judge Cripps would allow me to return home to my two-bedroom semi and my loving family.

As I strolled over to take a seat and relax for a moment, I heard Windy pipe up: 'Little Jimmy's here.' He gestured back towards the stairway and Jimmy bounced into view. He walked like he was black – he grew up on rap and hip hop and smoked dope like the government were going to start taxing it the next day. We shook hands and giggled like schoolgirls – we were showing our nerves. In fact, the last time I'd heard Little Jimmy giggle like this was when we went to Millwall in 2002.

On that day, we had travelled down to London with over 150 good lads and headed straight down over Westminster Bridge past Guy's Hospital to The Miller of Mansfield pub, as we knew that Millwall's lads frequented the place on match days. Once there, our numbers swelled as small bands of Luton lads made their way across the capital to join our gathering.

Millwall later claimed they didn't know we were coming, but I find that hard to believe. One of the MI2s, Black K, was living in Bermondsey at the time and had recruited two others from the baby firm to spray-paint half the area with the words 'Mig Crew are Coming!' K is a lunatic, one of the gamest lads I've ever met and without a doubt he was born in the wrong era. He would have loved the 80s, with the huge mobs of 300 or 400 hooligans clashing on the high streets of England every Saturday.

He'd shown this on 17 May 2002, when he got caught up in a night of violence on the South London streets around Millwall's New Den. Hundreds of their boys (and men!) rioted for hours following the final whistle, after a goal from Birmingham City striker Stern John had put paid to their promotion hopes. Of the 300 OB on duty that night, nearly half were injured and 16 police horses received wounds as Millwall tried to confront the Brummie supporters leaving the stadium.

The OB forced them away from the ground, but trouble still flared on a scale not seen in England for a while. At its height, the police could hardly cope and on many occasions had to beat a hasty retreat from pre-planned bushwhack points set up by the Southeast Londoners – although, as it happens, many of those involved in the riot were later identified as being from other parts of the country.

One of those picked out and punished was our K. On the morning after the riot, I opened my newspaper to see pictures of Birmingham players celebrating their famous victory, but also spotted Black K on the pitch in the background of one of the snaps. Over the following weeks, more reports followed showing graphic footage of mobs engaging the police on street corners and housing estates around South Bermondsey.

One report in particular caught my attention, as late one Tuesday night *Sky News* showed a mob of Millwall lads fronting a line of the Met. They weren't coming forwards, but held their position about 40 metres from the police, pelting them with rocks and bottles. It continued like this for a while and was looking like a stalemate when suddenly one lad burst from the crowd and closed on the Met. He calmly crossed the no-man's land and, once within throwing range, hurled his missile at the men in black. There was no mistaking him – it was Black K! The manhunt began in earnest as the tabloids were splashed with pictures of those involved and inevitably he was arrested shortly afterwards.

Before long, most of the offenders had been rounded up and everyone waited for sentencing, to see what kind of example the courts would make of them. The first person to be sentenced was a 38-year-old from Folkestone in Kent, jailed for two years and given a 10-year banning order. Young K soon followed and got 18 months. So, with K telling us Millwall knew we were coming and his Mig Crew painting skills evident as we exited South Bermondsey Station, I couldn't understand how they could say they never knew about it beforehand.

We marched through South Bermondsey in a tight formation at first but, as we became more relaxed in our surroundings, the group started to spread out, stretching for about 100 metres. The Met blocked us from entering pubs along the way and as we continued on more and more of them glued themselves to us. Eventually, they held us in a cordon a few hundred metres from the ground. But I didn't fancy staying cooped up like a chicken, so I sneaked through a gap between two phone boxes and headed on towards the Den with Baby B in tow.

We reached the ground and had a wander around the home supporters' area to check out the opposition. Within seconds we had attracted unwanted attention from various Neanderthal types who gave us all the usual threats, although no one actually came forward to get their hands dirty. Soon, we also got the wrong sort of company in the form of two very large Met plod, who informed us that we were in the wrong place and could do a lot worse than making our way round to the other end of the stadium. They fixed their eyes on us and seemed pretty insistent, so we agreed and backed off.

As we moved through the Millwall supporters around the compact stadium, we began to see more of the bulldogs, who even started to make animal noises as we passed. One of them jumped in front of us, his face contorted, and screeched, 'Ya caaan't cam darn 'ere. This is Millwall!'

I started to piss myself and not out of fear either! Between giggles, Baby B made a half-hearted attempt to grab hold of the big-mouthed baldy, but our friends from the Met soon intervened and pushed us back on track to the away supporters' section.

As we joined the crowds of Luton supporters at the turnstiles, we shared a laugh, mimicking the welcoming Millwall fan. Baby B likes to do impressions and had me in stitches as he aped the South London accent, albeit in his high-pitched voice. But B's performance was cut short as the noise of sirens and shouting drifted our way. It was kicking off! We immediately left the queue of happy Hatters and ran towards the sound along with 20 other Luton lads. I didn't know any of this lot, but recognised a couple of faces from previous games. I just hoped that they were up for it in case things came on top.

About 80 metres up ahead, we saw some of the Migs and MI2s from The Miller of Mansfield and, although they weren't running, most were backing off slowly. I couldn't tell whether it was OB or Millwall's firm that was pushing them backwards; I just wanted to help our lads hold their ground. So, along with most of those around me, I charged over at about 45 degrees to the action.

A gap immediately opened in the crowd and things became clearer. Millwall had come running down behind the Luton boys who were being escorted to the ground and steamed in even though well outnumbered. The police had tried to stop the fighting, but hadn't completely got to grips with the situation, so, when we came from an unexpected direction, things heated up again.

Within seconds, we had backed the Southeast Londoners off about 15 feet, but the OB came crashing into both crews and began to wrestle everyone apart. Some skinny idiot in a sky-blue tracksuit top then tagged me from the side. I double-checked all around to make sure I wasn't becoming an easy target by getting isolated from the rest of the lads and spotted Scottish Brian charging over in my direction, hot on the tail of one Millwall lad.

As I steamed into the enemy within range, I spotted a familiar bulldog-looking thug coming up on my right, his bald head bouncing with excitement. I don't think he knew I had spotted him and, when he was really close, I spun round to face him. He stopped bouncing immediately.

The Bermondsey boy obviously didn't want to row in front of the OB and risk a tug, so instead he just screamed at the top of his voice: 'Ya caaan't cam dan 'ere. This is Millwall!'

Deja vu! I could easily have put my fist straight into his mouth, but resisted the temptation and instead gave the cocky Cockney some lip. 'What the fuck are you talking about? We're already here, you fool! We've been here all day!'

My bulldog look-alike turned to his mates for support, but instead found Big Wayne – another massive Luton lad – closing on him. 'We'll fackin see ya at Landan Bridge then, ya mugs.' He obviously wasn't too happy with our presence in his manor today.

But the next voice to be heard was one of authority, as a younger copper gripped me by the arm. 'Any more trouble from you and you'll be spending a night in the cells,' he barked.

I didn't fancy this option so I straightened myself up, retraced my steps and entered the visitors' section.

The New Den is a neat and tidy all-seater stadium; it's modern by anyone's standards and helps present Millwall FC's new 'friendly' face. Their last ground, The Den on Cold Blow Lane which they left in 1993 after 83 incident-packed years, was something else altogether. It was cramped and crumbling and helped reinforce Millwall's traditional image around the world – grim and intimidating. For years, it was a breeding ground for violent thugs.

Inside Millwall's new upmarket stadium, I chose to move away from the rest of Luton's hooligan element and sat almost directly behind the goal. I had a perfect view of the pitch and couldn't help but admire the place. However, once the game got under way, it soon became obvious what the place lacked, especially compared to Cold Blow Lane – an atmosphere.

When I'd visited The Den in the 80s, it was a shithole, but the menace in the air was unmistakable. We had been packed in a corner of the ruin of a ground with only some garish bright-yellow fences keeping the scum at bay. Even though it was terrifying, it was a trip that had to be experienced at least once in your life and the hairs on the back of my neck stood to attention as that infamous noise echoed around the terraces throughout the game: 'Miiiiiilllwaaaaaalll!' As I sat in my shiny blue plastic seat, I found myself missing those 'bad old days' at The Den, but I bet most Millwall lads miss it even more.

Within a few minutes of the kick-off, Black K and the MI2s were smashing seats in full view of the Metropolitan Police positioned in our stand. The surprising thing was that the handful of seats stamped into pieces didn't get launched at the Millwall support to our left. Instead, many of the lads chose to hold their trophies above their heads and wave them at the locals, who glared back in anger. Maybe they wanted to take them home and stick them on the mantlepiece as souvenirs! I watched the Luton liaison officer standing tall with his arms folded across his chest and shaking his head in disbelief at the spectacle of five MI2s with their hoods up, waving slabs of plastic at Millwall. I had to chuckle.

In the second half, he came over and whispered in my ear that he didn't agree with what was about to happen next. Obviously, I enquired as to what he was talking about, but he just replied that he couldn't justify what the Met were going to do to me. I was confused; however, he quickly turned the conversation to other matters and gave the lads a bit of a heads-up by saying that he was impressed with our turnout for the day, although he doubted that we had enough to finish the job at London Bridge after the game. Of course, I argued the point. Within minutes of our liaison officer's departure, I discovered exactly what it was that he disagreed with the London OB about.

As I sat watching the match, two officers approached. They asked me to stand up while one of them spoke into the little radio attached to his shoulder and described my attire. 'Lime-green jumper, dark jeans and white trainers.' He waited for a response and when it came nodded across at his partner in crime. 'Do you want to come downstairs for a chat, Tommy?' he asked in a professional tone.

'Not really, mate, I've paid to watch the match.'

'Do you want us to nick you for obstruction or are you coming downstairs for a chat?' They were insistent and looked ready to wrestle with me if they had to.

As I rose, I felt that old feeling of dread run through my veins. We walked towards the exit leading to the area beneath the stand.

'What's going on, Yeti? What the fuck do they want?' It was my old mate Demus.

Demus had moved on from the hooligan scene some years previously, although a year later he was back on the scene at 'All Bar One' in London Bridge when some Bushwhackers entered looking for the Migs and to their surprise found some of the originals. A main player on the Millwall scene strolled up to the Luton crew seated in the rear and gave it the big one.

'Cam to play wiv the Millwall, 'ave ya, boys?' One of the Bushwhackers bottled Flower and it kicked off big time.

Millwall had entered giving it large, but ended up out-fought in a two-minute toe-to-toe that resembled a saloon scene from the Wild West. They were bashed silly inside the bar and forced to retreat. Some even left their trainers in their haste to escape, while Demus found another Cockney's bloodied tooth embedded in his knuckle. Dave M smashed three of the Bushwhackers in the doorway as they were breaking ranks to evade the violence and he had to ask them, 'Whatever made you cunts think we were playing?'

I gave Demus a bemused look, but assured him it was OK and continued towards the cold concrete staircase. Once we were downstairs, they informed me that I was going to be arrested for the handbags outside the ground, but not charged. I would be moved to a police station some distance away and then released later on. 'It's all about prevention,' Plod One explained.

I soon found myself being searched in front of a fat desk sergeant and sensed it was time for my ace. I pulled out my Royal Navy ID card from my wallet and stuck it right under his red nose.

'You're a fucking Matlot!' he screamed with astonishment. 'What the hell are you doing here?'

'For my sins, I'm also a Luton Town supporter,' I replied in a grand tone.

Soon I was on my way out of the New Den accompanied by a disappointed Plod Two, who'd been told to escort me away from the area and 'lose me'.

Once alone, I took the tube back to London Bridge and, while making my way through the streets south of the Thames, I called a few of the Migs who hadn't made it to the game. I told them I'd been ejected from the ground and that they might want to get a 'jog on' and meet me for a beer. I headed back to The Miller of Mansfield but, on finding it shut, turned around for Borough Station.

On the way, I spotted The White Hart, a small boozer with a single door on to the street. It was a tight little place with only one bar and a big screen at the rear showing the football scores. It looked perfect for a small mob to hold, even if outnumbered heavily. At the bar stood three lads who looked like they had served many a year on a Beirut paper round, if you know what I mean. I stood close to them as I ordered my beer and could feel them eyeing me up and down – sizing me up because my face was new in town.

I took my bottle of Beck's over to the table nearest the big screen and turned my back on the gorillas at the bar to avoid continued eye contact. I had to avoid a confrontation and buy time until some back-up arrived. I took my mobile out discreetly, placed it in my lap and started to text my mate Sick Nick, telling him where I was and to get a move on because I was a sitting duck. I watched the scores come in and suddenly a goal for Luton flashed up on screen. I couldn't help myself and shouted, 'Get in there,' gripping my fist tight and throwing a short jab. I didn't look to see the reaction of the locals.

Two minutes later, I felt better when Big Cliff, Sick Nick, Sinclair and Frank C arrived. They said nothing and went straight up to the bar, making our Baghdad paperboys look a little uncomfortable.

'I don't want no bloody trouble in here, lads,' came the direct order from the landlord who was serving the reinforcements with shaky hands.

Big Cliff agreed, making a witty remark that seemed to break the ice and even had our potential enemies at the bar laughing. Then the four of them joined me at the table that I'd found for our bit of South London socialising.

The door swung open again and I turned to check who'd entered this time. It wasn't good news, as a mountain of a man walked in followed by four others. They headed over to the bar and had a quick conference with the others. Then the big cunt nodded and gave us 'the look'.

I checked our little firm and gave each of them a quick once over. Big Cliff looked unconcerned and I knew he wouldn't back off if it came on top; Sinclair – his fat neck was already wobbling and sweat was flowing from his armpits as his blood pressure rose by the second. Would he stand? I wasn't sure. Sick Nick had been in the Special Forces and fought in secret wars – he had to be game.

And then I turned to check out Frank C. Where the fuck had Frank C gone? I looked over to the corner and clocked him with his head buried in a newspaper about as far away from us as humanly possible – probably checking the horse prices! 'Useless,' I thought. Pissed off, I watched as the Millwall lads started to make numerous phone calls. I reasoned that they were calling in reinforcements and decided to do the same.

Out the back of the pub, Big Cliff called up Baby B, who told us that Luton now had a huge crew of Migs and MI2s, plus some other old heads, and that they would make it to The White Hart in about 30 minutes. The race was on. Whoever got their lads to London Bridge quickest would win the day. If Luton were first, we could hold The White Hart no problem and would be in a good position to make a move on other Millwall pubs in the manor. But, if Millwall arrived sooner, we'd never take this little boozer with the sort of lads they would have defending it. Then the OB would just round us up, march us to London Bridge Station and send us back to Bedfordshire.

I decided to send Frank C to guide the rest of the crew in, because they could easily miss the place. He was happy to get a chance to leave the tense atmosphere that was building, because we now faced a potential battle with the local paperboys. As he left the pub, the Millwall crew stared at him and then at each other, wondering what was going on. But, within seconds, he rushed back in and shot straight over to me, speaking in a whisper to all of us huddled round our beers. 'Their whole fucking mob is coming up the road and they're heading in this direction.'

He looked terrified and had gone a horrible sickly grey colour. I had to act fast and buy time for our firm to arrive and save the day. Within a second, I had quick-stepped through the Millwall lads and out through the front door, alone. I was just in time, as I almost bumped straight into the Bushwhackers about to enter the pub, which would have meant disaster.

The fat cunt at the front of the crew turned to the rest and announced, 'That's one of them. He's a fucking Mig!'

A quick scan of their numbers and it was time to respond. 'Yeah, I'm a Mig' – it wasn't worth a bluff.

'Well, cam on then, let's go,' came from someone in the group and they all started to bounce towards me.

Again, I responded quickly to avoid the kicking. 'Is this how Millwall operate now – 20 on to one?' I was lucky – they stopped and began to question me instead. They wanted to know how many we'd brought down, so I lied. 'There's only 40 of us.'

I could see a couple still wanted to bash me there and then.

'Look, give us some credit,' I pleaded. 'We're trying to get what's left of our mob together. When the OB have gone home, we'll come back to The Miller of Mansfield and have it properly. But, if you kick off now, the OB will round us up and just send us straight back to Luton. It's your call.'

They accepted my proposal and started to head off to the Miller at walking pace.

'Mugs,' I chuckled.

As they moved in the direction of London Bridge Station, I heard a distant roar, which seemed to echo off the walls of the surrounding buildings in the street. At first, I couldn't see anything except the boys I'd just blagged running back towards the pub and then straight past me. One turned his head and shouted, 'It's your fucking lot!'

I looked back and saw Big Wayne, Jimmy and another Mig called Jay at the head of a herd of lads throwing bottles, slabs of concrete, bricks and whatever else they could lay their hands on. Jimmy spotted me and started to make his way towards the pub. For a second, I was well happy, as it looked like the day was going to end on a high note with us taking liberties around London Bridge, using The White Hart as our HQ.

My happiness quickly turned sour, though, as I watched the big Luton mob stop suddenly in its tracks and then start to back-pedal in disarray. I couldn't see what the lads were facing, but I knew it was coming from the direction of The Miller of Mansfield. I wondered what could have stopped such a big firm. It wasn't Millwall and I could only watch as a mob of Robocops steamed into my mates clubbing them to the ground. They were merciless and smashed our crew to bits, forcing them all the way back to London Bridge. Where a few moments ago there stood a fine mob of Luton, now there was only a sea of black uniforms and shiny blue helmets.

Jimmy, however, had escaped the onslaught and joined me outside The White Hart. I told him to get inside the pub with the others, so as not to draw attention from the OB now swarming the area. As I looked for signs of any other Luton that had managed to evade the police, I spotted our own intelligence officer less than 30 feet away and at this point thought it best to take a swift walk around the corner.

I crossed the road and made for a narrow path opposite, but quickly applied the brakes. Lurking down the path was a load of Millwall lads, including the boys I had mugged off earlier. I didn't wait around to see if they spotted me, but crossed the path entrance and headed off towards Borough Station.

I tried to use my phone to see who was where and what chance we had of getting a mob together again, but as I was dialling I heard my name being screamed out by more than one anxious voice. I turned sharpish and saw Jimmy, Big Cliff and the others all running in my direction. As they were toeing it, they beckoned me to join them and I knew by the excitement in their voices that it was time to get a sprint on. I followed my fleeing pals into the station and looked back to see a mob of Millwall closing behind us. There were far too many to take on and I didn't fancy a shoeing in South London from this lot. But, as I reached the top of the escalators, there was a commotion at one of the gates – Sinclair was so fat that he'd got stuck and was frantically trying to put his ticket into the machine to get the barrier to open. We literally kicked him through and hurried down the spiral staircase to the tubes below.

As we checked the platform, though, we realised that we were in a dead end and, if the Bushwhackers followed us down here, we'd be properly fucked. I checked the electric board to see when the next train was due… two minutes. Frank C was trying all the doors on the platform as his fight or flight trigger got the better of him and I'm sure he would have run down the fucking tunnel if it had come to it.

Standing in a straight line facing the entrance with our fists raised for battle, we held our breath for the longest two minutes I can remember. We kept encouraging each other that we would have to just fight as hard as possible for two minutes… one minute… and then, leaping on the train, we started to breathe again as we realised that we'd escaped in one piece. I looked at Jimmy and he was giggling like a schoolgirl, then I chuckled too and soon we were all laughing like schoolgirls as we realised how lucky we'd been.

But now, as we stood together in the Crown Court, Jimmy and I soon stopped giggling – this time we probably wouldn't escape so lightly.

5
You Won't Get Better Than This

Now, as it was nearly time for my co-defendants and me to face the wrath of Judge Cripps, I had to speak to my barrister and find out exactly how he wanted to play it today. We had all signed in on the court register and some of the lads were already deep in conversation with their briefs; Andy and Big Cliff were locked away in a side room, while Dave was sitting with his, having a coffee. I'd lost sight of Little Jimmy, but knew that he was about somewhere. Armchair Alan was standing with Mr Jones, a solicitor I'd used on several occasions before. I shook hands with him as I headed over to find my barrister and he wished me good luck.

I returned to the arrivals desk where two pleasant elderly ladies put a call out for my legal representative. They soon received a response and sent me to an office on another floor of the smartly designed court building.

I was expecting to be represented by a certain barrister today, and I had been more than impressed with him at earlier interviews, as he sounded really positive about my chances of being found 'Not Guilty' at trial. He seemed sure I had a self-defence case, based on my not being accountable for the actions of my friends, but still having the right to defend them. The only problem with this was that I had carried on long after rescuing my mate from a beating and then gone on the offensive big time.

My brief had mentioned something else in conversation too – in his younger days, he'd been an avid follower of West Ham and moved in the same circles as the infamous ICF. He had seen many 'incidents' watching the Irons, he told me knowingly, and reading between the lines I wondered if he'd done a bit himself.

I first contacted him after a recommendation by my old mate Marcus, who I met in Scotland. The two of them had been friends at school and both rubbed shoulders with some of the more notorious members of the Chelsea Headhunters, including the notorious Twins. My brief had watched the police video covering my day at Watford and enjoyed the footage so much that he gave me a great scene-by-scene commentary of the fight.

On a previous court appearance for Plea and Directions, it had been difficult for me to decide which way to plead, as I had the solicitor from my local firm telling me I was 'bang to rights', while my own brief was still insisting that I had a decent defence. I needed time to think it through, but I was keeping the Crown Court waiting and felt pressured to make a decision. I'd looked to my barrister to give me the courage to fight the case, but he just pointed me to the bottom line – if I was found 'Guilty', it would mean an extra six months on my sentence and I was the one who would have to serve the time, not him. That hadn't exactly filled me with confidence! And it didn't help when the local solicitor insisted that, in his opinion, the brief was wrong and a jury would doubtless find me 'Guilty'. I had to make a decision and even though I wasn't happy about it, I pleaded 'Guilty'.

So, as I strolled towards the meet with my barrister, I was looking at a damage-limitation exercise. But I felt sure that, with my background in the armed forces and the fact that I hadn't been convicted of any offence for a number of years, I had an outside chance of a non-custodial sentence – especially with my brief's enthusiasm and expertise.

However, looking around the carpeted office space, I couldn't see him anywhere. In fact, the only one other person in the immediate vicinity was a smartly dressed, youngish woman with a thick folder of paperwork tucked under her arm. She looked official, so I enquired if she knew where my defence lawyer was hiding.

As I approached her, she looked up and smiled sweetly. 'You must be Tom.' She went on to explain that my original brief was working on another case today and that she would be representing me instead.

I felt cheated. Fucking cheated, in fact. With respect, of course… I'd spent hours discussing my case with him prior to today and he seemed much sharper than the barristers that my friends and co-defendants were using. He had earned my trust and seemed to understand the way football supporters' and even hooligans' minds worked. In a way, he'd been my last chance of avoiding prison and not losing my job or hurting those who loved me.

MIG CREW

Whenever Stoke visited in the 80s, running battles were the order of the day. Our multi-race firm on the prowl before the game.

Luton reclaiming the pitch from Stoke's invading army.

Stoke's sizeable mob pursuing our firm, and keen as ever to go toe-to-toe.

MIGS! MIGS! MIGS!

Luton's younger Migs: The MI2's

Author Tommy Robinson ponders on his 25 years with Luton's MIGS

One of many small bands of MIGS that entred Shrewsbury on the eve of promotion 2002

The lads chill out and lay low prior to invading the Shrewsbury Terraces.

Aubrey Bailey: the man who changed the way we operated on match days at Luton.

Today the Hoollie scene belongs to a much darker world

Toast the old firm

My new guide through the court machine was certainly younger and more attractive than him, but now I could foresee only one possible outcome in today's proceedings, and it wasn't a good one. As we spoke, she tried to calm me. I was obviously concerned at the prospect of appearing before Judge Cripps without my chosen representative – someone who knew the ins and outs of my case and hadn't just given it a quick read on the bus over.

She started off by explaining that, although I would almost certainly go to jail, it might not be for as long as I had first feared. Slowly, I became used to her ways and we adjourned to an interview room to chat. As I sat down, I asked her a very stupid question, 'How did you know it was me when I approached you downstairs anyway?'

Her reply made me feel like an idiot: 'The video… er… of your offence!'

My face turned crimson; I could feel myself burning up and all my composure disappeared as she giggled for a bit, and then a bit more to nail the point. I hadn't felt so fucking embarrassed since I stood in Luton Magistrates' Court accused of handling stolen goods way back in 1985. It wasn't the actual handling charge that was the problem that day, but rather what I had been accused of handling. I had appeared in front of a bench comprising of three grinning female magistrates, after being caught in possession of £15 quid's worth of oral bronzing tablets – nasty suntan aids that usually turned users bright orange! This time, the pills turned me bright red instead and my two mates in the public gallery let me and everyone else know about it for months afterwards.

Once I had returned to my normal colour, our conversation turned serious when she started to run through the facts of the case, including each copper's statement against me. She very quickly started to look bemused and then began shaking her head in disbelief as she realised the extent of surveillance on us as we made our way to the Watford match that day in September 2002. I realised that here we were, minutes before a Crown Court appearance, and she was indeed familiarising herself with the finer detail of my case on the spot.

But then she made a comment that really got me scowling. 'This is incredible, the amount of effort they went to – I mean, it's not like you're Chelsea, is it?'

Now I was angry, not only because it showed that she didn't know her subject beyond the big names and big headlines, but even more than that because I was insulted.

I couldn't help but think back to 94/95 and the glorious Cup run that we enjoyed that season. The Mig Crew had bounced back after a few quiet years following a number of events around 90–91. We'd been going from strength to strength for a number of years prior to that, with the clashes with London clubs becoming increasingly violent, and many of the bigger names in the football hooligan world coming unstuck when visiting Luton, especially for night games.

But the onset of the rave scene began to bite eventually and many of our lads turned their energies towards dancing to a different kind of beat from the one that football violence offered. Somewhat ironically, it was around this time that the Mig Crew made a very bad decision. We decided to go on holiday to Ibiza.

For a number of years, we'd been doing the usual lads' trips to the Mediterranean in the summer months. Usually, around six or seven of us would head off and chase women around the bars of some Spanish resort day and night, while necking as much lager as humanly possible. But this time we travelled in numbers. Fourteen of us were due to rendezvous with another larger group in Ibiza and we hoped to have a mob of 40 Migs together for the holiday of a lifetime and in a way that's exactly what it was.

Our little combat crew of Migs set off in good spirits from Luton Airport (of course), but we should have realised that it was going to be a nightmare trip when, as soon as we'd landed, our rep informed us that we wouldn't be staying in our chosen resort of San Antonio after all. Instead, we would be lodging in the small and tranquil village of Es Cana in the north of the island. Although we really wanted to be in San An with the rest of the gang, the sun was shining and it didn't seem like the end of the world at the time. So we didn't kick up a fuss and trooped on to the coach heading to our replacement accommodation.

Es Cana turned out to be a pleasant family resort with whitewashed buildings huddled around a crescent-shaped bay of inviting deep blue sea – lovely no doubt, but not really ideal for a load of 20-year-old football lads looking to burn off some close-season energy.

As soon as we arrived, we poured straight off the coach and ran upstairs to our apartments. Within minutes, we all gathered back at the front of the hotel building, dressed in shorts and admiring our balconies now decked out in the flag of St George with the letters M-I-G-S displayed in full view.

As we admired the view, the Jew opened a bottle of poppers and passed it around excitedly to anyone who wanted a headache. It made its way to

Ging, who wasn't really interested, and was then lost for a moment in a flurry of hands desperately trying to catch the small brown bottle spinning fast towards the hard concrete road. All was saved by the quick-thinking Jew who snatched the T-shirt from around his waist, lunging out with surprising accuracy to catch the poppers in it. But he let out a cry of anguish when he noticed the wet patch appearing, as the fluid spilled on to his T-shirt. He unwrapped the bundle in a flash, while muttering about not wasting the stuff, and stuck his big nose into the damp spot. Wrapping it around his head, he began inhaling deeply over and over again. He looked like some old skinhead sniffing glue, standing there on the edge of Es Cana's main thoroughfare in the blazing Spanish sun with his eyes bulging and the damp T-shirt clamped firmly to his face.

But, then, his arms dropped in slow motion and he started to droop forwards. We all looked on in amazement as the shirt fell from his face and he looked around slowly at us all with big rosy cheeks, smiling like a clown. Then, bang! He fell face first straight on to the road. Luckily, some of the lads reacted quickly and hauled him to his feet before his head was squashed by a passing car. He couldn't stand unaided and it took Big Cliff and Flower together to straighten him up against the wall. His giant nose was smashed across his face and his eyes were rolling – he looked properly fucked... Great stuff, poppers!

When we'd tidied up our little friend, we moseyed on down to the seafront and, after an hour on the beach, found ourselves a clean-looking bar to relax and have a few sips of the local beer. Eight hours later and we were still in the same bar, but had made plans to take taxis to San Antonio and meet up with the rest of the troops there.

Once in San An, we soon found them at a bar named Sergeant Peppers and started to drink heavily. Some of the lads banged on the poppers, while others chose to burn some weed. We were having a great night, but soon got bored with our surroundings and decided to head on to the main drag.

As we strolled through the neon-lit streets, a few of the Juveniles, as they liked to be known, came running over to tell us that a load of Geordies had been giving it the large just around the corner from where we were to meet. One of our youngsters known as 'Horrible' looked like he'd taken a slap to his face.

Now, Horrible had a certain reputation among the Migs as a blade merchant and on a number of occasions in the past was said to have sliced up opposition supporters from clubs such as Birmingham City, QPR and

Oxford, although nothing has ever been proved. But now he was close to tears because some Geordie beefer had whacked him in the chops. As always, Horrible wanted revenge.

After a quick conference, we strolled towards the large group of lads who had apparently attacked our youngsters. A quick nod of the head and it went off. We smashed them. The ferocity of our initial attack caused such panic that they soon put 30 metres between themselves and us. One of their number lay unconscious on the Spanish cobbles and didn't look as if he would be getting up in a hurry. I noticed Horrible closing on his slumbering carcass, but we quickly pulled him away.

The Geordie lads rallied and came rushing back towards us with a roar, but were soon scattered back into the busy streets. As we pursued them, we turned a corner and to our surprise found a line of Spanish OB blocking our path. Foolishly, we now turned our attentions on them, hurling bottles and glasses, and for a second it looked as though they might leg it too, but, in fact, they steamed straight into us, batons flailing. We broke and ran in all directions. Luckily, I managed to find a taxi almost immediately and, along with G Lawla, Barty and Scouse, escaped the OB's attention and headed back to the safety of Es Cana.

The following morning, we all sat around the hotel bar devouring cheese toasties and bottles of ice-cold coke; no one had been arrested and spirits were high. But we decided not to head into San Antonio for a couple of days to let things cool down and to try a place called Santa Eulalia instead that night. We returned to our drinking den on the beach in Es Cana where we drank even more heavily than the day before and soon many of us were worse for wear.

By the early evening, the 14 Migs based in Es Cana were seated in a semi-circle facing the sea and watching the sun go down in good spirits, but Big Cliff was absolutely tanked. While everyone else in the group had been back to the apartment to change out of their 'Luton on Tour' T-shirts into casual evening wear, Cliff refused to waste valuable drinking time on 'looking pretty' and wore the same sweaty clothes he had been slobbing around in all day.

Santa Eulalia is a resort which, although not on the scale of San Antonio, has an abundance of bars and places for a group of lads to have a good night out, and that was our plan – although, if I had known what was going to happen, I would have stayed in my apartment with a good book and a bottle of San Miguel.

Initially, everything was cool and the lads mingled with whatever women were available. Big Cliff entertained all present with his struggle to stay standing while the alcohol in his blood and gravity combined to pull him to the floor. There were some other football lads from Essex in the bar, chatting about their love for West Ham and Leyton Orient. All was going well – maybe too well.

Barty and Scouse, two of the black Migs on the trip, had even spotted a way to earn a few quid, positioning themselves outside the bar and charging an entrance fee. They were making a tidy sum too, as the bar was quite popular, but, once word spread round to the rest of us, things took a turn for the worse when Big Cliff realised that he could make some cash and stumbled outside. Within minutes, Barty was whinging about our Cliff, as were a couple of Scottish girls who complained to the bar staff about the drunken doorman and his 'door tax'.

Soon, Cliff was bundled inside by the bar manager, who was only about four foot tall and it became surreal as this midget shoved him around the bar. Only the intervention of Ging and Demus stopped things getting out of hand. They managed to calm both the guv'nor and Cliff, who now positioned himself expectantly at the end of the bar.

I looked on in disbelief as he started to tap his fingers on the stone counter, slowly realising that after all the fuss he might not be getting any more drinks. Suddenly, his patience snapped and, having snatched an empty glass from a nearby table, he threw it on the floor. It exploded into a thousand pieces scattering everywhere. Cliff stomped outside in a huff and the place went quiet.

Apparently, size wasn't an issue for our midget manager, who came storming out from behind the drinks counter and headed straight after him. I couldn't help but laugh as the mini-barman dragged our drunken compadre back inside, produced a broom and tried to get him to sweep up his mess. It was becoming a circus act and soon the whole bar was whooping and cheering the freak show as our giant mate wrestled with the tiny Spaniard.

After a tough contest, which could have gone either way, Cliff emerged victorious, tossing the little man to one side before stomping out of the bar. We all followed, applauding our brave warrior as he stumbled triumphantly down the road!

The next bar we came to was the scene of probably our biggest mistake so far, or indeed since. It was set below street level and to gain access you had to descend a badly lit staircase enclosed by high concrete walls. As we approached the doors, for some unknown reason, two northern sorts with long legs and short skirts asked me if I was a footballer. Although I was tempted to play the part of the wealthy and successful sportsman and take full advantage of their attentions, I owned up to being a decorator and not being very rich at all actually.

During our little chat, though, my eyes were distracted by the somewhat different approach to socialising being taken by some of the others. In the doorway of the basement bar, a heated argument had erupted between my mates and the doormen. Neither side looked ready to compromise. I headed over to the scene to see if I could calm everyone down, but I didn't get a chance as the two tall bouncers slammed the doors shut, leaving us frustrated and deflated.

They didn't stay shut for long, though. Horrible and JB managed to drag them open again and tried to bundle into the establishment with Flower. Instead, they ended up in a shoving match with both the doormen and some local drinkers, all shouting in Spanish. As they pushed our lads back out and slammed the doors again, they all started to mutter, 'Huleo, Huleo…'

We didn't have a clue what they were going on about and looked at each other quizzically: 'What the fuck is Huleo?'

For now, we didn't know what to do with ourselves; a crowd of people had gathered around and we felt like we'd lost face in allowing ourselves to be fobbed off so easily. Nothing was discussed, but we all knew that we had to smash the doors down to prove we couldn't be mugged off so easily. Cliff wandered over to the entrance; he knew the score and started to bang on them with his big fist. Now we found out the truth about Huleo…

As Cliff thumped away, the door started to open, slowly at first, then a huge mountain of a man in a luminous-green vest stepped out. So this was Huleo, or Julio I guess – either way, he didn't look too friendly. The monster, who was even taller than Cliff, reached behind and produced another surprise from the darkness – a three-foot pickaxe handle! Then the sweaty giant raised the lump of timber in his gorilla-like hands and brought it down with a terrific thump straight on Cliff's forehead. Cliff's eyes crossed for a moment, as if he was trying to see what had hit him, and then he went down like a sack of shit. As I froze, transfixed by the blood gushing from the hole in his swede, somebody else reacted – Scouse.

Scouse is a tough character and as game as they come. Our paths had first crossed in my final year at school when our Stockwood Pringle Boys clashed with his firm from nearby Rotherham School. That time, all his mates abandoned him as he steamed into us alone and took a beating. But he had impressed us all and was soon on board as a member of the early Mig Crew.

As Cliff lay bleeding on the pavement and the rest of us hesitated, Scouse pulled out a blade and stepped forward to confront the giant Spaniard. The fat cunt in the green vest came to meet him, raised his pickaxe again and, without any hesitation, smashed it straight into his wrist – breaking it with the force and causing him to drop the cutthroat to the floor. Now Scouse was out of the game too and so the Jew was the next to face up to Huleo. Smack! The Jew's forearm was smashed by the Spaniard with the big stick. Fuck! He'd done this before.

The lads were backing off now – the sight of two of ours in pain and one out cold had shaken everyone and was seriously testing the old group confidence because we hadn't taken so many casualties in such a short space of time before.

Within a split second, Huleo had stepped in my direction and once again he was lifting the axe handle above his shoulders. For an instant, I wanted to cower away among my mates, but then something caught my eye. Sat on the floor down to my left was a fire extinguisher. I guess it had been used as a door prop until we'd turned up and now it was just sat on the deck waiting to be given a new job – I had one for it. Without a second thought, I grabbed the heavy cylinder, raised it to head height and smashed it straight into Huleo's face before he could split my head apart. If I'd delayed a second longer, I would doubtless have joined Cliff in the land of the fairies instead.

Now that the main player for the Spaniards was out of the game, we took the battle to the door staff who'd been goading us from behind Huleo's bulk. However, after a couple of punches, they melted and we soon had them on their toes and fleeing back into the bar.

Some of the lads followed suit, kicking over tables and throwing bottles and glasses at anyone in their path. The rest of us did our best to nurse our wounded warriors outside. This whole thing had happened in the space of 30 seconds – four people injured, a Spanish bar damaged and a lot of innocent people scared out of their wits.

We decided to disappear from the scene, not in disorder, but as a group. We simply strolled back up the stairs and turned right into the main drag with its bright lights and crowded bars. Once there, we thought it was all over, but we were wrong.

Unknown to most of our crew, three of the younger lads had helped themselves to the cash register at the now wrecked bar which had been sitting in a tray at the door to the bar. During the charge into the foyer, Horrible had grabbed it and divvied it up with a couple of the others before departing the scene. Now the Spaniards wanted it back.

They came charging down the road – maybe 30- or 40-strong with Huleo and his bloody pickaxe handle at the front. We decided to stand and have it, as there wasn't really anywhere to go, although, to be honest, the Spanish mob didn't look up to much anyway. Their charge soon fizzled out as they got nearer, aided by the rocks we launched in their direction. Huleo was trying to call his numbers on to battle, but their hearts weren't really in it. Sensing this, we steamed into their lines and for the second time in 10 minutes the 'home side' were running in panic. Even the bloodied Huleo forced his overweight body back up the hill at top speed, dropping his trusty club in his haste to escape. Lawla grabbed it and waved it in defiance at the fleeing Spaniards.

Once they had retreated out of sight, we continued on our way along the main drag. I was concerned for Big Cliff as he was in bad shape and covered in blood. He looked a proper sight staggering through the crowds of dolled-up partygoers, with his 'Luton on Tour' T-shirt and busted head.

As we strolled along, we met the Essex lads again and our account of the trouble had them fuming and swearing to join us if anything else happened. So now our numbers grew, and the further we walked, the more people were drawn to the sight of Cliff's injury.

Suddenly, our attention was seized by an even larger mob of Spaniards marching up behind us, led by Huleo. This lot was nearly 70- or 80-strong, but again poor in quality. We started to pick up missiles, as did our newfound allies and the singing soon started: 'E-n-g-errrland, E-n-g-errrland, E-n-g-errrland!'

Some of the other Brits had now started hurling stones at the windows of the surrounding bars and smashing streetlamps too. It dawned on me that a mini-riot had kicked off and I felt uncomfortable with the idea of being a rather significant part of it. But I didn't have time to dwell on the whys and wherefores, as the next sound I heard was sirens. While we rushed towards the mob confronting us on the hill, the police drove through the crowd at some speed.

Unfortunately, Lawla chose this precise moment to throw the pickaxe handle at the Spanish mob. It missed everyone completely and instead smashed through the windscreen of the police car, which lost control, slid on the dusty road and ploughed into a parked taxi. The furious taxi driver clambered out of what was left of his cab, as did his mates sitting in their cars close to the scene of the crash, and at the same time all our English allies disappeared into the night.

So now it was just 14 Migs – one with a split head and two with broken wrists – against Spanish OB, half a dozen taxi drivers and 80 or so fuming locals. Plus, of course, our old mate Huleo in his nasty green vest and just about to re-arm himself with his trusty caveman club. For two seconds, there was a stand off… we all looked at each other and then fucking legged it!

It was Ipswich and Forest rolled into one, as the fear of being the only one caught took a grip. I didn't give a fuck about any other cunt now, I just had to escape. Most of the lads shot off in one direction, but Ging and I chose a different route. As soon as we were away from the main drag, we spotted a taxi pulled up at a junction and hurriedly ordered him in French to take us to Es Cana. He agreed and luckily his French was as bad as ours, so then we pretended to be trying to speak English instead. 'The English, they go crazy!'

'Oui, er, yes… they all hooligans,' we agreed, shaking our heads in disgust.

'Why they drink too much? Why… they cause big fight?' he said, frowning, clearly pissed off.

When we were safely back in Es Cana and a good few miles from Santa Eulalia, we gradually regrouped in the dark streets around our hotel. I felt a sense of foreboding as I thought back to the evening's wild events. We'd definitely overdone it tonight and where the fuck was Big Cliff? The last thing anyone had seen of the battered big guy was him shouting at us all in a high-pitched voice: 'I'm bleeding for you lot, bleeding for you!'

No one had seen Scouse or the Jew either and they were both pretty fucked up as well.

The streets were dark now and there was a chill wind blowing in off the sea. Against our better judgement, we decided to head back to the hotel to get warmer clothes and also in the hope of finding the missing lads. However, as soon as I turned the corner to my apartment, I felt sick inside. There were three angry Spanish Police waiting out front. They jumped into action on spotting us and within seconds were bundling us towards the local police station, which was only a few metres away from our accommodation.

I found myself sat inside handcuffed to Ging, Demus and Lawla. The OB were very calm, but kept inspecting the pile of passports they had perched on their desk. They would open one, take a look at us, shut it and then laugh knowingly. If they were trying to make us nervous, it was working.

Then, one by one, our comrades were escorted in. It was largely a simple process with the OB taking down each name, checking the relevant passport and having a little conference. Then they would all nod before asking the latest detainee to sit with those of us they had caught earlier. Every now and then, though, one of our lads would try to sell the Spanish a dummy, but the OB's answer was always to grab their coshes and beat the truth straight out of them. This lot clearly didn't mess about.

At one point, they brought in Barty, who was a well-known womaniser. True to form, he put on the most pathetic innocent face and gibbered on about being in bed with his girlfriend all night. He tried getting all touchy-feely with the gavvers to convince them he was a lover not a fighter and, incredibly, it seemed like he might get a walk out.

But then this horrible cunt of a copper stepped forward and started scratching his greasy sideburns while scrutinising him with his head cocked to one side. Barty began to stammer now, as he felt this monkey-looking twat's doubtful eyes burning into him. He sensed danger. We all sensed he was in danger too – we knew their style by now.

'You'd better sit the fuck down before you get a beating, Barty.'

He shot us a dirty look and bleated, 'Excuse me? Do I know you? That's not even my name and who the fuck are you anyway?'

We were rolling around in hysterics now, but just ended up tightening each other's handcuffs in the process.

'They've got all the passports from the hotel in front of them, you mug,' cried Ginger.

'Sit down, Barty,' Demus pleaded now.

'Please, señor officers, I not know these,' was Barty's response in his best sitcom Spanish.

Monkey cracked him across the back of the neck.

'OK... OK... you got me,' said Barty and sat down.

Things then went from bad to worse, as the door leading from the front desk to our little gathering opened and in came another old mate. It was Huleo! I was sat close to a filing cabinet at the time and practically climbed into it, trying to keep my head down, mainly because I didn't want the fat bastard to recognise me, but also because his face didn't look too good at all now – his nose was broken and his lips were all swollen and bloody.

He spoke briefly to the OB, turned to face the rest of us on the bench and smiled as he recognised Scouse. After another quick word with the coppers, he pointed to my mate and said in English, 'This black boy, he 'ave the knife!'

Scouse tried in vain to protest his innocence, but was quickly clubbed into submission and silence.

Now we knew that we were properly fucked – clearly, there were no rules in an investigation at the hands of the holiday police. By the early hours, they had rounded up all the lads except the Jew, Big Cliff, JB and Chop. We were questioned repeatedly as to their whereabouts and obviously we had no idea, but unfortunately this didn't stop the filth trying to beat it out of us anyway.

A ray of light then appeared in our hopeless situation in the shape of Big Cliff, who was bundled through the open door and led up to the boss of the investigating team assembled in front of us. He looked in a really sorry state as he'd been taken to hospital and had his head stitched up with thick black thread. The wound was about four inches long and was mounted on a lump the size of a tennis ball – I kid you not. His 'Luton on Tour' T-shirt was completely stained red and both his eyes were blackening steadily too.

We all leaped to our feet shouting for him to tell the police what Huleo had done to him, but he just stared at us with glazed eyes and shrugged his shoulders as if to say he didn't remember a thing. We begged him to speak up, but it was no good – our last chance was concussed and didn't know what planet he was on let alone who'd hit him.

So we were totally done for and they soon locked us up in the dark below ground. Cliff hardly said a word and slept for most of the two days we spent in the dungeon; he was really ill, but the coppers couldn't have cared less. They were more interested in playing Spanish radio as loud as possible through the intercom into our cells and laughing like children at our protests.

These were low moments for all of us and, as we lay on the floor in those concrete boxes below Es Cana, we had plenty of time to reflect on how we'd ended up in this mess. I went over my actions and what the consequences might be if I was convicted of using the fire extinguisher as a weapon. It made me think about my family and loved ones and all the shit that I had put them through by choosing to belong to the Mig Crew. I even considered knocking the football firm on the head.

Then, on the second morning, a fresh face appeared at our cell door. It was a copper who wasn't quite as harsh as the others and actually seemed concerned with Cliff's head and Scouse's injured hand. We told him we couldn't drink the water they'd been giving us, that we had money in the apartment and if he was good to us he might be able to have some of it.

Things got lively again, as our new guards chose Ging and me to be taken out of our respective cells, handcuffed together and marched across the road to our hotel to get money for water and food. I felt so embarrassed as I was led up into the sunlit street in the same clothes I had been wearing nearly three days before. I hadn't washed or shaved since then either and God knows what my breath smelled like!

Ging and I were dragged into the hotel reception by our chains, and our passports were presented to the receptionist, who addressed the OB in Spanish before asking us how much money we required from our safety deposit box. We gave her a figure, which Ging had rather wisely suggested we keep on the low side in case there was too much left over for our captor's light fingers.

Then I thought I saw a ghost. About 10 feet away on our left was the hotel staircase, which twisted around on itself and had mirrored walls, so you could see to the top of the stairwell from the reception area below. As I stared into the mirror checking exactly how much of a mess I was, I spotted a familiar face looking back at me from up the stairs. It was Chop.

Chop had been on the run with JB since our battle in Santa Eulalia. Somehow, they had evaded capture on the night and had stayed free for nearly three days, but now they were in grave danger of getting caught. I looked at him without expression, as I couldn't tell if the rozzers could see my face and didn't want to give the game away. He seemed scared and his afro was really nappy and full of bits of dirt and other crap. He'd obviously been roughing it.

He crept closer and started to mouth words silently at me, but I couldn't grasp what he was saying. Ging had spotted him too now and nudged me gently to let me know. But I just kept still and let my eyes do the talking. Then came a mistake by Chop. I don't know why, but he edged even closer – too close. The filth spotted him and that was that – he was nicked. JB, meanwhile, must have seen Chop lifted and handed himself in too. Now we were all in custody apart from the Jew, who the police had freed because of his epilepsy.

The heat outside was intense – way into the 90s. As the crowds of holidaymakers enjoyed their sangria and ice creams on the beachfront, 13 lads from Luton sat below street level in the pitch black, thirsty, hungry and depressed. The British consul visited, but only stayed for half an hour. We'd been beaten and threatened by the officers on duty, and the four black Migs with us had been repeatedly racially abused and struck with force if they reacted, but he wasn't having any of it.

Our shopping trip ended up causing us even more problems. Ging, Chop, JB and myself had returned with boxes full of essential items: crisps, chocolate, biscuits and various drinks. However, we'd also managed to get two packs of playing cards and even a bottle of poppers into the cells by convincing the OB that it was for medicinal purposes.

Once we were back behind the steel doors of the concrete boxes, we handed out the goodies and upended the boxes they'd been transported in. Then, with the lights now on, we dealt a hand of cards each, started to sniff the rush and within seconds were laughing out loud and happy as pigs in shit (which, of course, is exactly what we were). Everything seemed so much more bearable now as we chatted and ate heartily, but our good spirits were to be short-lived.

As the sound of laughter echoed around the concrete walls, the steel cell door opened slowly and in stepped the one we called Monkey. 'What is this? This is prison… not holiday. You stop… you stop now… no more holiday for you.' He rushed round the cell collecting everything we had just imported from the outside world, handing out slaps as he went.

Once the boxes were restocked with their original contents and he was sure that he had everything together, Monkey ordered us all out of our temporary home and into the corridor. His next move was predictable. Gibbering in Spanish (no doubt insulting our nationality and parentage), he proceeded to line us up in a row facing the wall, kicking and punching each of us in turn.

This was meant to hurt, but he was certainly no Mike Tyson so we all burst out laughing. Monkey lost the plot now. He ran into our cells and started to swab them out with some filthy piss-stinking water, which he'd fetched from under the staircase. Then he separated us into two groups and pushed us back inside the cells. His final trick was to produce an industrial-sized can of fly spray, which he emptied into the cells. This, of course, caused us to all start coughing wildly and I almost threw up, as did a couple of the other lads. Content with his work, Monkey slammed the doors, leaving a pile of coughing and puking Migs behind him. He was smiling again now.

Sometime later, the door opened and we were led out to join the lads from the other cell. We were handcuffed together in a long chain and led upstairs outside the police station and into the sunshine. To our surprise, we found the Jew standing by a couple of police vans, which were waiting to transport us to court on the other side of the island.

A couple of hours later, we were brought before a judge in Ibiza Town and after signing statements – which of course we couldn't read as they were in Spanish – we were sent to the local prison to fester. Only the Jew was allowed to go free again.

We soon discovered that the Spanish had imposed bail conditions on us, including payment of £500 each as security to ensure that we wouldn't leave the country or that, if we did, we'd return to face the music. So now we were banking on the Jew arranging the payments and thereby ensuring our release as soon as possible. Inside Ibiza Town Prison, the screws split us up into two groups. The Juveniles were put on one wing, while the older Migs and myself were caged in another.

We spent nearly two weeks there, during which time the Juveniles had to fight in the yard every day just to hold on to their trainers and Flower ended up in solitary confinement. Meanwhile, I had to dodge an Algerian knifeman after calling him a thief. It was surprising how angry he got, considering that he was locked up for using stolen credit cards!

In keeping with the spirit of our stay at Hotel Holiday Nightmare, Ging organised a three-round, three-minute boxing match between our own G Lawla and a six-and-a-half-foot Moroccan in the sweltering heat of the exercise yard. It was declared a draw because any other result would probably have caused a riot. We even took control of one of the fire hydrants and blasted the screws, keeping them at bay for a while, before being banned from the yard for a few days as punishment.

One sunny morning, we were finally released and flown back to lovely Luton Airport. It was then the shit really hit the fan. My in-laws had put up my bail money so now they were fully aware of the arsehole I was becoming. Suddenly, I wasn't very welcome at family functions. Most of the other lads began to have similar experiences too and soon our secret little social scene was out in the open as people realised the Migs weren't just a schoolboy joke any more.

The following season Luton went on a Cup run, which was actually not unusual for us in those days. We'd drawn Bradford City in the third round, which meant we'd come face to face with a firm we knew very little about, apart from their name – 'the Ointment'.

They surprised us by coming down early and put it about town that they were here to give it to the Mig Crew. For most of the day, they went unopposed and gained in confidence. They strolled from pub to pub giving it large, not realising that the clock was ticking on their fun because Luton's mob was gathering in Hightown as people finished work and got their football heads on.

Not long before six o'clock, we made our way towards the town centre and The Heights pub. The Ointment had been drowning their sorrows in there for the last few hours and were so keen to meet us they even asked the landlord where the Migs were. What the Yorkshire boys didn't know was that he also ran the pub we used for big games. He was one of us, so to speak, and so now we knew how many, how game and how pissed.

We met them outside the Town Hall; they were 40-handed and came bouncing straight towards us. We stood our ground and then a couple of us pulled out whistles and started to blow. As the two rival mobs clashed on George Street, neither was really gaining the upper hand, but we continued blowing our whistles regardless, causing confused faces in the Ointment's front row. They gathered their numbers again, ready to charge and rout our little crew, but then they saw why we were blowing on our plastic whistles.

They were a signal for the rest of our lads to head to a designated meeting point. All too often when you try to move a football mob about, the OB spot it quickly because of the sheer numbers and then proceed to block its route, so we decided to split down into more manoeuvrable groups to avoid being quite so obvious. But, of course, this meant that we could find ourselves seriously outnumbered if we came across the opposing crew. The whistles cured this problem. So, just as Bradford's lads had started to feel confident in their superior numbers, they had to think again as Luton lads came pouring out of the shadows on all sides and converged on the battle location.

The Ointment quickly changed their attack position to a defensive one. Scouse came in from one side and was soon trading punches with a tall mixed-race lad. As they battled like two deer locking horns, I joined Maz in an attack on the right-hand side. This didn't go too well initially, as we became isolated from the main mob and soon felt the weight of half a dozen Yorkshire lumps bearing down on us. They forced us back against the nearby buildings and we didn't get to throw too many punches until one of them slipped, lost his footing and ended up on his arse. Soon another joined him, as I landed a clean one under his chin.

The Bradford boys panicked now, as they realised that this was a battle they weren't going to win, so they turned and broke in a total mess. We gave chase and soon the Ointment was smeared everywhere. The last I saw of them was a pair of feet hanging out of a taxi window as they dived in to escape the onslaught.

The next round brought us a dream tie against QPR. This lot were our bitter enemies and, on their day, both mobs could claim results against the other. However, as it transpired, the lads travelled to Shepherds Bush without me and many of the other main players. It was just one of those things that happen sometimes. For whatever reasons, we didn't send the right force down there and the price was paid accordingly.

Once they reached White City, the Juveniles and a ragged collection of other 'up for it' lads decided to enter the South Africa Stand and try to get a result in the ground. So, as the Rangers lads entered their section of Loftus Road, they were greeted by around 40 lairy Luton in their seats. Unfortunately, it started to get nasty, and our lads, many of whom just weren't ready for the level of hostility they'd provoked, backed off and ended up letting the side down. The Met eventually removed the Luton contingent, which probably saved the day and prevented a rout of our up-and-coming youngsters.

After the game, the disheartened Luton group made its way to St Pancras to board the train home and, while they were waiting on the concourse licking their wounds, what looked like a good opportunity for revenge appeared. A group of QPR lads were standing under the arch leading out on to the Euston Road and beckoning them outside for a row. There were only 10 of them and the bait was too sweet to ignore.

So Luton's mob went for it and chased after the fast-departing West London lads. It was a mistake. No sooner had the 40 or so Luton exited St Pancras hot on the heels of their prey than a mob of nearly 150 Bush Babies came charging from across Euston Road. Luton ran in panic.

Back inside the station, a small band of the Juveniles and original Migs made a stand at the ticket barriers and held up the Rangers firm for a minute or two, but eventually the weight of numbers had them backing off on to the platform. Now the battle really turned vicious, as makeshift weapons such as brooms and trolleys were smashed into limbs and heads. During this heated battle, a Luton lad called Touch charged into the QPR group with a luggage trolley and then disappeared under a hail of punches, where he was stabbed.

After the return fixture at Kenilworth Road, revenge was the order of the day. QPR came in their usual style: small bands of game lads, well dressed and sure of themselves and again numbering about 150 altogether. What they met that night was an army of locals and Migs who gave no quarter and, by the time the match kicked off, seven Bush Babies were already in hospital with stab wounds or having had ammonia squirted in their eyes.

It wasn't just football, it was hate and, although there have been clashes with QPR since, they've never been on the same scale. The national press reported the clashes in detail and focused on the stabbings, which resulted in some unwanted police attention for me, as I had been arrested on the night of the game myself and accused of wounding one of the Rangers lads. The police had their facts wrong, but charged me anyway.

In the draw for the next round, we got Portsmouth, which meant a chance to test ourselves against a firm with a big reputation in the football hooligan world – the infamous 6.57 Crew.

On the morning of the tie, the front doors came in. 'Operation Spoonbill' moved rapidly into full swing and, by the end of the day, many of the Mig Crew were behind bars. Charges were handed out and some of the lads remanded. Across the country, other firms were being similarly 'dawn raided' and charged with football-related crimes. The police were using the standard approach of hitting possible hooligans' houses at the crack of dawn, armed with a sledgehammer and a TV camera crew.

They would highlight the Casual clothing and any other paraphernalia that they could get their grubby little mitts on, as if providing proof of an organised and profitable crime gang. Then, in the evening, they would wheel out the decorator's paste table covered in a white cloth to display the stash of confiscated weapons like some horde of buried treasure. Of course, they always failed to point out that the bottles of bleach were from the kitchen and the hammers and craft knives from your dad's toolbox in the garden shed.

But all the Luton lads were acquitted and up and down the country trials against the likes of Wolverhampton Wanderers' Subway Army, Chelsea's Headhunters and the Leicester Baby Squad had only minimal success in gaining convictions.

A conviction is one thing, but the fear of one is quite another and, when you're looking down the barrel of a six- or seven-year sentence for Conspiracy to Cause Affray, it hits home. So, with the Ibiza 'holiday' plus the dawn raids and of course the option of dancing the night away to the sound of house beats instead, the Mig Crew passed into a cycle of decline.

It stayed like this for a few years. But then in 1994 another Cup run came along. We played Newcastle in the third round and, after we had sent the Geordies packing with some top-drawer football, which hadn't been seen at Kenilworth Road for a few years, we were due to take on Cardiff City at Ninian Park on a Sunday.

Thousands made the journey from Bedfordshire to South Wales and among the travelling army was a detachment of the original Migs, myself included. We were back together for the first time in a couple of years and it felt good. One thing was for sure, we weren't in Cardiff just for the football. To prove the point, we drove straight past the ground and headed deep into the tightly packed houses of an estate about two miles from Ninian Park, where we found the perfect spot for a confrontation – a working men's club full of Taffies.

We came into one side of the bar and the action soon started. We managed to hold our end without too much difficulty, but the Taffs wanted to take it outside and so we kindly obliged. There was a skip full of builders' rubbish just across the road, which we soon emptied and used to our advantage, so the Cardiff lads wisely retired straight back into the boozer and left the OB to sort us out instead.

Luton won the game 2–1 with David Preece scoring a blatantly offside winner after Swansea-born John Hartson had celebrated our first in front of a stadium packed full of Cardiff headcases 'Doing the Ayatollah'.

For most of the match, we exchanged missiles with our Welsh enemy and waited for the final whistle, which when it came was the signal for them to invade the pitch. We all scaled the fencing in anticipation, ready to face the onslaught. Half a dozen Luton lads even jumped on to the pitch in their eagerness, but were immediately hammered by the stewards. Fighting then broke out between the massed ranks of Luton supporters and the same heavy-handed stewards. Meanwhile, the Cardiff lads launched an attack on the first Luton to try to exit the stadium, using CS gas to cause panic among the normal fans as it all went Wild West outside.

Next came West Ham at a packed Upton Park on a Tuesday evening, when 4,000 Luton supporters were seated in the newly opened Bobby Moore Stand. After a pulsating evening's entertainment, which somehow ended 0–0, we made our way to The Denmark Arms in East Ham where we had a beer with a few Eastenders and no trouble at all. The replay was a fantastic occasion with the Town winning 3–2, thanks to a Scott Oakes hat-trick, which got me so worked up that I invaded the pitch as the third hit the back of the net and ended up with a £150 fine for my troubles.

Now we were in the semis and needed to dispose of the mighty Chelsea to get to the Final, which was most unlikely. So, in a way, we all knew this was to be our final both on and off the pitch. The game was to be played at Wembley, which made the occasion that little bit different to if it had been played at Stamford Bridge. I know which I would have preferred.

The Mig Crew put the word out that we would be meeting at The Moulders Arms and the doors would be open from seven in the morning. We'd made contact with the latest version of the Chelsea Headhunters and arranged to meet them at West Hampstead.

At 1.30, we marched over the hill at West Hampstead with over 200 of Luton's finest boys, not just the Mig Crew, but a mixture of old faces including some of the Castle Bar and the Hockwell Steamers. This firm was probably as good as we could get, if not the largest gathering we could muster at the time. It would take something special to shift it one inch, let alone to take it.

The scene that we came upon was one of another 200 lads having a pop at a couple of police vans and not doing too badly either. One thing was obvious, though, it wasn't the Chelsea mob we were due to meet, but more Luton lads.

A decision was made to about face and head straight down to the Underground. This was done so quickly that half the firm didn't even realise and headed on to join the other Luton crew. The lads that had turned sharply on their heels and made their way down the staircase leading to the trains had one thing in common – they were all Migs.

At the head of our breakaway firm was a legend in his own time, DP. In my opinion and that of many others too, DP was the main player at Luton for many years. He's a big lump of a black fella with a history that would fill more than one book and I have watched opposition firms crumble at just the sight of him heading in their direction.

Once on the tube, we headed to Kilburn, as we'd heard this was going to be a staging post for the Chelsea mob before it headed on to West Hampstead. At Kilburn, we streamed off with menace on our minds. Another train pulled into the adjoining platform containing hundreds of Chelsea 'shirts', but with a few lads mixed in too. We were going to ignore them but, when the doors opened, they started to give us verbals, so we steamed straight on to the train and handed out digs to those asking for it.

During the commotion, one of the lads, Buzz, sparked up a CS Gas Stick and launched it into the blue cunts on the train. However, he'd misjudged its strength and soon the whole of Kilburn Station hung in a gas cloud. I saw DP rubbing his eyes too, as the CS burned into them. Then the OB arrived, clutching handkerchiefs against their faces, and charged into the haze on the platforms. One particular woman PC tackled Buzz and rather impressively wrestled him to the deck, where she set about handcuffing him. He looked up at us for help, but there was no way anyone was going to touch a female officer.

The main body of Luton now found themselves facing a huge wave of police rushing on to the scene and used Chelsea's reputation to good effect by telling the first officers on the scene in dramatic tones, 'Chelsea are animals! They've attacked our train and now they're battering everyone down the far end.'

The Met bravely reassured us of our safety and went storming off down the platform in search of the Chelsea thugs.

Meanwhile, we nipped out of the station, took a right and spotted the proper Chelsea firm holed up in the pub outside. There were loads of them in there, crammed right up to the windows, so they saw us instantly. We charged forward and the windows went in.

Chelsea started to fight their way out into the High Street by launching bottles and half-filled glasses of beer and they certainly won the initial engagement, as one particularly hard cunt in a red sweatshirt decked Windy with a slamming blow. We fought for every inch, but they had the momentum and it briefly became a scrum without a ball, as they forced us back. DP then stepped in and smashed the lump in red, who dropped immediately and took a good shoeing. The tide had changed. Now we battered as many of the West Londoners as possible, as they retreated back where they'd come from.

Somewhat inevitably, the OB came pouring back out of the station, so we legged it down Kilburn High Street knocking out any Chelsea in our path. It was quite funny seeing one after another go down so easily, although I have to admit they weren't all proper boys. Ten minutes later, we were on a double-decker escaping the scene. There were about 30 of us on one bus, including big DP who was laughing his head off at how shit Chelsea had been after all the hype.

On the pitch at Wembley, we didn't fare so well as Luton lost the game 4–1 in front of a capacity crowd that was at least two-thirds blue. While the Chelsea fans celebrated, a small team of Migs headed to West Hampstead to locate a boozer to house a decent-sized firm in readiness for the mob of Chelsea that would appear at some point.

During the train journey, DP and I had a chance encounter with four West London lads who I was sure I recognised. They didn't say much, but asked where to find us that night. We made it simple for them, suggesting that they should leave West Hampstead Station, turn right and head up the hill towards the village. We would be in the first pub they found open and would stay there until closing time. By about 8.30 that night, we had 80 Migs getting pissed up in a tight, but well-lit pub on the main drag.

Around this time, one of the notorious Chelsea Twins walked in and enquired if we were the Migs. The reply was a confident 'yes', so he asked if he and his compatriot could have a drink and a chat and we duly obliged. Once the pleasantries were over, we asked how many were coming to West Hampstead.

He looked up at the ceiling and seemed to be mulling over whether it was a good idea to tell us Chelsea's strength, but then announced, 'About 200 and I'll tell you now, chaps, these are top boys... You won't get better than this.'

DP bit straight away. He told him to get the fuck out of the boozer and get them here now. The Chelsea face didn't look too comfortable and a bead of sweat appeared on his forehead before trickling its way down his tanned face. He rose without a word and left with his sidekick in tow.

As the Migs gathered outside West Hampstead Station, we tooled up by grabbing bottles of beer out of the many surrounding off-licences. The battle was sure to come, but would it happen before the Met turned up?

An hour passed and the bottles were empty, and by now many of the lads wanted to give up waiting and head on back to Luton for last orders. We argued and were gutted when many of our best lads, including The

Wolf, left for home. This guy was someone we were desperate to keep with us for the party, but he wouldn't believe that Chelsea were really coming – half the lads felt that the visit by one of the Twins was actually a sign that the Headhunters weren't coming today. In the end, half the firm left and boarded the train to Luton.

The rest of us watched as two more trains stopped below and then headed on north. And, as our thirsts were building and time was ticking on, we finally strolled down on to West Hampstead Station to catch the next train home. As we stood discussing the day's events and where to go clubbing once safely back in Luton, they came. We stared in utter disbelief as hundreds of bobbing heads appeared on the bridge that crosses the mainline tracks. It looked as though they wouldn't stop coming. It was sobering to say the least.

How did we react? We charged up the platform stairs and tore straight into them. It was mental as they came charging along to meet our sudden surge, but soon found themselves outgunned on the frontline.

DP, Nigel, Freddy, Andy, Ging and a host of others joined me in the fierce toe-to-toe battle on the stairs and it was such a buzz seeing the fear in the eyes of our infamous foe. We were dragging Chelsea cunts down into the pack behind and then they were being launched on to the tracks. In the midst of the battle, I looked at the faces in the two mobs and there couldn't have been more of a contrast – we were loving it and they just looked stunned.

I saw our mates from the train earlier as we battled along the top of the staircase and they didn't want to know. It was turning into a rout now, especially as those who couldn't fit on the stairs were using the bottles purchased earlier to good effect on Chelsea heads. Just as we reached the street outside, the OB arrived on the scene and battered us back with batons until we were penned in at the far end of the platform. We celebrated like we'd just won the lottery.

What a contrast between the feelings I felt running through me that day and the ones my new brief had just caused with one little comment: 'Its not like you're Chelsea, is it?'

She didn't have a clue and, to be brutally honest, most football lads don't either. We aren't the famous CFC, that's for sure, but we'd shown that on the day reputations count for fuck all. What counts is togetherness and belief in the group you're attached to.

So, Chelsea, you won't get better than this, eh? I beg to differ.

6 Catching the Shady Express

Up and down the country on Saturday mornings, week in and week out, you'll find thousands of lads jumping out of bed early, having a quick wash and then climbing into their favourite clobber. They come from many different backgrounds and you won't be able to stereotype them into one social group, no matter how much some people try to. They have one thing in common, though – they like football violence.

I have read many people's views on what makes a football hooligan tick and, even though some of the literature is interesting, it's never 100 per cent accurate. It can't be, because football lads change with the times and never stand still. In recent years, the law has changed too. When I left school and was still a baby in the hoolie world, if you were arrested for fighting at the match, you would expect a fine at the most.

I'd been arrested at Coventry City in the mid-80s in a ground that had recently been made an all-seater on the orders of a certain Jimmy Hill, who was their chairman at the time. He believed that seated stadiums would prevent trouble as plastic seats made unsuitable terrain for brawling. What Mr Hill failed to understand, however, was that we would fight on a bed of nails if we had to.

So, as I connected with the back of the ginger lad's head at Highfield Road that day, I didn't even notice the plastic ripping my shins to pieces. As blows rained down on my own head too, all that mattered was that I was buzzing. I only realised my shins hurt as I was being dragged along the pitch by two OB and knew I was on my way to the cells.

Two weeks later, five of us pleaded 'Guilty' to the traditional football offence of Threatening Words and Behaviour and I took my £250 fine on the chin like a man – the punishment fitted the crime. That was nearly 20 years ago. Today, I was awaiting sentencing for throwing the same kind of punches, but this time the chances were that I would be going to prison. Like I said, the law has changed – the question was, had I?

My new barrister remained cheerful as we chatted about today's hearing. But she moaned about the previous brief's notes and handwriting, eventually coming to the decision that she would go her own way completely.

'What's your main aim for the day, Tom?'

'To stay out of prison,' I replied as firmly as possible, holding eye contact to help reinforce my plea for freedom.

'Looking at the previous sentencing for this incident, I don't see that as a realistic possibility I'm afraid.'

In the days prior to my hearing, another group of our lads had been up before Judge Cripps and all 14 of them had been banged up. My brief described the case of one of the lads who had been caged. Alf was in his early twenties and of Italian descent and his only crime had been to run on to the pitch at Vicarage Road before the game, then run off it again shortly afterwards. He didn't hit anybody and didn't approach anyone in a threatening manner. He said he acted alone.

The prosecution accepted that he had no previous convictions and was of 'good character'. Judge Cripps then listened to his fiancée in the dock as she explained that they were getting married in the New Year and had a joint mortgage too. Alf was self-employed and clearly a thoughtful, hardworking partner. Cripps just sent him straight down for eight months and banned him from football for seven years.

Unsurprisingly, on hearing this, I felt somewhat deflated. My brief started to look for some positives to take into court – one being that I had served my country for seven years in the Navy and had recently been sent to Sierra Leone on a humanitarian operation. She said the court would definitely look favourably at this. So maybe things weren't as bad as they seemed.

There was another difference between my case and those heard previously – I was pleading 'Guilty' to Affray, while the lads caught on the pitch had been charged with the more serious offence of Violent Disorder. So now I was ready to face Mr Cripps and, as I left my legal representative sitting alone in the cramped magnolia-coloured room, I felt a wave of optimism pass over me.

Catching the Shady Express

Then I saw Armchair Al with a look of dread on his face. He'd just finished chatting with his solicitor and didn't much like what he had heard; he started to mumble about the fact that we were probably all going to prison in the next few hours. I had to laugh. Even at this late stage, he still couldn't accept the possibility of a custodial sentence.

'Fucking hell, Al, you knew the risk when you joined up with the firm that day.' I was only telling him what he needed to hear. 'Grow up a bit and stop whining!'

But he wasn't happy and shook his head. 'Why did I listen to you cunts? I shouldn't even have gone.'

Armchair had picked up his nickname from the MI2s, when, in one of the many arguments at Luton between the younger lot and the elders, he'd made the mistake of joining in. 'Why don't you fuck off back home to your armchair and slippers, Granddad?' And so he was re-born.

As he griped about facing up to the consequences of his actions at Watford, I reminded him about Plymouth at home the previous season, when he punched through the window of a van full of Argyle lads and claimed to have sparked one of them out in the process.

He started to laugh, as he knew his argument was just plain hypocritical. But then he was at it again, claiming that we wound him up too much on the day and even made a last-ditch attempt to get us to stop calling him Armchair. 'You fuckers didn't call me that when Plymouth walked into The Barrels that day, did you, you cunts?' he pleaded, puffing out his chest.

He was referring to a Third Division game in February 2002 when Plymouth were racing us for the title. Plymouth had sold their full allocation of 2,000 tickets and helped make up a crowd of 9,585, which is a big gate for us nowadays. I'd managed to get a seat for the Maple Road End along with loads of the lads.

The morning prior to the game, a small clan of Migs, including Flower, Mixer, Armchair, Shit Hair, Manton, Sick Nick and myself, met in The Barrels for a pre-match drink before meeting the rest of the boys at The Old English. As we were waiting for our taxi, a coach pulled into the pub car park.

Now The Barrels is way outside the normal areas where you might find visiting supporters coming to Luton. It's near Stopsley, close to the A5, which leads to Hitchin. From there, you can either head north towards the A1 or out towards East Anglia, so you would only really expect supporters from Cambridge or maybe Norwich to use this route and certainly not fans from Devon in the deep South West.

The doors to The Barrels flew open and in walked 50 blokes of all ages, shouting, 'We are top the league – said, we are top the league' in strong yokel accents. We were sat at one end of the otherwise empty boozer and couldn't believe what was happening. We didn't react violently to the incursion, as we were heavily outnumbered, but also because we couldn't decide if this bunch of bumpkins were hostile or just regular supporters. Their dress code didn't help, as some had club shirts on, while others had Stone Island jumpers squeezed over their ample frames.

We lined ourselves up in a defensive position ready for any onslaught and Flower reached for his gas. Yet, after their initial rowdy outburst, on spotting our shady-looking crew, the Plymouth boys huddled together and silence descended. I'm sure they knew that they had the numbers to take us, but they also realised it would have been a bloodbath. Maybe some among them just weren't up for that kind of action, but for whatever the reason the attack never came. What did come, however, was our black cab. We walked out calmly and set off to The Old English, leaving the Plymouth boys to relax.

There, we joined the mob of assembling Migs and waited for contact from The Central Element boys. We'd set up a bushwhack by sending them to a boozer close to where we would be drinking ourselves. This spot, The Melson, held a crowd of MI2s. The idea was to draw The Central Element out of their watering hole and into the open by offering them the Babies as easy pickings. Once they'd engaged our youngsters, we would hit them hard from behind with proven Mig chaps. This would have left the Plymouth crew scattered in small numbers, three miles from the ground on the wrong side of town, where they would have been terrorised for the rest of the day.

Some old mates of mine arrived at The Old English at about one o'clock. Icy, Neil K and Jonesy are all from Wrexham and had come down to witness the potential clash of two top Third Division mobs. I met Jonesy at an earlier game when Wrexham had brought a tight firm of 30 lads to Luton. They had managed to evade the OB, get themselves into our town centre and were plotted up in The Saddlers Bar.

I rated them for this, as bigger clubs and those much closer to Luton don't often manage to do it. Usually, it's because they don't actually try very hard. All too often, you have to listen to all the chat from so-called 'good mobs' about how they have this many or that many and they're going to do this and that, only to see a large escort surrounding 100 posing lads arrive at Luton at half-past two. QPR have been particularly guilty of this in recent years.

As Jonesy and the Wrexham lads sat drinking, I turned up with Windy to see what their plans were. They didn't have any firm plans apart from getting to Luton and mobbing up. They were told where to go for a row and where not to go if they wanted to avoid the OB, but unfortunately they ignored this advice and, instead, chose to kick off near the ground with some of Luton's other football lads.

When I received the news, I was so pissed off that I jumped in a taxi with Big Cliff and headed down to where Jonesy and his boys were being held up by Bedfordshire OB. It was pissing down and I was quickly soaked through as I leaped out and stormed through the OB, to let Wrexham's Frontline know exactly how disappointed I was. I spotted Jonesy at the front of the escort and headed straight over to him to tell him what a letdown him and his firm were.

Two weeks later, I was pissing it up in The Sports Bar after another home game, when Jonesy walked in and came over to apologise for what had happened. To stroll into a boozer in a rival's town on your own and make yourself known takes some balls and he won my respect on the spot. Soon I also met a lunatic named Icy and then Neil K followed. They're all sound lads and proper football boys.

As The Old English swelled with Migs, we became increasingly impatient because Plymouth's firm seemed very disorganised and disjointed. We'd received conflicting calls, saying they had numbers ranging from 30 to 300. In any event, we just kept on pointing them towards our trap, hoping that they were keen enough to take the bait.

At around two o'clock, we began to see a pattern emerge from the Plymouth contacts. They were all converging on The Nine Bar in the town centre. The place was surrounded by CCTV and was where the OB stuck most visiting fans these days, as it's close to the train station and easy for them to control. To us, on the other hand, it meant game over.

At this point, many firms would know they were beaten and just give up. I have to admit that at times the Migs have done the same. Not on this occasion, though. Instead, we told the Babies to head in the direction of The Nine Bar and try to keep the OB occupied. At the same time, we sent a runner to The White House, which was just a few minutes from The Nine

Bar and contained over 100 other Luton thugs. We asked this lot to come out of the boozer and give the police another distraction. We hoped that all this combined commotion might create enough of a diversion to allow the Mig Crew to storm The Nine Bar and get at The Central Element inside.

We needed a route that would keep us hidden from the OB until the last minute, so we headed through the bus station, across Guildford Street and into the multi-storey car park. There, we made for stairwells leading directly on to the road below, which would give us access to the side door of The Nine Bar.

Initially, we moved like ghosts and no one saw us pass through the grey streets of Luton, but then we came to Guildford Street. The Nine Bar was also here, about 150 metres up the road from us. I suspected the OB would have spotters covering this potential angle of attack. But we were pleasantly surprised to see no OB on Guildford Street at all, so the way looked open for a sneak attack on the Plymouth fans.

'Looks like the other lads have drawn all the plod away,' someone shouted from the rear.

We started along Guildford Street, zipping up our hoods or wrapping dark-coloured scarves over our excited faces – getting caught on CCTV wasn't an option. But, just as we thought we might get the confrontation we'd been hoping for all morning, things took a turn for the worse.

A handful of OB came running round the corner of the target pub and stopped, gesturing back in the direction from which they had just appeared. This meant that they had more colleagues waiting to repel any assault so we quickly returned to plan A and headed in the direction of the multi-storey car park. There, we hid in the darkness trying to regain our breath. The adrenaline was flowing and we knew we had almost reached our prey. As we filed into the stairwells and descended to the next level, we spotted the OB through the grimy car-park window – they were racing around from the town to cut off our advance. What now?

We had three choices: one, a full-scale charge at the OB lines; two, get back to Guildford Street and find another way to get at the Plymouth mob; or the final option was to stay put and hope the OB wouldn't spot 80 lads in hoods and baseball caps hiding on the dimly lit staircase. We chose to stay put.

As I peered through the glass, Luton's police spotter came into view. He was marching towards our position while staring through his big bins at the multi-storey car park – obviously, he'd heard reports on his radio that a group of us had run inside. He had a troubled look on his face and moved uncomfortably while holding his hand close to his ear. I watched as he came closer still and half-expected him to spot us lurking in the shadows.

'He's as blind as a bat, the stupid cunt,' was one of the more polite comments made by the lads waiting patiently for him to pass.

Then, just as he was almost upon us, he stopped, rubbed his forehead again, before turning and heading back towards The White House. He'd missed us.

Now we got on the mobile to Plymouth's lads asking them if they'd make a big effort to get out of the pub and into the road, as we were close by and they would have a chance of an off within the next few minutes. Next, we took a chance and the piss at the same time. Knowing there was a pile of OB, including the Met's Robocops, waiting in between The Nine Bar and us, we had to cross the road ahead to try to evade being rounded up. So, as our spotter sauntered back towards his colleagues with a bemused look on his face, I decided to stroll out into the open and simply pray that he didn't turn around.

The lads all followed suit and, as our mate from the Old Bill walked in the direction of The White House, he didn't see our sizeable crew passing just feet behind him. His colleagues did, though, and started to wave frantically at him to turn round. But he didn't have a clue and we all pissed ourselves as he ignored them, shouting in an authoritative voice, 'They ain't in there – they must be somewhere else.' It was hard not to run up behind him and boot him in the arse!

As we left matey and his radio, we passed between the library building and the Strathmore Hotel, both close to the green in the town centre, took a sharp right and headed towards The White House. By now, everyone had realised that we probably weren't going to get to The Nine Bar, but hoped Plymouth's firm might have made it into the road. Then, as we approached, we saw a sight that got the heart racing.

Straight ahead, only 30 metres away, a mob of over 100 lads were calling us on for a battle. They outnumbered us comfortably, but it was the perfect invitation. Scarves and headgear were adjusted as we spread out in a wide front and started to jog towards the ranks of lads standing outside The White House. The jog became a sprint and clusters of thugs crossed the road to meet us – battle was imminent.

The first to get dropped was a skinhead who fell while negotiating the traffic blocking his progress. Then one of the Migs punched another lad, connecting cleanly twice and causing his rival to drop to the pavement. I started to size up a fat cunt who was calling everyone forward to join the conflict now breaking out in the full view of the OB. As I closed on my target, I noticed the OB charging at us with batons drawn, but I also started to feel that I recognised the guy I was lining up for a smack. Then suddenly it dawned on me that we were fighting Luton lads in full view of the law. It had to be because we were all hiding our identities and they thought we were Plymouth. Soon all was revealed as the cry of 'Migs, Migs, Migs' filled the air.

The Luton lads now retreated across the road, laughing as they went and we followed them into The White House. The conversations were humorous and loud, with the other local lads praising themselves for standing in the face of a charge from the infamous Mig Crew. The OB, meanwhile, breathed a sigh of relief when they realised what had happened.

Now the Migs were housed in the same boozer as the other Luton boys, there must have been over 250 hooligans all wanting to get at the Plymouth mob. However, as is often the case nowadays, we waited in vain as the Devon boys were escorted through the streets to Kenilworth Road by a huge police presence, including horses and dog handlers.

A tense atmosphere at the match was broken when Matthew Taylor was brought down in the Plymouth box and Nichols converted the resulting penalty. It was as much as the Town deserved, until Howard headed home from a corner with only minutes remaining.

Plymouth's Central Element did eventually find some action in the streets of Bury Park. While trying to evade Bedfordshire Police, they bumped into the local Asian gang – the BPYP – and fought a running battle with them for a couple of minutes until the police halted the action. Before the OB arrived, one of the Plymouth lads was stabbed bringing a long day to a sad end.

The fact that we never met their crew head on was a bit of a disappointment as I'd been out on the piss in Plymouth, or 'Guzz' as we called in the RN, and had always looked for signs of football lads in and around the town centre. I'd never seen any evidence, but had heard a lot about them from other Matlots during my time in service. I admit that we didn't travel down to Plymouth for the earlier fixture at their place, but this was because they were carrying out ground improvements and limiting the tickets available to visiting fans. So, when the day was over, I felt deflated.

It was totally different to how I'd felt earlier in the season when Swansea visited. The Welsh lads came to town totally unannounced. A lot of the lads prefer proper notification as this gives everyone time to prepare, although I don't mind either way. Instead, they just turned up in vans during the match with about 30 to 40 lads. The South Wales boys made their way to the Newt & Cucumber, one of our boozers in town, and bumped into Windy who was alone. He made the call to us at the game and soon a small band of Migs was making its way back through Bury Park to see what the sneaky boyos were up to.

Within seconds of the first six or seven of us arriving at the agreed pub, my attention was seized by 30 lads coming up King Street towards us. It was the Swansea crew. There wasn't a copper in sight as Shit Hair, Baby J, D Gentle plus a couple of others ploughed straight into them and traded blows. I took on a bald-headed lump in the centre of the road and, after blocking his feeble haymakers, smacked him straight in the jaw and then backed him up with a right to the forehead. I jeered at him as he fell backwards on to his arse.

To my left, I heard a few slaps go in and spotted Baby J curled up with his hands protecting his head and two Welsh cunts stamping on him. I turned 45 degrees and charged across to help him. One of them went straight over as I connected with the back of his head and then, as he fell over Baby J's body, he knocked his mate over at the same time. I didn't bother to touch them as they struggled to get back up and instead helped the young MI2 to his feet.

Now the Swansea firm started to melt. As we sensed they were losing their confidence, we went for the kill, and with one big charge had them running back down King Street in panic. We didn't bother chasing them.

After this incident, there were a couple of other skirmishes later that evening, but nothing worth reporting. Swansea had done their bit, though, and made a top effort – now we had to return the compliment.

As our successful 2001–02 season drew to a close, we had a decision to make. Our final three away fixtures were Swansea in March, with Hull and Shrewsbury Town in April. Each one was equally important, but for different reasons. While Swansea had come to Luton and a return trip was due, Hull hadn't bothered back in November, but they were known to have a good home mob. Shrewsbury was our last away game of the season, so we had to do that one and, besides, we'd heard the Border Firm were well worth a dance. We couldn't ask the majority of the lads to make all three trips, so it was a straight choice between Hull and Swansea.

I wanted to go to Swansea as did half the lads, but many wanted Hull because they would be a bigger scalp. We spoke to some Yids who'd been up there recently and they informed us it was over-policed, so we might not actually get much action. We considered taking it to the Silver Cod, but felt we might get backed off there so we decided that it would be a waste of our efforts. Also, with any trip to Wales always proving eventful for an English mob, we agreed that it would be Swansea first, then Shrewsbury and the EBF a couple of weeks later.

Transport became an issue with long journeys for both games. Cars and vans would be one option, as they allow a lot of flexibility, but on the downside you never really know how many lads will turn up on the day. From past experience, we had found that it's best to get an early commitment to an away day in the form of cash up front, as this generally guarantees an appearance.

For Swansea, we decided on a coach for the Migs and vans for the MI2s, who were going to head into town first to do a bit of spotting. The opposition were known to drink in The Glamorgan, The Jacks or The Garibaldi on match days, so our aim was to take one of these boozers and hold it until home time. Alternatively, we'd plot up somewhere the OB would never expect us and let Swansea bring it to us.

We arrived at 10 in the morning, while the Babies had arrived half an hour before and been pulled over by the OB. They'd been lucky not to get banged up on the spot as they had various weapons stowed on board, along with the Mig Crew battle flag and other dubious bits and pieces. They called us, giving clear instructions of where the OB were set up to catch us, and it soon became obvious that we were going to struggle to reach any of the target areas without the OB joining us and spoiling the fun.

As the Babies tried to talk their way out of trouble, we stopped our coach on the ring road at the edge of town and told the driver to disappear. Once we were all off, we headed into an estate situated on a raised area above the main route into Swansea town centre. At the top of the steps, there was a working men's pub with a selection of tables and chairs arranged out front and, as it was a lovely sunny day, we chose to stick around and get pissed. Soon, most of the lads were catching some rays as

Catching the Shady Express

they discussed the day ahead. The rest of us sat in the boozer, mingling with the dockers who started to appear around midday. Some of these were rough lads and were well shocked to find a mob of English boys pissing it up in their favourite watering hole.

Not long afterwards, the rotten-looking barmaid shouted over that there was a phone call for the Luton lads and, rather bemused, one of the boys followed her to the payphone. He returned and said it was for me! I stumbled out back to the phone and raised the receiver to my ear, half-expecting to hear one of the lads out front start taking the piss in a bad attempt at a Welsh accent. But, instead, the voice on the other end belonged to a proper Swansea lad called Ross. 'We know you're there, Tommy. Just sit tight and we'll be down to see you soon.'

I put the phone down.

Meanwhile, the sunbathing Migs were laughing as two Welsh bobbies ran round in circles after a bunch of kids who'd been launching stones at the traffic passing down below the estate. Once they'd given up the chase, the two plod turned their attention to the 20 or so lads burning in the sun: 'Who are you lot then?'

'We're from Ipswich, officer. It's a stag do. We're out in Cardiff tonight and thought we'd stop off for some refreshment at this fine establishment.'

The OB nodded sarcastically and left.

We informed everyone that Swansea knew where we were and that we should stay put until they arrived. We waited patiently for about an hour, but no one appeared apart from two nervous young Stone Islanders, who didn't hang around for long. However, the beers were flowing steadily and everyone was looking forward to the action that was bound to come our way at some stage.

The Babies had now reached The Glamorgan and already had the better of a small skirmish with some of the Jack's Army in the back streets, although they admitted that the numbers were in their favour.

Then a small unmarked police car pulled up outside our pub and it was our very own football spotter who stepped out alongside his opposite number from Swansea OB. He shook his head and told us they'd found our coach, so now we had a straight choice between a three-mile walk through hostile territory to the ground or for our driver to come and give us a lift.

We called their bluff and started to walk off towards the city centre – it was a sunny day after all and perfect for a stroll. Inevitably, though, we had

OB all over us within minutes and, after they rounded us all up, our coach appeared outside the pub. We were herded on board and after a short journey parked right outside The Glamorgan for the next stage of our OB-assisted pub crawl. Inside, we joined the other Luton lads and, of course, the MI2s, who'd also brought an element of Tottenham's youth firm with them to South Wales.

From here, it was clear that it would take a special effort to get through the police lines to meet the Welsh boys only a couple of hundred metres up the road. We made an attempt at 2.30, as over 100 of us stormed towards a garage across the road, only to be forced back by the local plod. I managed to slip through, though, and met up with Ross to have quick chat, all of which was filmed by the ever-present police video department of course.

As we entered the Vetch at three, we positioned ourselves down in the left-hand corner closest to the Swansea lads. The Welsh boys gave us the traditional hand signals calling us to come forward, but our younger lads had a new trick up their sleeves. They produced golf balls with St George's crosses and the words 'Luton Mig Crew' printed across them, which were hurled at the tightly packed Welsh terrace. The locals responded with an angry surge towards the pitch, knocking over the advertising hoardings in the process and forcing the OB to hurriedly redeploy themselves to force any would-be pitch invaders back into the stand.

Just after half-time, a large group of us tried a different approach, attempting to smash our way out of the ground and make our way around to the back of the stand containing our rivals. But, after a fruitless struggle with the heavy iron gates and the OB hitting us from behind with batons, we gave up and returned to the terrace for the second half.

With the sun still shining, we celebrated wildly as Matt Homes scored a rare goal and good old Steve Howard added a third, before Swansea grabbed a consolation in the last minute. After the match, the Luton players stayed on the pitch to celebrate promotion with their fans, but we had other ideas. As soon as the exits were open, we stormed straight out, only to be greeted by a heavy police presence intent on forcing us back to our transport and on to the road home as quickly as possible.

However, 20 or so of us broke through and started to pick our way through the tightly packed streets surrounding the ground. We came across a couple of small pubs that were filling with locals and hesitated while we considered nipping in for a beer. Then a gaggle of screeching women pointed us towards a group of Taffies who looked like they wanted to battle at first, but then quickly decided to get on their toes. We followed them, as did two mounted police officers who'd spotted us breaking away from the escort.

As we trailed the banshees, we turned a corner and there at the end of the road was Swansea's mob, but also more mounted police. We were sandwiched by the cavalry now. Fair enough, it wasn't exactly the battle of Waterloo, but facing OB on horseback trying to run us down from both sides was no fun either.

Scouse managed to slip his slender frame through an impossible gap to stop himself being knocked to the ground, but Dibble was sent flying into some rubbish bags. As the dark riders were splitting us up, a group of lads down one side of the road started to call us to join them. A quick assessment of the situation revealed that they were Swansea, trying to get at the escort of Luton fans passing their position on the other side of the street. It gave us a shot at a quick result, because the police would doubtless be chuffed to see us heading back towards the rest of the Luton support and our coaches. So, as one, we jogged off towards these Swansea boys.

As we approached, they became even more animated and turned their backs on us to gesture violently at the visiting herd passing by. They really did think we were Swansea as well and I don't think it had even crossed their minds that we might be Luton coming from behind them. When they did realise it, I wished I had a camera. They were so shocked that they just burst through the OB in front of them and straight into the Luton fans they'd been calling on to fight only moments before. The Chief managed to clip one as he leaped through the police line like an antelope. The poor old Taffy didn't know he had even been smacked, because as soon as he landed he was thrown straight into a front garden. Then, to add insult to injury, two OB steamed him as well!

That was the end of it. Although it hadn't gone off as well as it had at home, we'd made the required return trip, had a good day on the piss and seen Luton promoted out of the bottom flight to boot.

The game at Hull was next up and, although the Migs had decided not to put a mob together for this trip, a handful ventured north to have a nose. Little Jimmy even arranged to meet a Hull representative called Marc in the town centre to let them know none of the Migs would be on duty. As they sat chatting, the atmosphere suddenly turned hostile and he was warned to disappear quickly, as a mob from a boozer only two minutes away was heading over and there was no guarantee of his safety. As Little

Jimmy and co headed off, they caught sight of this menacing crew approaching and didn't hang around for a closer look.

It seemed that we'd underestimated the importance that Hull's firm placed on the occasion. We were the two top teams in the division and pride was at stake, but we failed to give it the attention it deserved. Some Luton lads found just how up for it the local lads were while drinking in Five Ways, when a local crew bowled straight past the OB and began intimidating the handful of lads sat inside.

One old face from the Migs with the Luton contingent that day was Demus. He had taken his son to the game and watched with frustration as the Humbersiders put it about to all in attendance. He told me afterwards that we'd made a mistake not travelling up and, with the Town winning 4–0 as well, there was no doubt he was right.

The Shrewsbury game was the last in a successful season, so thousands of Hatters journeyed to the picturesque county of Shropshire to see our boys take the game to them. In the home end, a small band of Migs, including Flower, Windy, DM, Mixer, Melv and Daggers, took the battle to the EBF. The poor Border lads had just fought their way into the ground after being attacked by the rest of Luton's hooligan element outside, only to find a quality detachment of the main lads waiting for them on the open terrace.

The battle was furious, with the numbers heavily against our lads, but no one could claim the upper hand that day. The sight of a huge gap opening on the terraces was a reminder of the 70s and 80s that didn't go unnoticed by the local press, who called it 'a return to the bad old days'.

Luton earned a 2–0 victory and so the season ended on a high for us, although not for Shrewsbury as the defeat meant that they missed out on a play-off spot.

On reflection, it had been an eventful season in England's lowest league. When we had originally been relegated, I wondered if there was much potential for trouble at any of our fixtures in the twilight zone. Swansea and Hull always looked the best bets, but one fixture that came as a complete surprise was Mansfield, when we mobilised the whole firm on a cold day in November.

I have to admit that I didn't even know Mansfield's Shady Express existed. Baby B had bumped into two of their lads – Ryan and Palmer – when on the piss in Athens watching England, and had stayed in contact with them since. As soon as I was told that Nottingham Forest lads would be with them, I was sold and the trip was on.

Catching the Shady Express

At seven-thirty in the morning, we had over 100 game lads, including both old faces and many MI2s as well, packed into three carriages on the Inter-City to Nottingham. Windy had gone ahead by car to Nottingham so he could check for any OB presence in the station and guide us to the platform for Mansfield with the minimum of fuss.

Ryan had promised us a welcoming committee, but as usual we bent the rules by turning up a little earlier than agreed. In fact, we'd told him we would be arriving at midday, but instead arrived at just before ten o'clock. At the last station before our destination, there was a big old unit of a lad dressed in the regulation Stone Island jacket and dark baseball cap who soon spotted us and was straight on the blower. He politely declined our invitation to travel along with us for the rest of the journey to Mansfield and scurried off the platform.

Now they knew we were coming and, as we poured out of Mansfield Station, all the lads were bubbling with the possibility of a mob being close by and launching an immediate attack on us. We adjusted our hoods, scarves and headgear, lids were removed from the gas canisters and we were ready.

We marched down the slope outside the ageing station and turned right, hoping to find a boozer to get us off the streets and out of the public eye. Instead, we bumped into a pair of dopey-looking coppers looking for something to do with themselves. They tried stopping us for a chat and clearly didn't like the sight of 100 lads, faces hidden, wandering towards the town centre.

Now they knew we'd arrived and time was against us, so we had to adopt a different approach. We split the boys into more than one mob to stretch the police resources and hopefully create enough confusion so that at least one of our groups could confront the local crew. In the centre of the market town, a boozer stood out due to its elevated position looking down on the main drag. It was the perfect spot to put a firm and send out a message too, so the lads filed in and we set up camp.

As soon as the boys were comfortable, I set off on a reconnaissance mission with Windy, armed with the name of Mansfield's mob's current boozer. As the pair of us left base camp, we passed our two resident bobbies outside, but they didn't bat an eyelid and were too busy ogling the passing ladies doing their Saturday shopping.

Within five minutes, we had found our destination and also five lads perched on barstools around a crescent-shaped table. They watched us approaching across the open-plan pub with blank expressions on their faces. Windy and I said good morning and asked if they already knew we were in town – they did.

'What time do you lads get up in the morning?' asked one of the Shady boys.

'We left before seven, mate. You have to get up early if you want to be any good at this game, old chap!'

The conversation established that we were in the right spot, but they wouldn't be ready for us for a couple of hours or so. They felt confident they would have enough to confront us by then, although they clearly weren't expecting us to travel in such big numbers.

'Don't worry, lads, nothing will happen until you're ready – I give you my word. Trust me.'

As Windy and I left by one door, we didn't see another group of Luton lads who'd also organised a scout party approaching from the other direction. A few minutes later, they entered the same boozer and kicked off, running the Mansfield lads out the back of the building. In the midst of the skirmish, Fred D was struck with a glass thrown by one of the Nottinghamshire boys and soon his face was covered in blood.

Windy and I heard the commotion and spotted the police heading to the scene, so we ran back to join 20 other lads also trying to get down the road. The OB were having none of it, quickly wrestling Dennis E to the floor and arresting him with another of the chaps. Fred D meanwhile stood on the sideline having his injury attended to by another OB.

As confusion reigned, more of the lads arrived and were hurriedly advised to break up into small teams and hide in nearby pubs. Windy and I picked one right on the corner and, along with half a dozen other Luton lads, tried to blend in with the locals.

Peering through the doorway, we could see a shoving match developing between Nottinghamshire OB and our mates. As usual, it looked like the police were winning. This was OK for us, though, because when the scrum passed we knew that we would be free to stroll back to the Mansfield boozer. The noise outside subsided and all seemed to be going according to plan but then, as if by magic, the Migs police spotter appeared at the doorway to say hello. And, within moments, we were being frogmarched back to join the rest of our buddies at the first pub.

The scene inside was mental. During our excursion, another mob of lads had arrived to join the Migs, so there was now a massive crew holed up together. The lads were either trying to escape through the kitchens or arguing with the OB blocking the narrow doorway. I asked to use the cashpoint because money was getting low and another of the Luton OB escorted me to the machine and back – as if I would try to slip the net!

Luton's mob was caged in the pub until 2.30 and then the mood of joviality changed abruptly when the plod decided it was time for us to make our way to the ground. Some were happy with this, but many no longer wanted to go to the game because they were having such a good piss-up. And, of course, by staying in town, the chances of a row were greatly improved. Some even pointed out to the OB that if they were to go to the ground now they might actually be breaking the law, as it's an offence to enter a football stadium when pissed.

On this occasion, though, the letter of the law didn't matter much to its upholders as they stormed into the establishment, smashing pint glasses and manhandling us out of the door at speed. They herded us on to the pavement in a tight formation, kicking and abusing us all the way to the ground. Big Wayne took exception to one cheap comment too many, attacked the officer who'd made it and was arrested on the spot.

Once the unhappy escort reached the ground and was lined up outside the visiting supporters' sections, it soon became apparent that Notts Police had underestimated the level of support making the trip north from Bedfordshire because the away end was already full. Now they had a moody mob on their hands and nowhere to put them.

As the OB discussed their options, we made our own decision. Just to the right of us were a couple of turnstiles marked for home fans, so we swarmed through the gates into a rickety old stand that wouldn't have looked out of place in our own state-of-the-art stadium! The OB reacted, but too late and, by the time they'd fought their way through the back of our mob, so many had already clambered through the turnstiles that it was obvious that they wouldn't have a chance of getting us out.

We marched into the cramped wooden stand and positioned ourselves level with the halfway line. The Mansfield supporters, meanwhile, all moved to the side of the stand and many were led to a section behind the goal. Then, stories started to filter in that, as we'd jokingly predicted, many of the boys had indeed been arrested for being drunk at a football match, despite having had no choice in the matter

The noise level in our section hit the roof as Mick Harford and Joe

Kinnear walked across the pitch and took up their positions in the dugouts immediately in front of our gathering. Mick Harford even raised a clenched fist to us and we returned the gesture with a threatening roar.

The game didn't go quite as well, though, as Chris Greenacre and his Mansfield team tore into the Hatters. By the 63rd minute, we were 3–0 down and we'd seen enough – it was time to leave. The Migs and the rest of Luton's hooligan army headed towards the exits, only to be confronted once again by Nottinghamshire OB and their batons. But this time we didn't run.

One of the MI2s launched a bottle at the OB storming towards him, felled one and sparked a battle with the local police that spilled on to the pitch and into the national papers. They charged forward and then backed off to regroup as the temporary fencing separating our stand from the rest of the Luton contingent was smashed to the ground, almost taking me with it. Pete stood on the pitch trying to marshal the lads to charge across and confront the few Mansfield lads sitting in the stand opposite, but only Scottish Brian was prepared to join him as the conflict with the OB continued.

Eventually, the police restored order to the ground and made the obligatory token arrests. We were then escorted to the train station and, after a couple of breakout attempts, were sent packing towards Nottingham.

Nearly all of the cases against the lads arrested in Mansfield were dropped because of insufficient evidence. If the OB's top brass had studied the CCTV footage of the day thoroughly, I guess they might have been ashamed at how their frontline handled things.

The lads who were arrested never moaned about it, though, and took the treatment handed out like men. They knew they had put themselves in a position of risk and didn't want to be hypocrites because, let's face it, they were hooligans.

So, as I stood in Luton Crown Court listening to Armchair Alan whining about the unfairness of his case and the severity of the sentences in the days leading up to our own appearance, I couldn't help but think how unfair the OB had been so often in the past. I almost felt like having a moan as well, but at the end of the day football lads know the risks involved and make their decision before they leave the house. This is not a soap opera and we are not acting – real violence has real consequences.

'Shut up, Al. You should know the fucking drill by now – if you can't do the time, don't do the crime, mate,' I snapped back and let my mind return to that day in Mansfield, sitting next to Shit Hair, as the Inter-City slowed to a stop in good old Leicester.

7 Someone Slap That Baby

At the far end of the court rest area sat a group of people that I took to be a family. They were all smartly dressed and included two youngish women, one of whom held a baby, an elderly chap who was half-asleep and a guy about my age in a dark-coloured suit. The bloke in the whistle was obviously the one facing justice today and he looked as nervous as a sheep in Wales. When I compared them to our motley crew, I almost felt ashamed, as we didn't look like we had a care in the world.

The loudspeaker began rolling out our names: 'Armchair Alan, Tommy R, Big Cliff, Andy P, Little Jimmy and D Gentle – could you please make your way to Court Two.' Then I heard my name called again and turned to see Monty, an Asian mate of mine, rushing towards me with his hand outstretched. I shook it and he wished me good luck in his usual off-key manner. 'Good luck, you gypo – make sure you write!'

I began to laugh, but suddenly someone started to cry instead. And when I say cry, I mean make some real fucking noise. It was the baby with the anxious family and she had started up as they were walking past us. 'Another bad omen,' I thought.

'Someone slap that fucking baby,' Monty exclaimed, not giving a damn if anybody heard him.

I stopped laughing, shook my head in embarrassment and was about to have a word with him about his big mouth, when I remembered that I had once used the same words myself. I returned to my memories of Mansfield.

As our train back from Nottingham pulled into Leicester and Shit Hair rose from his seat, I asked who else was getting off. Not many it seemed, as most were now either fucked from the heavy drinking before the game or shaken up by all the wrongful arrests and just wanted to get home as quickly as possible. Nevertheless, I exchanged pleasantries with the two Transport Police who'd travelled with us and strolled off the train behind Shit Hair.

I was actually feeling a bit worse for wear myself. As an older member of the Migs, all the boozing and battles with the over-touchy Nottinghamshire OB had taken it out of me. And, with the gap between pissing it up and now being well over three hours, I was sobering up, but gaining a thumping headache at the same time. There was a cure to be had, though: a touch of the old 'hair of the dog'. So, as Shit Hair and I climbed the grimy stairs at Leicester Station in search of the nearest boozer, we had a small band of 15 volunteers, mainly MI2s, in tow.

Outside, we headed straight over to a traditional-looking pub called The Hind. At the entrance, we came across a crowd decked out like regular football fans, except that I couldn't place the club colours of red, green and white. It was only on entering that we read the flags, scarves and club crests and realised that it was Leicester Rugby Club supporters who'd packed the place out tonight. The rugby boys were in high spirits, singing away happily and didn't pay much attention to our sorry-looking group as we filed in.

Once we'd hit the bar, we managed to grab some seats and were soon back on course to having a good night out, as we joined in some banter with the rugger buggers. Within an hour, we were well on our way to being pissed again, as our noise level began to match and then exceed that of the locals. Soon all you could hear was songs about Shit Hair drowning out all their 'swing low, sweet chariot' stuff.

I noticed many of the rugby fans leaving slowly now and, as I waved goodbye to some of these good people, I spotted a rather different-looking chap lurking outside. He wore no colours, but was dressed in Aquascutum from head to toe and was peering in at our group while jabbering into the mobile clamped to his ear. I jumped up and moved towards the door. He slipped out of sight immediately, but I called after him and managed to get him to stop. 'Who are you then? Leicester? Or is it QPR?' The West Londoners were playing at Nottingham today and we had hoped to bump into them at some point. Indeed, as we fought with the OB at Mansfield in the morning, reinforcements had been bussed in from the Forest v QPR game to help out.

Mr Aquascutum turned out to be Leicester, of course, but swore blind that he was not Baby Squad and had never heard of SH or the Wongs either, although the look in his eyes suggested otherwise. I had to get more info out of him and, noticing the joint in his hand, I invited him to come and join us in The Hind so he could meet the lads and have a puff with the smokers in the crew.

He accepted and my new mate from Leicester was soon chatting and laughing wildly, as Scottish Brian and Sick Nick demonstrated their individual breakdancing styles. Nick took the crown as he did 'The Worm' on the pub floor, to roars of approval from rugby boys and the lads alike. I hoped that Mr Aquascutum would soon be relaxed enough to answer some more specific questions about where the Baby Squad might be found tonight, but I was wrong and, within seconds of me starting the interrogation, he had disappeared into the night, never to be seen again.

We carried on pissing it up until sometime after nine o'clock, when we had to think about getting the train home. Baby B and Mickey had already been across to the station and discovered that the last train to Luton was at quarter to ten, so, unless we fancied paying for taxis or stopping all night, we needed to get the last round in and down our Gregorys quick.

By half-past nine, the 15 of us were stood swaying on the southbound platform, awaiting our sweet chariot back to Luton. The only others about were half a dozen rugby fans and a couple of lads who looked like they might well be football chaps as they had all the right clobber. The Stone Islanders quickly denied affiliation to any football team and, although we were sure they were West London boys, no one bothered them because bullying isn't our thing.

In fact, there were another few lads further down the platform, but in my drunken haze I hadn't spotted them. As I stared aimlessly up at the dark night sky through bleary eyes, I was suddenly brought back to my senses by an unannounced smack in the face. I managed to stay upright – which was no mean feat considering the state I was in – and registered that I had received a blow of some sort. Alcohol is a great painkiller, but I know a punch when it hits me and this didn't really qualify.

I looked around and saw a pair of likely lads standing near by on the stairs to our platform. One was gesturing for me to come forward, so I obliged, but was grabbed instantly and bundled roughly into the side of the staircase. I started to fight back, until I realised that it was actually a copper who had hold of me. 'Calm down, lad. Just let it go and get home to bed.'

'So you saw what happened then? Why the fuck should I calm down?'

But, before he could answer, a bottle smashed against the wall near to his head. I looked up and saw my assailant smiling, well pleased with himself. Not for long though. 'What sort of punch was that? It was a fucking girl's slap, you nonce.'

He looked a little taken aback.

'When I get this cunt off me, you're fucked' I continued, still struggling with the transport plod.

As I tried to reason with the copper, the prick who'd hit me approached again with two of his mates and one of them launched another bottle in my direction, but missed once more.

I'd had enough now, so I slipped my mate from the Transport Police and bounded up the stairs alongside Baby B, Black K and Baby J. 'If you've come to fight, then let's fight, you cunt!'

The wankers started to run now. But, as they backed away, they also encouraged us to keep following them. Now I knew for sure that they were football lads and most likely Baby Squad come to give us a send-off.

'Someone slap that fucking Baby!' I screamed at the young MI2s, who were gaining on the Leicester lads now heading for the ticket barriers at top speed.

The chase moved through the ticket office area into the main station forecourt. Here, the BS boys turned right, sprinted down an incline and out under an old arch leading on to the main road into the city centre. We rather naively followed them. As we came out into the road, things suddenly turned sour. In an instant, what had been even numbers became three facing 10, with more pouring out of a boozer only yards away. It was an ambush! A quick glance told me that Baby Mickey had managed to join our party now, so, although we were outnumbered, there was enough of us to form a battle line between the two legs of the arch into the station.

The Baby Squad soon felt confident enough to come towards us, but hesitated from actually engaging in any combat – choosing instead to make lots of noise and dance around like they were on drugs. I decided to test their resolve and steamed into them throwing my arms around wildly, in an attempt to back them off far enough for the MI2s to gain the confidence to take the battle to them as well.

I needn't have worried, though, because as soon as I moved the other three were straight in with me. But fair play to the Leicester lads – they didn't break as I'd hoped and instead fought as one, dealing with our limited assault quite comfortably. I have to admit to taking a few heavy blows to my drunken head and, unlike the girly slap on the platform, I felt them.

More lads from the pub were joining our adversaries and we were getting out of our depth now. If any of us went down, we would get a proper beating, so I decided that we should head back into the station and fetch the rest of the lads to even things up a bit. We didn't turn and run, but instead walked back steadily, trying to stay facing the pack of hyenas trailing behind us. But, foolishly, a couple of the lads turned their backs. At this, a roar went up from the Leicester boys and they charged into us. I managed to drop one as he tried to stop himself being pushed into us by his mates behind, but at this moment the two OB from the platform finally appeared and got stuck in. This was actually a relief and allowed us to hurriedly muster some more of the troops.

Shit Hair and PM led the relief party over and quickly got the gist of what had happened. So now we were 12-strong and on the warpath again. Our attention was drawn to two of the Baby Squad boys standing beneath the main arch leading directly into the station. They looked keen enough, so we strolled across the concourse towards them and, as we closed, they didn't back off at all. In fact, the better dressed of the pair stepped forward confidently, with a broad smile on his face. 'You can't just come to Leicester and act like you…'

Before he'd even finished, he was smashed to the floor by Shit Hair and, after dropping with a groan, he just lay on his back staring up at the vaulted ceiling. He didn't appear to be smiling any more.

Two young girls ran screaming from across the busy carriageway to his aid and we were off, jogging out of the station in the direction of the pub that the BS had appeared from a few minutes earlier. It wasn't far and, within seconds, we caught sight of the Midlands mob still prowling about. We called it on and started to deploy in a wide line. The Baby Squad did likewise, with numbers probably twice our own and a few more besides.

'Let's fucking do this!' The order was given and we stormed towards them while keeping the rigid line formation.

As we neared the Leicester firm, many of their boys started to break ranks and run away. About half of them stood for the initial clash, which went heavily in our favour, with one of theirs felled like a tree in a storm. He stayed down and the Baby Squad backed off, looking as though they would melt. But, true to their reputation, they rallied and launched a charge back at us and so began round two.

This time, we split them into three splinter groups, with one of superior quality to the others. It was on this mob that we focused our attention and within a couple of minutes we'd pushed them back to the intersection leading to the city centre. Now the Leicester lads knew they were beaten and, as we scattered the few remaining odds and sods, this lot remained at a distance on the other side of the busy dual carriageway, inviting us into town to 'meet our main lads'.

We were buzzing and about to take the invite, when I was grabbed by a huge chap in a suit – a doorman from the pub where the Baby Squad had launched their bushwhack. 'Why don't you take a look up and say cheese, you stupid bleeder!'

Cameras! It was like fucking Hollywood down there. I thanked the Good Samaritan and he nodded back with an eyebrow raised.

My senses returned quickly now and I raced down the road to call back Shit Hair, as he was already bowling off into Leicester city centre like a Tasmanian Devil. It was no easy task either because he'd lost the plot completely by then. However, once I told him that the last train home would be leaving any second, he swept his hideous orange hair back under his Paul & Shark cap and joined the rest of our group in a head count.

Once satisfied all were safe and sound, we started the short walk back to the station, passing the two lads that had been decked minutes earlier en route. One didn't look too bad and was sat up rubbing his head, but the other seemed in a worse condition, with a gathering of concerned locals doing all they could to sort him out. Maybe not one for the grandchildren, I know, but we've all been there.

We bundled on to the platform to see if our getaway train had left without us. But, thankfully, Scouse, Scottish Brian and Sick Nick had held it up by refusing to let the automatic doors close, despite the protests of the other passengers. As it pulled away, most of the lads were happy with their performances in the battle outside the station, but one comment too many upset Brian and Nick and soon some of the lads were at each other's throats, instead of Leicester's.

As I sat watching my mates push each other about, I wondered what might have been regarding the recent battle. Although it was a good row and had come at the end of an exciting day in Mansfield, battling with the OB and doing our utmost to take it to the Shady Express Crew, I still felt a little down. I had too many fond memories of our clashes with the Leicester Baby Squad from the 80s. So fond, in fact, that twenty years later I was back in the same place, still chasing the buzz from those early days. The youngsters wouldn't have wanted to hear me say it, but old-timers like Shit Hair knew – things were serious then. And one name sprang to mind in an instant – Paddy W.

Ironically, in a town with so many Irish folk, Paddy was actually a West Indian yout'. He was tall and skinny, with the biggest smile of any football lad I knew. In my opinion and that of many others, Paddy was a legend in his own lifetime. Perhaps more than any other, he embodied the rude-boy Casual style that we loved so much at Luton.

On most Saturdays, he would take his seat among the crew gathered in the old Maple Road and get everyone up, singing and dancing to all sorts of ridiculous songs from our own 'Sing a bit louder now – ooh!' to a dodgy version of 'Dr Beat'. We would watch him move through the crowd, taking time out to greet and chat with each and every member of the firm individually. His goal was to make us all feel part of something; to feel part of a family so that we would always come back – and we did. Without any doubt, Paddy W was our leader at the time.

Paddy's favourite game of any season was Leicester City, home or away. And he alone ensured that transport was provided at an affordable price for each of the away fixtures, so that not only the older lads, but also the younger ones like myself, could travel with the mob on the day.

My first encounter with Paddy had been in a seedy little drinking hole in Hightown known simply and affectionately as Molly's. He was the resident DJ at the time and kept the place rocking with soul tunes like 'Touch Me' by Fonda Rae. Shit Hair had introduced us at the bar and we hit it off immediately.

Then, a while later in October 1984, we played Leicester City in the Milk Cup at Kenilworth Road, in front of a poor crowd of just over 8,000. This included a handful of loyal Leicester fans who had to endure a poor performance from their side, with Gary Lineker alone justifying his wage packet by scoring a late consolation goal. The only sour moment for the Town fans was the sight of one of our heroes, Paul Elliot, being carried off the pitch with a broken leg.

While Leicester were getting the better of the early exchanges, I noticed three lads sitting huddled together in the Wing Stand. I didn't recognise them and went sniffing. They turned out to be from Leicester and, although not part of the Baby Squad, were 'lads' and guaranteed there would be a substantial welcoming committee put together by the time we arrived at Filbert Street in December.

When the day finally came around, I was champing at the bit, as I'd heard more about the Leicester trip than Christmas. Apparently, we'd be taking hundreds of lads up there and mayhem was planned both outside and in the ground. I'd even been shopping with my mate Chemist, one of the more dapper Migs, and bought a new Lacoste jacket and a pair of Diadora Golds especially for the occasion. The transport would be leaving at 10 in the morning from Guildford Street, just up the road from Strokes, a club spread over two floors, where by now Paddy had become the main DJ. His success was plain for all to see.

Come the morning of the trip north, I strolled down from Hightown with Winston and Chemist in tow. We bounced along, eyeing each other's garms to see who looked the best and, though I hate to admit it, in those days it was nearly always the Chem. We passed the train station, hurrying down the stairs into Guildford Street to see how many had turned up and weren't disappointed – it was an amazing sight.

Parked on the side of the road were two coaches with 'Dinsey Tours' emblazoned along the sides. For years I actually thought it said 'Disney' and enjoyed the jokes about us being a Mickey Mouse firm! Crowded around one of them was a mob of well over 100 lads all jostling to get in. Paddy stood at the door nightclub-style and was keeping everyone back who wasn't on his list of those who had paid up front. The other coach was already full.

As our youthful threesome approached, Paddy quickly spotted us, beckoned us to the front of the queue and soon we were sat up front with about 20 of the original Migs. It turned out that, in his wisdom, Paddy had anticipated the big turnout and arranged for two box vans to be made available as well – at the right price, of course – to cart the remaining lads to Leicester. And there weren't many that turned down the offer.

By midday, our convoy, which now included a few cars as well, edged its way into Leicester. Without any real target to aim at, we decided to park between the station and the ground, next to Nelson Mandela Park. The mob disembarked and, apparently without any guidance, began to stroll towards the ground. I was pissed off that we'd gone wrong already – we should have been heading in the opposite direction, towards the city centre.

However, all became clearer when Paddy explained to me that the aim was to find the ticket office and get seats in the Leicester parts of the ground. This sounded good to me and, after a short walk, we reached Filbert Street. Paddy collected a tenner from each of those who wanted to go on the mission in the seats and, after disappearing for a few minutes, he returned with tickets that would gain us access to home territory and hopefully lead to a full-scale battle later in the day.

As Paddy was distributing them, his name was called out from across the street. It was Mickey D. Now, Mick was a Ricky Hill look-alike and knew it only too well, sporting those jheri curls with pride! He'd just been for a stroll round the ground and had some interesting news. He'd bumped into three Burberry-raincoated Baby Squad, who assured him that they would get a firm together in 10 minutes flat and have them heading in our direction for a quick off, before the OB spotted us. Mickey also said that they didn't know the true size of our crew.

On hearing this, Paddy had us gathered around a blind corner and ready for battle in an instant. He stood out in the main road with a group of mainly black boys, including Mickey D and his hair – probably less than 30 chaps in total. This was just a show for the Baby Squad and would hopefully cause them to drop their guard, so that, when the main herd charged, it would be to maximum effect. Paddy positioned himself to the rear of the handpicked bait, so as to keep control on when to push the button and release us. Now we waited.

It didn't take long for the body language of our allies to change from relaxed to tense. We couldn't see what was making its way towards them, but it was certainly enough to make some of them shoot worried glances in our direction, to ensure that we were still in position to strike and save their skins. As the seconds passed, we jostled with each other trying to gain a favourable position from which to charge and almost spilled out into the open, such was our eagerness to get into the Baby Squad.

Suddenly, Paddy gave the signal and we charged around the corner making as much noise as possible. The roar was magnificent and had the right effect, as all we could see were scattering Leicester lads, heading in blind panic back to wherever they had just come from. We didn't pursue them, though, as the victory was ours without a single punch being thrown.

As we began to follow signposts towards the city centre, I was a bit disappointed at what had just happened. Although the Leicester lads had been run, one thing still troubled me – there were only about 30 of them. What would happen when we met a firm of equal size?

Then, as we headed on towards town, we happened upon another mob of Leicester on a large wasteland area near the hospital. They stood on one side of the flat concrete space and we were on the other, about 80 metres apart. It wasn't going to be easy to get to them, though, as there were remnants of old fences and other obstacles between us. The Leicester lads didn't try too hard to come at us, as we outnumbered them quite heavily again, but at the same time they showed no signs of backing off either. It was up to us to do the donkey work, so we started to pour across the no-man's land separating our two Casual crews.

The OB chose this moment to make their presence known and came steaming from a road behind the Baby Squad. There were loads of them. And they had dog handlers with them too – something that caused panic among many a mob back then. I chose to scramble through a gap in the fence and almost fell on my arse as I tried to negotiate a pile of rubble blocking my path.

Unperturbed, I charged on and caught sight of a mixed-race lad, dressed in a Burberry jacket, of course, moving towards my mate Winston. He didn't see me coming and I caught him on the side of the head with a rather sloppy punch. But this lad's reaction was not quite what I expected – he swivelled round to face me and lumped me straight in the mouth causing my lip to explode. He was a bit more experienced than me and would have followed up his assault, but for the grace of God and the speed of Norfs' feet, as he kicked my rival straight in the nuts, sending him to the floor, a look of extreme pain contorting his face. As this hard cunt curled up on the deck, I considered sticking the boot (or rather Diadora Elite!) into his head, but Winston beat me to it and stamped on the poor bloke's ear.

Out of the corner of my eye, I saw a flash of black heading at speed in the direction of the melee and knew instinctively that it was OB – time to go. I ran back in the direction of the hole that I'd just struggled through, but it was no use, as what looked like a bus queue of lads was waiting to do the same thing. Instead, I headed across the concourse and followed those who had slipped between two meat wagons parked on the kerb.

As more and more police arrived on the scene, they forced us on to the pavement in a big pack, while small groups of lads continued to fight it out on the far side of the wasteland. As we watched, we jostled with the OB, who returned the compliment by kicking us in the shins and letting the dogs snap at our calves.

Eventually, the police managed to separate the fighting factions and brought the rest of our lads over to be escorted to the ground with us. As we lined up outside the turnstile, though, I thought the OB were a bit thick as they didn't flinch when over 100 lads from Luton entered the same section of the ground that had housed the Baby Squad on my visit to Leicester the season before. It had to mean war.

Unfortunately, I was wrong and it didn't mean war at all, as, within seconds of bowling into the stand, we realised that this area had now become available to away supporters anyway. The Baby Squad were sat next to us in the same stand, but separated by a fence and a line of stewards. We could see more Leicester lads above the terraced end of the stadium, on a double-decker stand high in the dark sky. 'I'll sit up there, the next time we play here,' I thought.

As the game ebbed and flowed in the cold winter air, stories began to circulate of a Rasta among Leicester's thugs. Apparently, he was game and more than likely their 'top boy'. Gypsy John said he wanted to try to knock the bloke out afterwards, but I just wanted to catch a glimpse of the bloke who co-ordinated such a well-dressed and organised firm.

Mick Harford scored a late, late equaliser that stunned the home fans and we duly surged up the fence and tried to climb on to the pitch, only to end up with bruised and battered hands, because of the Leicester's OB's effective use of their truncheons. Only one of the lads managed to get over and he was duly arrested for his troubles.

After the game, we were held in the seats and continued our funky football singsong, which had been accompanied by customary swaying from side to side throughout. Paddy conducted the singing from the front of the stand in his own inimitable style. With the Migs it wasn't just about violence – we had fun and sometimes it felt like a blues dance transported to the football.

About 20 minutes later, we were allowed out on to the streets and joined a large group of other Luton fans heading for the train station. We wormed our way through the streets of Leicester led by the OB, who stopped us repeatedly and made us wait while they attempted to force the local lads out of our path. From the accounts they gave, there was a really big mob out to get at us now and it was in our best interest to stay put.

We moved along silently until we reached Mandela Park again, where the OB became confused, as a huge mob of Leicester suddenly came rushing in our direction from the adjoining street. The plod had just started to split the Migs from the coaches and the lads from the train, so chaos briefly reigned and we seized our opportunity. We broke from the escort in a massive pack and hurtled towards the local crew. For a few moments, they thought we'd stop, but once they realised we meant business they started to break and run. But the Leicester OB did their stuff and once again they arrived just in time to get between the two mobs and force us back across the park towards the waiting coaches and vans. With the adrenaline still flowing, we climbed up the steps of the manky old Dinsey coaches and were soon under escort, heading to the M1 and home. Paddy had us all up singing and dancing again and everyone had a wicked grin on their face all the way back to Luton.

In May of the following year, Luton played Leicester at home. After our own exploits, we wondered if the Baby Squad would make an appearance for this game and they sure did. A while beforehand, though, a friend of mine, Mark, had decided to travel down to Ramsgate to see a lad that had moved away from Luton some years previously and I agreed to go along, without realising who we were playing that weekend.

So, on the day in question, I was still beating myself up for missing it all as we strolled down Hightown Road towards the train station to set off for Kent. When we reached the bridge, we spotted John, the tough gypsy boy, who told us that he'd just passed through the station and had an argument with some Leicester lads there. We quickly agreed to join him and investigate.

Approaching the ticket area, we saw half a dozen smartly dressed lads standing casually with their hands behind their backs, like they owned the place.

I sauntered up to one and asked, 'Where's your fucking firm hiding then?'

As his mates closed threateningly round me, I unzipped my kit bag and pulled out the broken end of a hockey stick, keeping it well hidden behind me. As my target grew more confident and looked knowingly across at his boys, I smacked him straight in the cheek causing a massive lump to appear almost instantly. At this precise moment, John landed a big one on another of the Leicester scout party, while Mark tussled with a third. Then, just as they looked as though they might fancy their chances, I produced the jolly hockey stick and offered them all a piece of action. At this, they backed off into the station only to reappear with a copper in tow, complaining that I was tooled up. Mark reacted quickly, though, and passed behind me to sneak the homemade club away before I was arrested.

After the OB had let me go, I headed down to the bus station to rejoin them, but John had disappeared and now only Mark and myself remained. So we sat in the café and had a coffee, giving the Leicester upstairs in the train station some time to disappear before continuing our journey, as we were damn sure they would be looking to give us a proper slap. I felt extra proud of myself, though. I had been fighting demons for the past few days because I felt I was letting the lads down by missing such an important match. Now I'd done my bit and landed the first blow of the day, so all was cool in my eyes.

Slowly, we turned the corner that leads from the bus depot to the stairs up to the train station bridge and, as we did so, I shit myself. Just 20 feet ahead and led by a lanky dread was a mob of over 100 Baby Squad rushing the other way towards the town centre. We froze, didn't utter a word and did our best impressions of lampposts.

The angry mob of Leicester chaps just kept on pouring down the stairs from the station. They were moving at some speed and that's probably why they didn't spot us standing there rooted to the spot in terror. Then they were gone. Mark and I looked at each other in disbelief and hurried up to the station and on to the platform even quicker than the BS had just left it. I didn't relax until I saw Luton disappearing behind me through the windows of the speeding carriage.

On returning two days later, I discovered it had kicked off big time in the town, with the Baby Squad doing Leicester proud and taking the battle to Luton. During one of the clashes, it was claimed that the dread leading the Baby Squad had gone toe-to-toe with our Aubrey B, in front of equal-sized mobs. Apparently, the two crews had actually stepped respectfully aside to let the two top boys square up. As the big rasta loped into position, though, Aubrey didn't wait to introduce himself and decked him as he was still bouncing. With Leicester's main man on his arse in front of them, Luton had put the visiting mob on the back foot. But there was no question that they had come looking for it and earned proper respect from our firm in doing so.

With another season set to start in August 1986, I was by now a decorator and accustomed to hearing my Geordie boss bleat on about the great North Eastern tradition of producing 'special footballers like Chris Waddle and Peter Beardsley'. I buried my head as deep as possible in my paper as I heard him warming up for another round of it.

The fixtures were out and I couldn't help but smile when I saw our fixture for the opening day. As far as smaller clubs like Luton go, it's important to get the season off to a good start, both on and off the pitch. The club want to get three points in the bag early on and with football crews it's not dissimilar. If you can get a fixture that kicks off properly on the first day of a new season, then the chances are that the stories told over the following few days will get many lads on the fringes stirred up and into action at the following matches.

Luton's first game of the 1986/87 season would be Leicester City away. In the days leading up to it, the lads' phones didn't stop ringing, as we tried to ensure that as many as possible would be making the trip up the M1. There was a bit of a concern, though, as some of the boys had now started to watch London clubs and run with their firms as well as, or instead of, the Migs. If you went down to Arsenal, you would often find GM, Winston, Aubrey and Chemist with the Gooners. Norfs could be seen at Chelsea, Catlin at West Ham, and so on.

With Luton being so close to London, it was inevitable that many people followed clubs from the capital. But it was also cool to be a Cockney or for people to think you were. So, even though we had our own thing going on and were tighter, funkier and downright heavier than some of the Home Counties crews that followed the big clubs, we suffered heavily at the hands of fashion.

After some fighting within the firm over this, there had been a split of sorts and as a result the Migs could no longer muster the same numbers as in previous years. Still, we had found some able replacements to fill the frontline. One of these was Lawla. Although young and inexperienced in football violence, there was no doubting his abilities as he came from a boxing background and reminded many of Freezing Frank, a respected character in the Migs. One thing was for sure – he was game and had the bottle required to stand in the face of overwhelming numbers, as we were to find out only too well on this trip to Leicester.

I had to smile as we travelled north on the Inter-City – we had a collection of good lads today, including Demus, Ging, Flower, Freezing Frank and many more besides. It made my heart race to think that we would soon be on the streets of Leicester and battling with the Baby Squad again.

The previous season, we'd forced a tidy mob of them back up the stairs inside Winston's Bar – a favourite haunt of theirs, near the clock tower in the city centre. We had arrived early and set up, keeping plenty of glasses at hand for the inevitable. They never even knew we were downstairs as they gathered up at the bar. When they did realise they had a mob of Luton in their sights, they pushed each other towards us in a shambolic effort and ended up being showered in glasses, bottles and a few chairs for good measure.

Outside, the streets were narrow and we needed an escort to the ground as our small band of 40 nearly came unstuck, but not before Demus had decked one of the Baby Squad, nearly breaking his hand in the process. Our only real injury had been a certain Swanee, who was glassed by friendly fire during the exchanges inside the pub. I think anyone who was there would have to admit that we gained a result of sorts. However, once the Baby Squad got their act together, it was a different story and we were more than happy for the police presence.

This year, we hoped to do a bit better and certainly had a bigger crew on board in spite of our split. After we reached the city centre, we headed towards the Corn Exchange by the market and, within seconds, a running battle had broken out. Once again, we'd caught Leicester on the hop by arriving early and took the battle to the few lads available to us at the time. We ran them through the market, straight past Gary Lineker's family fruit stall with its lairy sign, but soon had OB all over us and were moved to some shitty pub on the outskirts of the centre, with two vans of plod for company.

The rest of the day leading up to the game was uneventful, but we fulfilled one ambition of mine as around 60 of us managed to get tickets for the double-decker stand behind the goal. We marched proudly in and strutted across the seats giving it the large one, in the hope that some of Leicester's mob might be close. We weren't disappointed either, as we soon found ourselves tussling with a small crew, but it was a little bit one-sided as we forced the locals back through sheer weight of numbers. I grabbed one of the shaken-up Leicester lads, pulled him backwards over a row of seats and then moved on, while others administered a bit of a kicking to the poor sod.

We took our seats right behind the goal, but just five minutes after kick-off the local Bobbies arrived and forced us back into the top corner of the stand and wouldn't let us move – even to the toilets – for the rest of the game.

Then, not long before the final whistle, a small band of Baby Squad appeared at the back of our section – how they got past the OB, I will never know. However, instead of kicking off, they signalled that they wanted to talk. Their spokesman wore a navy-blue Lacoste jumper and had a really confident manner about him. He didn't seem to give a fuck that he was surrounded by our whole mob and told us that, if we left the ground via the Main Stand, we would find the Baby Squad waiting outside.

After this, the band of five lads spun on their heels and left, giving us hand signals so we knew exactly which exit to take at the end of the game. I couldn't wait for the match to finish now. Freezing Frank was as keen as I was to get outside for a rumble and in no time we had a dozen lads running down the steep steps and out behind the Main Stand.

At first, the place looked pretty deserted with no OB in sight either and a quick glance back revealed a steady stream of Migs following us through the exit. Then, Freezing Frank pointed across to some railings that enclosed the club car park. 'They're here!'

Behind the handrails stood the same lads who'd given us the directions and they were calling us forwards to meet their mates. Without a second thought, we stormed over to exchange punches with them and, although the fighting was furious, it was none too effective, as we still had the barrier between us. So, I clambered over the fence alongside Freezing Frank and Lawla and carried the fight to the enemy, sending the Leicester bods reeling back from our more powerful blows.

But the scuffling didn't last for long as OB arrived from behind and pulled me to one side. I thought I was definitely going to be nicked, but surprisingly they just gave me a verbal warning and ordered me back over the barrier to join the mob of Migs gathering behind Paddy and Demus. Once we were all together, Paddy suggested that we head under the back of the Main Stand and through into the car park to continue the fight we'd started. We marched in a tight formation through the tunnel and emerged close to the Luton Town team bus and a couple of handicapped people's minibuses.

There, the expected battle started for real. Leicester came charging across the club car park in their hundreds and didn't wait to dance about or exchange pleasantries. Instead, they ploughed straight into us, knocking some of the lads to the floor almost immediately. I was hit on the head by a stone that came flying over the heads of the heaving ranks of their army of thugs. We were in trouble and being backed up heavily, as punches came at us from all angles. As they swarmed all over us, we started to break up and fall apart.

It was about self-preservation now and I was looking for an escape route when I spotted Lawla out on his own and receiving a sound beating from a group of them. But I could do fuck all now, as some cunt had hold of my jumper and was trying to knock my head off.

Then, above all the din and the chaos, a lone voice seemed to rise up and grab everyone's attention. It was clear and firm – the voice of authority itself: 'Watch out for the knives! They're blade merchants!'

To this day, I can't tell you if it was one of ours or one of theirs that shouted it, but the words had a dramatic and immediate impact, as both sides took a step back to see who had the blades. The Leicester lads called off the attack and backed off in the direction of the club car park, while we withdrew rather gratefully to a gap between the Luton team coach and the two minibuses parked nearby.

There was an uneasy stand off, as if people were double-checking their respective mobs for signs of anybody injured by a knife. I was just thankful for the rest and a chance to work out exactly how bad a position we were in. It was certainly worse than I could have predicted at the start of the fighting. From a mob of nearly 60 outside the ground, we were now down to 15 or 20 tops. Things didn't look good. In fact, I wasn't sure if we were going to come out of this one standing.

Then, as I was beginning to lose heart, Lawla steamed straight into the ranks of Leicester standing only a few feet away. It was suicidal, but I followed his example and thumped the first one of them I could get my hands on. I ended up on the floor, but bounced back up like I was made of rubber, in case one of the East Midlands bad boys fancied sticking a blade in me. Once back upright, I walked towards the ranks of Baby Squad with hands outstretched, offering a row to whoever fancied a go, but no one took up the offer. The fighting looked like it was about to stop – maybe we'd actually called their bluff. Unfortunately, it was just the calm before the storm.

At first, we had looked good, standing in a battle line and backing each other up – Flower was on one side of me, and Lawla the other. We felt we couldn't be beaten while holding firm between the parked vehicles, with the walls of Filbert Street to protect our rear. We looked the part and now we were proving to a big city crew that we *were* the part too. Then they stoned us.

We stood there for what seemed like an eternity while the Baby Squad rained down missiles and stones from the car park floor from every direction. One hit me in the mouth and I felt a tooth move in my jaw. Then it went really pear-shaped, as from the right of us a group of 30 menacing and older-looking lads came storming through the crowd. This lot meant business – believe me, you could tell from their expressions alone.

I saw the threat to our stability these new arrivals had brought and along with Freezing Frank and Ging decided to try to hold them up. I clashed with a bald cunt who started to knock me about, then an Asian lad joined from my left and added to the blows that I seemed to be collecting for fun now.

It was too much and I turned to join my fleeing comrades. As I fled, I felt some bastard get hold of my hair and try to hold me back by it, as yet more Baby Squad closed on me. I yanked so hard that a patch of hair and skin became detached from the back of my head, but I was away and didn't look back. I didn't really have a way out, though, because Leicester had completely cut off any escape routes. So I joined the rest of our lads fleeing into the narrow space between the Luton team coach and the Main Stand.

Our attackers continued their vicious assault, until we were literally grappling with each other to get behind the coach. I tried to pull Shit Hair back so he could take a few slaps instead of me and maybe get some of his blond locks pulled out by the dark roots as well! We ended up stuck behind the Luton team bus, but, instead of feeling down about the bashing, we started to laugh our heads off and sing Mig songs to lift our spirits.

The police turned up and ordered us out of hiding. Of course, we pretended to still want to have a go at Leicester, but in truth I don't think anyone apart from Lawla really wanted to battle on. And he was only raging because he'd just lost his new gold sovereign ring in the fighting.

Our small band of battered Migs headed back towards the end that had housed the majority of Luton fans for the day. As we reached the crowd of a couple of hundred waiting to be escorted to the train station, we spotted many of the lads who'd run in the initial clash and left us to fight a rearguard action. They looked a bit sheepish and all I can say is that to this day they know exactly who they are.

Someone who actually didn't mind being slated at the time was none other than our leader Paddy. 'They ripped my jeans, guy! There's no respect for man an' man's status up here!'

There was blood flowing from a wound to his knee and he took the piss out of himself further, admitting that he had to get on his toes as he'd been taking a bit of a shoeing on the floor and thought he might lose his hat as well!

No one could have known at the time, but this season was to be a particularly bad one for Leicester City Football Club as, come 9 May, they were relegated. We played them again, later in the season at Kenilworth Road, in the New Year, but there was to be no repeat of the scenes of Casual violence that had marked these matches, as Luton's ban on away fans stopped the Baby Squad from travelling in any force.

But someone from Leicester who did come down that season was John Williams. This transplanted Scouser was one of the Leicester University sociologists who were the principal commentators on football violence in the 80s and who along with Eric Dunning had written one of the first ever books on the subject – *Hooligan's Abroad*. They were now writing a report on the away-fan ban at Luton and Williams had been brought down to Kenilworth Road by Tuse, someone who I'd met when Paddy and the boys were still sporting designer tracksuits and deerstalkers were all the rage.

Tuse wasn't like many of the lads at the time in a couple of key areas. For a start, while most of the firm at that time came from the rougher parts of Luton, he came from nearby Harpenden, which is a pretty exclusive and expensive place to live. Nevertheless, he mingled with the chaps and was soon well known and you'd never have realised he hadn't dragged himself up on the dark streets of Hightown or the estates of Hockwell Ring or Lewsey Farm. He wore the garms with a particular liking for Aquascutum and could often be seen with his better-looking twin, Glen D from Bedford.

On his first trip to Leicester, he'd found himself in the thick of the action when he became isolated with DP and John A by the canal behind Filbert Street. They came under attack and managed to hold the line even though vastly outnumbered. With his new Cecil Gee shirt ripped from his back, big DP had completely lost the plot, which is not a pretty sight I can tell you, and ended up chasing more than 20 Leicester lads into our escort as it reached the canal. For a second, we thought they wanted it, but they just ran straight past, pursued by a topless DP, muscles bulging and raging about how much his shirt had cost him!

But, a couple of seasons later, Tuse became a law student at Leicester University and had got to know not only the sociologists, but also our

Someone Slap That Baby

friends the Baby Squad, who'd recognised him in town after our coach trip with Paddy back in 1984. So now he was a good source of information and feedback to the battles we regularly had with them and allowed us to gauge our growing reputation in the Midlands.

He told us more about the big dreadlock from the Highfields area who led the Baby Squad at the time and also about the various Asian lads, including his new mates, the Khan brothers, who were some of the main faces in their firm and as game as they came. In Luton, we have a huge Asian community too, but very few watch the Town play on a Saturday and only Sinbad and Monty ever chose to get involved in football violence.

So, accompanied by a battered-looking Tuse, who'd had his jaw broken by a Leicester rugby player the night before, the Scally sociologist had watched Luton stuff Liverpool 4–1. Mr Williams presented me with a copy of his book and met the Migs to discuss our part in the away-fan ban. Of course, I didn't have any answers, but explained that the violence at Luton was getting out of hand, as it escalated season after season and the stabbings were a regular occurrence nowadays. Over the years, our town had become one of the battlegrounds of choice for the discerning football hooligan – Millwall had just been the icing on the cake, and allowed them to bring in the ban with no opposition.

So the Migs got a write-up from the original hoolie book author and commentator, but unfortunately the Football Trust Report was hardly a bestseller with the lads and it would take another 20 years to get it together to write the story properly. My copy of *Hooligan's Abroad* subsequently became a media star too, though, when it appeared on TV sets alongside a bottle of bleach and a couple of craft knives, after being confiscated during police raids for Operation Spoonbill!

Then, ironically enough, it was our chairman David Evans's away-fan ban that brought us back together with the Baby Squad soon afterwards, when, during the 1987/88 season, Luton Town were drawn against Coventry City in the Littlewoods Cup. The tie was due to be played at Kenilworth Road, but this would be a problem because, after the ban, the ground no longer had proper segregation and Coventry were entitled to 3,500 tickets for their fans.

David Evans had made it clear that he wouldn't allow the streets of Luton to be turned into a battle zone again and certainly wasn't about to allow visiting supporters into Kenilworth Road without segregation. So, rather than run the risk of being thrown out of the competition and losing money as had happened the previous season, he negotiated to have the second round tie played at Filbert Street. Thanks, Dave!

On 27 October 1987, I travelled up the M1 in a hired Ford Fiesta along with Winston, Horrible and Norfs. Three more cars followed closely behind containing Flower, Nuggy and the Juveniles – our younger mob. That night, we clashed with both Coventry and Leicester lads. Coventry weren't too much of a problem and, after the initial battle, which ended when three of our party pulled out blades, Coventry's boys ran to the OB for assistance.

Leicester, though, were a different proposition and we found a big crew of them drinking close to the ground. Despite only having a token force available, we called it on in a narrow alleyway just across the road from where they were gathered. I watched from behind a lamppost, close to the mouth of the alley, as up to 40 lads bowled towards our position. Horrible noticed something about this mob: 'They've got Asian fellas with them!'

He was right – a tall, light-skinned Asian lad was at the head of the mob and he certainly didn't look out of place, dressed in the proper gear and walking with the swagger that only football lads can carry off.

We backed into the alley and tooled up with handfuls of ammo to throw. Then things got nasty with bricks being thrown at point-blank range and car aerials snapped off and used as whips. I was tripped during the clash and took a couple of kicks to the back of my head, as I struggled to get up again. Slowly, the Baby Squad's superior numbers began to pay dividends and we were forced back down the pathway and out on to the streets behind. We tried to herd them in the alley, but were soon on our toes as none of us was prepared to risk being caught alone on the lonely and dark streets of Leicester. Sadly, this was to be my last meeting with the Baby Squad for many years – Muslim Casuals and all.

Now back at Luton Crown Court, I finished shaking hands with my Hindu mate Monty, knowing that perhaps he was not of the same calibre as the Asian lads who'd fought against us on our trips to Leicester. Then I turned, gave my name to the usher and strolled into the courtroom taking my place next to my mates behind the glass shields.

Now we were ready to face a different and even more fearsome foe than the Baby Squad – the law.

8 They Soon Knew They'd Met the Luton Blacks

When you're awaiting judgment for a crime that you know full well you've committed, your mind goes through the process of preparing for whatever punishment you might receive. You always imagine the worst-case scenario, but still cling to the hope of escaping with only a slap on the wrist. I'd thought through all the possible outcomes of my court appearance and always spoke as if I was certain to be sent down for a good stretch. It was my way of letting everyone know that I'd be OK, no matter what the judge decided I deserved.

But in truth, it was only a smokescreen. I was gutted at the prospect of spending time behind bars for slapping a few Hertfordshire idiots in the twisted belief that I was performing some kind of civic duty. When I thought about all the time I would waste sat on my arse in jail, the most depressing aspect was not knowing what I could have achieved had I not been locked up.

I was already close to deciding once and for all that enough is enough and that I wouldn't return to the firm. But I was also aware that once again I might not learn my lesson and could end up back in court facing another prison sentence in a few years time. How could I make sure that I learned from all this and didn't slip back into bad habits?

Plenty of Mig Crew members had been imprisoned in the past, but one in particular springs to mind. I first met Dibble, or Dibs to his closer mates, during some inter-school fighting as a teenager and we immediately became friends. He was a cool customer until he got excited and then he was a total liability.

As my teens rolled by and I drifted into the football hooligan scene, I saw more of Dibs. He hung around the town centre with the gangs of black youths that gathered every Saturday when Luton were playing at home. I first saw him joining the battle with the ICF around the Strathmore Hotel and Central Car Parks – clearly a man with little fear and a lot of energy for the fight.

Then, against QPR one season, I spotted him being chased by a whole herd of police officers following a clash with Rangers lads at the West Side Centre. The chase was like something out of the Keystone Cops, except that our man Dibble had a leather belt in his hand that he'd just used to great effect on some poor West Londoner – which, of course, is why the OB weren't giving up on the chase. Eventually, he was caught and sent down for his part in the fighting that day. It was his second prison term for football-related violence, the first being some time earlier, following clashes with Tottenham thugs on Dunstable Road.

The Yids were renowned as the best-dressed firm in London at the time and one of the most formidable opponents of the era. We never really had much success against them and, out of all the London clubs that visited, they were the toughest nut to crack. Their numbers were always impressive and I'd go so far as to say that, apart from Millwall, they brought the biggest mob I ever saw at Luton.

A large presence of smartly dressed Cockney lads usually drew many extra local thugs out of the woodwork, in the hope of robbing the visitors of their expensive garms. Dibble had been part of a group of which maybe half wanted the row, but the rest were there purely on the rob. As soon as the Tottenham boys put up a decent fight, the muggers melted away, leaving only Dibs and a handful of others to save the day. In his desperation to take the battle to the Yids, he removed his belt and aimed the buckle in their direction – his trademark move.

It cost him his liberty at a time when prison was not the usual sentence for a football-related offence. Then, most recently, he got 10 months for his part in the televised pitch invasion at Watford, which took place on the same day and at almost exactly the same time as my own offence outside the Moon Under Water. Why hadn't he learned? What motivated him to keep on going back for more and risking his liberty every time?

As I thought of Dibs, I remembered my own first football-related offence and wondered why I hadn't taken anything on board since then. I was convicted of Robbery at Bedford Crown Court after taxing a Watford fan before a match in the old Second Division. I appeared alongside

Taking a casual look into the Kenny

Author getting nabbed at Vicarage Road

LUTON V. WEST HAM 1980 All kicks off in the Oak Road as the ICF enter. Look particularly at the huge West Ham support filling the Kenilworth Road as Luton's youngsters,

displaced from Oak Road, sprint across the pitch to escape the fighting. The Maple Road also breaks out into violent clashes but holds its own.

LUTON V. CHELSEA 1980 Same as West Ham, same season but this time Luton do a

little better and manage to hold on to half the Oak Road, as Chelsea take the fight to Luton.

LUTON V. OLDHAM 1981 Luton fans storm over from the Maple Road (Triangle) and launch attacks on the travelling Oldham contingent, who desert the Kenilworth Road

terraces to seek refuge under the stand after Oldham gave it loads of verbal earlier.

LUTON V. ARSENAL 1984 Arsenal and the Gooners try it on in the Oak Road. An end now known for being pure Scarfers, but they came unstuck when the MIGS from the Maple

Road sprung into action and forced the Gooners back. The pictures of Gooners on the pitch after the fight clearly show them sporting sore heads.

The Maple Road Triangle was where Luton's hardcore stood.

You had two leagues, one on the pitch the other one of it.

LUTON V. SHEFFIELD WEDNESDAY 1981 Scenes of destruction: Sheffield Wednesday's team bus and many other coaches were smashed up in the fighting in the car park.

Luton's most famous supporter, comedian Eric Morecambe, with officials check his car for damage.

There's a bit of history with us and Leicester. Above: Luton fans at Leicester in 1959, and below: Leicester's Baby Squad during the 80s.

'Said, we are top of the League'. Plymouth's Central Element arrive in Luton, 2002.

Forest Executive Crew: A right rough old mob of seasoned football thugs.

We made a mistake in not travelling up to Hull, the City Psychos are known to have a good home mob.

The most impressive firm to come to Luton was always Tottenham.

The most famous riot in British Hooligan history: Luton v. Millwall, 1985

Starsky, another of Luton's black firm, and we both escaped with fines and some stern words from the evil-looking judge.

Unlike me, Starsky learned his lesson and began the complicated process of removing himself from football violence, showing that a little willpower can change a man's life. Unfortunately, I suspected that it might take something more than that to make me stop. I also wanted to know what explanation a decent member of society, who paid his taxes and raised his children almost single-handedly, had for getting sucked into what is typically assumed to be a white racist's environment. Here is what Starsky told me:

I'd been going football since I was around 13 and will never forget the noise when I first jumped over the back fence and climbed up a ladder to get into the Oak Road. The singing, jumping and shouting – it was one big buzz. As a Junior Hatter, I turned up every other week for the sum of a mere 75 pence and soon noticed that alongside the match there was another game involved with the occasion – the one played by the local hard boys. They were known as the Maple Road and also the Castle Bar. These boys loved their football, but they loved a fight as well.

I remember when we played West Ham in the early 80s, I was 14 years old and all you could hear was 'United... United' – it was West Ham in the Oak Road. I was at the front of the terraces and Luton were getting a right kicking, so we had to get on to the pitch to escape. West Ham had come to take our end and by damn they did, but as I looked to my right the Maple managed to hold on to their section – 'You'll never take the Maple!'

All this commotion made your heart speed up to rocket pace. That was it for me – I'd tasted it now and wanted my own piece of the pie. But I was still young and would have to prove myself to get anywhere near this firm.

I noticed a big black Luton guy who had a lot of respect from the people around him, throwing some heavy punches over in the Maple. I found out his name was Tony. He seemed to be pointing to the exit and clapping, then you heard loud and clear, 'We'll see you all outside!' It was like a church choir.

If you went week after week, you got to know the main boys who liked to put their hands up and soon got accepted. I'd also heard about a guy called Aubrey B, from his cousin Macca. He was an Arsenal Gooner, but lived in Luton and eventually we met up. By this time, we'd grown in stature, both physically and within the crew, and were loving everything that was happening around the football.

We had a nice group of boys with us now. Not all went to the match, but they were always ready to link up after the final whistle. The usual place – the home base for the Luton Blacks – was the Arndale Shopping Centre. It was all good! The Maple Boys were still active and the Castle Bar too, but they appreciated that the Luton Blacks were now also a force.

One memorable battle was against QPR. We decided to hit them early as they had history with Luton. Aubrey B was going to lead the Luton Blacks around the back of the town and lay an ambush. This guy knew precisely what to do and when to do it. And another thing I noticed, his clothes were well particular – Fila, Giorgio Armani, classic Lyle & Scott and also Diadora Gold trainers, like Bjorn Borg the tennis chap wore. This was a big part of the football changeover from local hard cases on the terraces to running with a proper firm. You had to be game, but now it was just as important that you looked right.

We were mobbed up and ready – Macca, Dibs and the Just brothers along with a good 25 or 30 others. The Rangers had landed so me and Macca confirmed the news of their arrival to Aubrey B.

He told us, 'Split up and go round the corner to wait.' So we waited. Then Aubrey stepped out and spoke to them in a relaxed manner. 'Do you want the off?'

He was so calm that it didn't matter that Rangers outnumbered us – we had a game plan. As they came closer, we let them have it. They were keen as well, I'll give them that. But, once the rest of our boys came round the other corner and got stuck in too, they looked a bit shocked – we were all black! But that's how it was. I remember Dibs getting stuck in and the Just brothers were at it too. I was in there like a jackal. After all, they wanted it and so did we.

Aubrey was well happy. I suppose with us lot being the younger ones we needed a guide and he was willing to fill that role. But all the boys could put up a fight and he knew it. The Farley Hill lot were no soft touch, with Jamie and the Duval brothers. Our lot were known as 'Town Boys' because we came from near the town centre. Then there were some Hockwell Ring lads, including the King brothers, who were getting involved as well. Our numbers were growing all the time.

They Soon Knew They'd Met the Luton Blacks

Whenever a visiting team showed, you could guarantee that the Luton Blacks would be there to greet them. Any club that had football boys knew about us now and as a result certain firms came looking for us. Things got really interesting once reputations were flying around. You also noticed that you had more respect because you were running with the firm. Sometimes after a brawl, we'd end up at a late-night blues party where we could have a good burn and drink and dance with some girls till morning.

One thing you have to remember – we liked to fight, but we liked other things as well. Our families were all from the West Indies and, whether it was Jamaica, St Vincent or any other island, a Caribbean upbringing raised you up rough and ready. We were prepared to defend our patch and weren't faking it. We were young rebels with a cause now. We knew we had to be on our toes to survive in this game and it wasn't easy. But back then there weren't many cameras and, apart from a certain local sergeant called Jock McKenzie, the OB weren't too clued up.

West Ham were next – in a night match – so hopefully we were going to see both the Under-Fives and the infamous ICF. It would be a good test for us all – 'let's see who are the true warriors!' In the meantime, pass the spliff, some curry goat and a cold beer.

As one blues dance ran into the early hours, Macca came in and told us stories about them: 'Yo! Them boys got to get a beating. Some of them have to run all the way home!'

It was time to put our heads down – West Ham are coming to town and Luton have scores to settle with the East End boys. We all headed off in different directions, knowing full well that we were going to have to be at our best to finish on top.

Days were ticking by slowly before the encounter and as it approached you could only imagine what would happen. Word had spread that West Ham were coming looking for the Luton Blacks in particular. Some of the soul boys in the firm had caught some scouts out clocking the lay of the land. West Ham had a good rep so we knew they'd do their homework, but Leppy couldn't resist giving one stray a dig just to send him on his way. Maybe he hoped the victim would work hard to pay it back. Leppy was a soul boy, but he could fight – I should know as we've had some tear-ups in the past.

The night before the match we decided to meet at Breakers – a bar up a side street in the town centre. All the main boys were there. Some were out-and-out villains, but today they were here to discuss defending their hometown at any cost. Aubrey B came in, dressed in new gear as usual. Macca and myself bought some drinks. More boys arrived and soon the place was packed out – it was obvious that everyone who came down really wanted it. As the drinking got going, you could tell we were all ready and soon Leppy shouted, 'Let them come!' Typical, always ready.

And now the banter starts flowing. 'Remember when you lot got run by the Cockney Reds?' That was big-mouth Jamie – a die-hard Man United supporter who would never run, even when well outnumbered. As Bob Marley once said, he would always live to fight another day. One of Aubrey's boys, Grumpy, also liked the Gooners, but was a Luton Black as well. I can't relate to running with more than one firm myself, because I'm a Luton Black and that's all I've ever wanted to be. But each to their own.

All the boys were here now – Boogie, a totally game chap who loved dancing to the reggae tunes; in step as always, the Just brothers; then a big roar went up as Tiller showed in the pub – he only comes when he's sure it's on. Time was moving on and everyone was merry, with more boys arriving all the time, including some I hadn't seen before. Brownie confirmed who's who – it's always good to have someone who studies these things. It's something they are born with. Brownie was an observer and always remembered a face so he was useful to have around. He was also never alone and usually brought a good number of boys with him.

Breakers is the kind of place where you could gain a rep or lose one, but not everyone in there that day was a football boy. Some were what we called 'rude boys'. They could deal with most problems and would watch out for some of us if we got in over our head. We were brave, but young and needed some kind of guidance. We respected these guys and they understood that. The rudies knew what we got up to, but they still had time for us and would say, 'Mind how you go, my yout.' They knew we were on a slippery slope, but we had a 'no care' attitude.

Tom, the bar manager at Breakers, was well under the cosh and who wouldn't have been in his position? Some of the right hustlers made sure everything was sweet for him and so for a small price this was our den. It was last orders, but not everybody wanted to leave and no one was taking any notice of the landlord. He called to one of the men that helped him out and the big guy roared, 'You all have to leave… NOW!' He turned and smiled. 'You have to know how to talk to them, Tom!'

The landlord must be thinking, 'Why did they come to this bar? Why did they pick my place?'

We all began to move and I noticed a few of the Town Boys start a little ruck with some Hockwell Ring. But it was just their way of keeping themselves sharp. The only thing was, someone got their nose bloodied, so we joined in to even the sides up. Even though we were all one, we would often test each other to see who were top boys and this time round the Town lads came out winners. It's been the other way round before, though, so there's no love lost.

Everyone went their separate ways. The soul boys were going for a boogie down North London at the Electric Ballroom in Camden Town, so they all piled into motors and headed for the M1. Macca and Dibs were on a promise from some girls they'd met at a blues party. If it was those girls I saw them dancing with, they can keep them. A good steady walk home was the safer choice! And, anyway, I wanted an early night to be ready for the big day tomorrow.

The Duval brothers lived not far from me so we walked together. The breeze was cool, just what you need when you're a bit tipsy. The older brother was well drunk and itching for a fight. You could tell by the way he was bouncing and screwing out anyone that walked towards us – we hoped he'd be like that tomorrow. We kept him steady to make sure he'd still be around for the big showdown. You know how it is – the last thing you want is to get nicked for something silly the night before an important match.

They made it to their door and struggled to open it, but finally cracked it and fell inside. I stepped up the pace and was soon outside my gates, then through the door into the bathroom, washed up and in the sack. Oh no! Bedroom spinning, up at a dash, head over the toilet… you know the rest.

The morning had come and I was still a bit drunk which wasn't too bad as we weren't meeting up with the rest of the boys till one o'clock. I wanted to nod back off, but time passed too quickly and I soon heard my mum scream out, 'Someone at the door.'

It was Macca with a huge smile on his face. I leaped up and soon we headed out to meet the rest of the boys. It was time, and that's what Macca's big grin was all about.

We headed up the hill and spotted Aubrey B in a motor. He hooted to us, making sure we saw him and after a brief chat we knew where to link up. One thing about this football thing, I like to know that there's good boys around who won't leave you in a tight corner. Aubrey put our minds at rest on that score. As we stepped up the pace and approached the Arndale, we knew we were guaranteed to run into some faces.

It was just past midday and there was already a crowd inside the front entrance, so we started to mingle and prowl about like a pack of wolves. At that time, the OB never had as many cameras so the odds were better for you to avoid their gaze. As you looked in each other's eyes, you saw that we had one thing in common today... we were here for aggro.

Then, as we hung near the front we heard a scream: 'They're here! The Under-Fives are here!' It was Wild Bill – take it from me, he was wild!

We saw about 30 boys in half-cut Pringles, Fila tracksuits and more gear, but they hadn't spotted our mob because we were inside the shopping centre. Macca was urging us to take it to them, so the ones that were well into the game led an attack and I ran at them with Leppy, Jacks and the Duval brothers. As we got close, they looked a bit hesitant – but we weren't and smashed right into them. They soon knew they'd met the Luton Blacks.

The West Ham were all dressed well, although I don't think they were the main mob. But who cares – we still done them and the thieves in our pack robbed them silly. Them clothes cost a lot of cash! I honestly thought that they plain lost their bottle and just took a hiding. Wild Bill knocked them all over the place and after the battle we couldn't stop laughing. As far as we were concerned, we turned that Under-Fives lot right over and it was a good feeling because we'd been waiting for them to come to town for some time. But it was still early and they would soon relay the fact that they'd been done back to their main mob.

As we returned to the Arndale, we walked with a bounce in our step – proud that we'd been in the thick of the action. We were all buzzing now – hanging near the front and keeping alert. In this game, things can change at any time... and so it proved. At about half-past two, more West Ham came from nowhere. All you heard was an almighty roar.

Those bastards in claret and blue had surprised us and steamed right in. Some of our mob ran, but many stood and fought back. This time the fighting was fierce and spilled into nearby shops.

One guy called King held it together for the Luton Blacks. He was heavy handed and laying some big punches on those West Ham boys, but, that aside, the Cockneys were game and evened up the score. Earlier, we had slapped them silly – this was different. As the fighting raged, we regrouped and charged. We had to stop them claiming the upper hand. Rollings was taking a kicking, but he was still up and at them again. We held our own and gave them back some of what they were handing out. I respected the way they had come right back at us so quick, but I'm sure they also respected us because we'd stood our ground.

Now we started to gather momentum and push them back – Aubrey kept encouraging everybody and giving us confidence: 'Let them have it! They're not used to taking it… we can do them.' We needed words of wisdom, because some hadn't experienced this sort of heavy action before and it was a testing time.

Suddenly, above the din of the battle Macca shouted, 'Babylon!' And who else but Sergeant Jock McKenzie came running in to restore order.

Jock was a tough Scotsman and a real character. He knew most of the Luton boys and wasn't shy to give you a slap to keep you in line. It seemed like he really enjoyed his job chasing football hooligans around. He lead his men into action and quickly set about dividing the two firms and restoring order.

Once things calmed for a second, I checked around. There were some of the Castle Bar and Maple Road boys standing with us, looking worse for wear, but with big smiles on their faces. The other Luton lads had joined us to take on West Ham and it was a proud sight. So we had got what we were waiting for and, unlike some clubs, West Ham never disappointed.

One thing I learned from the Under-Fives and the ICF was the importance of being well organised and fighting as a team. This meant you could never take them lightly, particularly at a night match. You looked at some of the faces in that firm and clearly saw the fear in their eyes, but in others you could see only anger. What gave this lot their edge is that a man can be dangerous with either and a football firm was better off with both.

As we started to move off, the West Ham lot kept glaring in our direction and you knew there would be more to come later, so we bogged them out. This was key, like two boxers once the bell's gone at the end of a round. The communication was with the eyes. Both sides knew they'd stood their ground, so both sets of egos were running high. Aubrey B, Jacks, the Just brothers and Wen huddled together for a talk. I overheard them saying they would head for Bury Park when the match got under way. Looking back now it was like chess masters sharing some of their best strategies and it wouldn't be too long before us pawns were told the next move.

Right on cue, Aubrey B headed over to us and set the tactics. This time he gave Dibs and Macca the scouting job and, within seconds, they both had broad smiles. In a way, I was relieved that it wasn't me, because the ICF had already done some of Brownie's boys when they were out scouting earlier and left their famous calling card as a reminder too. But for now Dibble and Macca were just thinking they'd moved up a notch and enjoying the moment. The rest of us headed on to Breakers for a game of pool and a drink.

As the night drew in, we all felt a chill. We were waiting for Macca and Dibble to make their entrance and you could see the concern on some of the boys' faces. The time was drawing near. It was dark outside now and you couldn't see much, but so many thoughts were running through our minds. Do the ICF know where we are? Would they rush the pub at any moment? We needed the scouts to come back with some information. It was one big build-up and getting more tense by the minute.

You could hear someone saying, 'I bet they've been done over.' That had to be Augustus John. He had this weird name – I think his mum named him after some film star. He had more jokes than Tommy Cooper and at that time you needed someone to take the tension out the air. 'I reckon Macca's found a girl and he's gone to get busy.'

Everybody started laughing because we all knew how he loved to chase girls. But I was sure he'd be back. Augustus just kept on cussing like his mum would curse him.

More relaxed now, drinks were passed around and we got merry. Then the doors swung open and the two so-called scouts came strolling in like they were starring in some old cowboy movie and Aubrey quickly called them over to the corner. Brownie and his merry men were here too, so we had good numbers – a mix of the same old

They Soon Knew They'd Met the Luton Blacks

characters and some new recruits. It's like everything in life, if you hear about something all the time, you want to experience it for yourself. And that's why they came – you hear about so-called 'names', look up to them and hope that you can be a name yourself one day.

It was time to move out of Breakers and defend our patch. Aubrey took some main boys like Wen, Jacks, Wild Bill, Joe Lou and the Just brothers and headed towards the ground. No one I knew was actually going in to watch the game... only the odd few did. Aubs had left Dibs and Macca to organise us lot and, in a way, it was a big step up for them. But I was more than willing to back them because I knew they were real.

Macca called us together and told us what he'd seen. 'They're firmed up at the back of the West Side Centre. They've got good numbers, so we have to spilt up and try to link later or we'll be too easy to spot.'

Someone else spoke. 'They're out to get us now... they want us badly, I'm telling you.' Dibs was making the most of his new cameo role as well and good luck to him.

We were all ready. Now we were on our own, away from the more experienced boys, but that was the only way we would flourish – by making our own decisions. We walked around to the back of the football ground by a quiet route. We were at home and had to make use of any advantage available to us. This West Ham mob had a very good record and wouldn't want us to ruin it. We had around 30 boys stepping together. When I looked back at the crew, I felt strong just walking with them, but we were never really about great numbers – it was more about heart. As we got closer, you could feel a tingle, like some kind of sixth sense.

Up at the ground, Macca and Dibble decided we should hang back so as not to stand out. So we just leaned back on some walls and watched what was happening around us. We noticed unfamiliar faces, but because it was a night match no one was 100 per cent sure who was who. Leppy was certain he'd seen an Under-Five that he slapped earlier.

Then we heard, 'Come on then, West Ham' and turned to see the big black guy I'd seen when I first went to football.

At first, we just watched, as there was still a while before kick-off and then slowly they came out to confront him. By damn! It was the West Ham mob ready to turn Luton over in their own end! We stood up and backed it, but the Cockneys just kept coming out of the crowd. We scuffled with them, but the old Maple Road boy had gone on the missing list so we were right in it and the ICF mob soon saw us off. We'd upset a hornets' nest and they just kept on after us.

I remember a heavyweight guy known as the Bear sprinting like an athlete to escape the onslaught. Dibs had been right when he said they wanted us! We drew back and tried to hold it together. Although we were on the run, Macca had a plan. He knew we needed more heads and was taunting them into a trap, so the scene wasn't all doom. We turned and faced them again at the West Side Centre. We were outnumbered, but battled hard. They were good, though, and began to gain the upper hand. That is, until Aubrey B and co came running in from the side and the ICF backed right up. Big DP was in action as well and it was quite a sight to behold. He was a legend among the Luton Blacks and more than lived up to his reputation that day.

We had held our own and I could see the surprise on the West Ham lot's faces as they lost control of the battle, but that's how things can turn. That's what made these guys get involved in this game; it was a feeling that takes you to the edge. You could see them pointing out Aubrey now – he ran with the Gooners as well and was a face in football circles. They looked confused, but Aubrey had grown up around us, so he was one of us first.

That was that, they'd been shook up and would see us in a different light from then on. We had a fair battle and it was just them and us. West Ham had some top boys hurt that day, but even when they were outnumbered they still ran into us. Them boys came right in and never stepped back at all. They'd proved themselves on many occasions before and done so again in Luton tonight. But the Luton Blacks came out on top and I won't forget Aubrey B, Dirty Harry and DP jumping for joy because we had got to their main boys. It was like getting through to Napoleon at the battle of Waterloo.

Now, though, it was time to make an exit because Jock McKenzie had got wind of the trouble and was tearing around like the Sweeney with his siren wailing and blue lights flashing. The last thing you wanted was him getting hold of you when he was on a mission.

It was over, so the Under-Fives and ICF moved on. No doubt they'd be back again, but it was a day we would never forget. Fighting was part of our upbringing and it was in our nature to defend our patch. But

They Soon Knew They'd Met the Luton Blacks

this was different, it was like you were looking for it, but so were they. It was serious.

We started to head back to Breakers, the bounce in our step clear to see. After all, we had given a good account of ourselves. Macca, Brownie and Georgie were still hyper and discussing the day's events, like they'd just come out of the movies. They were young boys in their prime and probably not thinking any further ahead than next Saturday. From then on, the Maple Road boys would salute us and we returned their gestures. They were there before us, but it was our time now.

We soon got back to HQ and the usual chat centred on who got run, who got nicked and who stood their ground. Anyone that was there and had been in the thick of the action received a warm greeting on their return. They might have taken a hiding or spent some time helping the police with their enquiries, so we were there to lift their spirits and, of course, to drink some too. Sure, there were some pitfalls, but you had good odds of having a great day before coming back to base and getting involved in some camaraderie.

As the night ticked away, you would get the usual rivalry from your own boys. Lewsey boys would chant Hockwell Ring for running and it would be chucked straight back. One man in particular, Treats, was always at it, but he had a right because he was there all them years ago when it was scarves and hats with teams' colours on. Now it was Pringles, Fila, Nike, Armani and much more besides. It was all about fashion and, if you looked better than the other firm, you felt you were better than them. It was similar to military tactics. If you looked the part, you would stand out from the rest, so you had to keep up with the latest gear.

Also, the girls were into it as well – so they only wanted to be with someone who had the right clothes and the right chat. That got more of us involved, because, if you're getting attention from the opposite sex, you play up to it. It was one big ego trip, but that was only part of it. To be an all-rounder, you had to be seen to be involved in the confrontation and that made it the complete buzz.

After all the banter and the usual ego-tripping, Breakers was more crowded than usual, so you could guarantee there was a function going on afterwards. Jacks, Wen and Wild Bill explained that there was a blues party with two sound systems in one arena and most of the boys were off to the event. Well, at least the ones who like to listen to reggae music and get close to some fine-looking young ladies.

That was right up our street and a good way to unwind after all the charging around, so Wen and Jacks made arrangements that we could ride in free later. It was a nice gesture as they were seen as senior to us and I suppose it was their way of letting us know that we did OK. Sometimes, the older guys in the firm found it difficult to tell us that we were up there now, but that was cool with us. We knew. So, as they left, Macca, Dibs, the younger Wallot brothers and myself tagged along.

When we reached the dancehall, the bass was hitting hard through the walls. Wen and Wild Bill ushered us to the front of the queue, which was going way back, but we weren't about to ask questions. They had a word with a man who stood at least six foot five and had a face you wouldn't want to look at twice. His presence alone was enough to make you wary. But after a little negotiation we followed behind Wild Bill without paying, which meant a hell of a lot because money was not in abundance. You felt a bit special just walking up like that. Everyone could see the beaming smiles on all our faces as we stepped through.

Inside, though, you were definitely not at the football. You were here to unwind and take it from me this was not the place to cause trouble. There were too many rude boys in here. They could dish it out, and they had no time for any youth that was off the rails. This was where we could dance to some sweet reggae and soul music. Along with some food, of course – curry goat, rice and peas and a Heineken to wash it all down. It was good to see the boys eating, drinking and laughing together. It wasn't all about fighting, but that's what had brought us together in the first place when we had to defend ourselves. Of course, not all our community saw it like that, but anyone who liked to chant bad language at my people soon changed their tune when they saw the rude boys.

As the music pumped from the speakers, we were given a request. A tune was played for the 'rude boys in the corner' – an old ska track called 'A Message To You Rudy'! We all erupted and started beating the walls and anything else that would make some noise to show our appreciation. It made you feel something inside. In a way, we saw it as recognition and for some of us that's all we had, so we had to make the most of it. The blues party went on into the early hours of the morning. Some of the boys left with numbers after chancing their arm and girls seemed to be around all the time now. You know the saying 'girls like a bad boy', and I can surely vouch for that. They all seemed to know who certain members of the crew were and would often spill drinks to get our attention.

The morning had come, we'd ridden the rollercoaster and it was time to call it a day. We said our goodbyes to Jacks, Wen, Wild Bill and the rest, thanking them for a great night. Macca and Dibs were almost too drunk to walk because Christos had given them some white rum. Being a Jamaican, that was his tipple, so he was fine, but them two were in trouble and looked like they were keen to cause some as well.

After a drunken stagger, we finally got to the cab station and ordered a ride. But Macca's drunken swearing offended the controller. An argument followed, someone raised their hands and suddenly the cab boss was spark out on the floor. The other cab drivers waded into us. What a sight – earlier, we had proved ourselves against the ICF, now we were all drunk and taking a hammering off some cabbies!

Next thing, sirens and you know the rest... in the back of the van all the way to the station. The Wallot brothers were well heated and abusing the police who nicked us, but the rest were too busted to get involved. We reached the police station, were hustled out of the van and, as luck would have it, bumped straight into our unfriendly football plod, Jock McKenzie. But he had a huge smile from one ear to the other now, like 'look what the cat's dragged in'. So even Macca shut up and we were led to the cells.

One thing about being in a cell – time stands still. Unless you're drunk, of course, when like Macca and Christos you just sleep it off. The Wallot brothers, meanwhile, made a nuisance of themselves purely to wind up the police. After about five hours, though, they let us go without charge. We had trouble waking up the rum drinkers, but eventually they raised up their weary heads to roars of laughter from everyone. Even Sergeant Jock McKenzie had to laugh and was heard to utter in his strong Glaswegian accent, 'Can't hold your drink, wee lad?' Later, though, he commented on our battles at the football and let us know that he had his eye on us. We humoured him in case he had a change of heart and put us back in those luxury beds again!

When you look back, we would fight together, eat and drink together, socialise and even get locked up together. There was a special loyalty that grew over time. You could feel the unity. It's hard to describe or imagine – you just had to be part of it. It was hard for anybody new to be accepted. He would have to pass through 'quality control' first – like when you take your car for its MOT. And, at some point, he would have to prove himself, just as the newcomers did against the ICF and Under-Fives that day. It was healthy, though, because knowing that new faces were around and wanted to make a name for themselves kept you on your toes.

You had it or you didn't and it wasn't about size or even about being a good one-on-one fighter. You had to have the bottle to step to it even when the odds were against you and in our case that meant most of the time, as the majority of clubs had more support. We could still give them trouble, though, because we shared a bond that made us strong and over time they had to bring a lot of boys to tackle us. We would always take out even numbers – especially if they were half 'fronters'. We had to get our direction together though as there were more boys from across the country claiming that they'd met the Luton Blacks. Word had spread.

Starsky had shown to me that colour was no barrier to anyone who found themselves brawling on an open terrace or up some shady backstreet in the defence of their town's reputation. I already knew that job description and social standing meant little to a fully paid-up member of the football hooligan world.

On the positive side, though, he had been as deeply involved in the scene at Luton, but when the consequences grew too much he managed to put it all behind him. Surely, this time could be my turning point too and never again would I be stood defending Luton and calling out to some West London thug, 'EIE... Migs! Do you want some?'

One thing was for sure – once this day was over, I had to avoid ever finding myself back in court and facing jail again.

9 Herding the Herd (Another Bloody Replay)

I like to think that it takes a lot to worry me, but, as Judge Seldon Cripps entered the courtroom, I suddenly felt very nervous indeed. I took a second to check the expressions on my co-defendants' faces and to a man they looked as worried sick as me. The judge stopped for a moment and peered disapprovingly over his thick glasses at our party lined up next to the Group 4 security guards. Then we remained standing as he took his seat. Game on.

We were each identified to the court and our relevant defence counsel noted. Then the charges were read out and one by one our pleas were given. We'd all entered pleas of 'Not Guilty' to Violent Disorder and 'Guilty' to Affray, five months earlier at St Albans Crown Court and the CPS had gladly accepted them. On that day, which seemed like an eternity ago now, we had been promised full credit for our sensible conversations with the prosecution. Judge Cripps had seemed happy that justice would be seen to be done and at minimal cost to the taxpayer too.

The proceedings today opened with the prosecution presenting the background events leading up to the arrests and then suggesting their case would rest on CCTV footage alone. Fucking CCTV! I could remember the day I had come across it for the first time. It was back in March 1986 when Luton had been on another impressive Cup run, this time in the FA Cup. In previous rounds, we'd beaten Crystal Palace at Selhurst Park in front of a 9,886 crowd that included the then England manager Bobby Robson. It was a good day out too, as we fought 40 on 40 with the almost aptly named South London firm the Nifty Fifty!

Next, we beat Bristol Rovers, before being drawn against Arsenal in the fifth round. Now at the time Arsenal were making quite a bit of noise around the country and had been documented taking a sizeable mob, known as 'the Herd', to the likes of Millwall, West Ham and Aston Villa. At Luton, we knew all too well about the Herd's success, because we had a number of lads that moved with it.

One of these was Aubrey B – the man who changed the way that Luton operated as a firm after the early 80s. Aubrey was an ex-Yid who had switched to Arsenal after being left by his boys to take a kicking from the Gooners and they were only too happy to have this new recruit on board.

He was, and by all accounts still is, a bit of an eccentric and never one to conform to the standard hooligan dress codes at the time. Sure, he would wear the same labels as the rest of us and maybe even wear the same style in trainers. But then he would go and do something that was almost revolutionary at the time and throw the colour pink into the equation. We would all buy classic white Lacoste T-shirts from Lillywhites on Oxford Street – Aubrey would buy pink. We would all buy clean white Nikes and he'd appear in pink joggers! Aubrey had his own rules.

In the early 80s, if two mobs came face to face and one considerably outnumbered the other, it would usually mean a charge from the bigger crew and the smaller one getting on their toes. Aubrey showed us a better way. We would send lads ahead as scouts to feed information back to the main mob and this would decide our approach to the confrontation ahead.

For example, if we had numerical advantage, we would hide the majority of our crew and only give the opposition a small show. Meanwhile, the main mob would get into position to ambush or bushwhack them. It might seem an obvious tactic to get the upper hand, but it also allowed us to establish the moral high ground. If you were in the larger firm and you simply attacked the other crew, they could always suggest that you outnumbered them and that was the only reason you kicked it off. However, if you only showed them a small group and they still chose to engage in a battle, then they immediately lost any moral defences and were fair game for a good hiding.

The flipside to this was that, if our scout reported that we were heavily outnumbered, then we would play a different game – we'd raise the stakes and 'tool up'. This was a decision not to be taken lightly. If you tooled up early in the day, the weapon of choice had to be small enough to conceal about your person, so as not to draw any unwanted attention from the OB as you wandered about. But if you left it too late – say when you were

Herding the Herd (Another Bloody Replay)

under attack from the other mob – then you could only use whatever you found in the heat of the moment and that might not be enough.

So, by sending out scouts we could establish the relevant information and still have plenty of time to find the right materials to use against the opposition. I know that these days lads don't tend to tool up at all and many will say it's uncalled for, but in the mid-80s most firms had lads who were more than happy to do a bit of cutting. And, if it came to it, the whole crew would launch anything they could get their hands on at a rival firm as well.

We were no different and no worse than any other crew in this respect, although some have claimed otherwise. Somewhat ironically, the changes that Aubrey brought to our tactics at Luton were to come back and haunt him, when during our 1986 Cup run we played Arsenal not once, but three times. Somewhat controversially for such a face in Luton, Aubrey decided he would bring the Gooners to visit with full instructions on how we operated and where to find us. However, I don't think even he could have envisaged the carnage that would ensue over the following weeks.

The first game was to be on 15 February at Kenilworth Road. During the weeks beforehand, one of Arsenal's top lads – a certain Ross – had been drinking in Breakers with some of the surprisingly numerous Luton boys who followed Arsenal. This was our favoured pub at the time so he'd been getting to know the lie of the land and even brought other Gooners with him on these days out. By the time the game came around, he doubtless had some ideas about how he could bring a mob to Luton and smash us on our own patch. But he underestimated us even more than the weather forecasters miscalculated the severity of the winter that year.

On the morning of the 15th, I made my way to Breakers through the snow, to see how many had turned out for the visit of Arsenal and the Herd. It was a good feeling to bowl into Breakers and see over 150 good lads, dressed for the weather in heavy jackets and ski-hats, already getting fired up for the action.

At around one o'clock, a message arrived. It seemed that the Herd was heading our way with numbers estimated at close to 400. We finished our drinks, covered up and left to face the Gooners.

We headed to the bottom of King Street, turned left and made towards the Town Hall. As we approached, we bumped into a few Luton lads moving at speed in the opposite direction. 'There's fucking hundreds of them passing The Studio right now!'

We approached the Town Hall and checked the large green that fronts the Library Theatre and the Strathmore Hotel. There were shoppers everywhere but, as we watched, a gap began to appear in the townsfolk – something was causing them to move aside in a hurry. Then we saw the Herd.

On first sight it looked impressive – 300- or 400-strong, well dressed and with a mix of races. However, a more detailed inspection showed that the mob included a lot of younger lads. They hadn't spotted us yet, though, so we had a chance of catching them off guard with a charge through the shoppers.

Without anyone making the decision, we leaped into action as one and stormed through the crowds straight at the massed ranks of Cockneys. The look of horror on their faces was plain to see. They turned and ran. I don't know how many we had, but it was enough to put the Herd on its toes in panic. We chased them as far as the corner of the library and the blood bank, with a fair few taking slaps en route. I jumped on to a bus along with another Mig and we administered a few punches to the handful of Gooners who'd sought refuge among the passengers.

Because of the sheer numbers involved in the running battle, it was inevitable that things would eventually grind to a halt, so that those involved could take a step back and establish the true state of affairs. We regrouped in front of the library, while the remainder of the Gooners were split, with half of their mob at the front of the multi-storey car park behind the library and the other bigger group over by The Studio or The Nine Bar, as it is now known.

One of the Luton Gooners now made an attempt to rally them, rushing forward and shouting instructions to his now disheartened mates, but it proved fruitless and they didn't pay any attention to him. We started to gather in front of the beleaguered Gooners and would have charged to finish them off, but the OB finally arrived and forced us across the grass towards the Town Hall.

So round one was over and it was a clear upset – the Migs had backed up the Herd and that was that. We knew there was still a long way to go, but we'd struck the first blow and many of the Arsenal firm would now be doubting both themselves and those who had been giving it the big one on the train journey up to our place.

We headed towards the ground and decided to split the firm in two, so that we could keep the OB on their toes and also maximise the chance of running into the Gooners again. The group I was with consisted almost

Herding the Herd (Another Bloody Replay)

entirely of Migs, while the other was more of a mixture of the firm and other Luton lads. Ging suggested we head towards the Oak Road End, which housed Luton's singers and beer boys, as he'd heard that Arsenal were going to try and take it. The plan was to confront them outside the turnstiles, before they'd even managed to get into the ground.

This threat to the Oak Road was a real one too, as a year or two previously Arsenal had managed to get around 80 lads on to the packed terrace and, within seconds of the kick-off, it went mental. That time we'd forced them back towards the back of the section and sent them packing thanks to our superior numbers. The result was really theirs, though, as they had caused a major disturbance and done so on our patch.

Shortly afterwards, another equally serious disturbance took place at the other end. As the Arsenal lads were being escorted around the pitch and on to the Kenilworth Road terrace, a huge gap opened in the right-hand section of the visiting fans.

'Fuck! Look at that... Luton are in the Kenilworth! They're taking it!'

I couldn't believe it – a tight knot of 50 chaps had the whole Arsenal section backing off into the four corners of their pen. For a moment, I felt a surge of pride as I thought I was witnessing Luton having a go back at the cunts. But it wasn't to be. It turned out that the train taking West Ham's ICF and Under-Fives to a game in the Midlands had been stopped by a points failure near Bedford, so they'd immediately changed course and turned up at our place to have a go at Arsenal instead. As resourceful as ever, after stealing a coach and crashing it, they pretended to be Gooners heading for Luton and the local OB were only to happy to bus them out of the area at top speed.

So, after the embarrassment of realising that we'd been singing 'We're proud of you' to West Ham, at least it was fun to watch Arsenal get a taste of their own medicine as they stopped crowing about their victory in the Oak Road and scattered.

So today we were determined that no one was going to get another cheap result by having a go at the scarfers in that end of the ground. We strolled up Oak Road itself, but there was no sign of any Arsenal fans or their firm. We walked the full length of the street until we came to Maple Road, where we hovered for a few moments discussing our next plan of action.

After a brief defence council, we decided to head towards the Bedfordshire Yeoman to see if there were any Gooners having a sneaky beer in there. It seemed the obvious place to plot if they were planning on infiltrating the home section. It was a wasted effort, as we found nothing but regular fans drinking together and sharing a friendly singsong. So we headed back to the top of Oak Road where we received a report from one of the younger lads. Apparently, there was a bit of a scuffle taking place at the junction of Oak Road and Dunstable Road, and Luton were getting backed off.

Now this was where we had developed as a firm from the old days of charging around like headless chickens. I walked into Oak Road with Norfs, Les and Ging and checked out the scene, while the rest of the lads stayed round the corner, packed up against the wall adjoining the ground on Maple Road. As we watched the fighting on the lower part of Oak Road, it was clear that Luton had a game crew including Shit Hair and Nigel P down there. But they were being forced back by a larger firm of 50 or so Gooners that included Ross, Denton, Miller and our own GM.

It was a hard call to make, but, even though they were getting pushed backwards, the Luton lads seemed to be handling themselves all right. So we decided to allow things to progress, in the hope that the brawl would eventually spill all the way back to our position and the 70 lads gathered round the corner.

The plan went like a dream and suddenly the action was too close to hold the lads back any longer, so we stormed around the corner screaming out, 'Migs, Migs, Migs' and making our trademark monkey noises. Arsenal began to break ranks and fled back down the Oak Road in disarray while we steamed into the few that stood. One of the Gooners who didn't panic and run was Ross. After backing off initially, he turned and planted one on our Ging. Les was straight over to help and, after a few wind-mills, Ross quickly followed his routed mates.

They only stopped running once Luton OB arrived at the scene and I reckon we would have ran them all the way back to the train station and down the tracks to London if the coppers hadn't turned up. Unfortunately, Ging was left with a broken nose and to rub salt in the wound Les had been nicked for his part in the brawling outside the Oak Road turnstiles. Still, we'd got the better of the North Londoners once again.

The game was a bruising encounter as well, which suited our Mick Harford and it was no surprise when he scored in the 39th minute bringing the scores to 2–2. This was how the game ended and it was announced that the replay would be at Highbury on 3 March.

After the match, we gathered outside Maple Road until we had a large enough firm to continue the battle with the Gooners. All the main players were at the meeting point and the mob of lads that set off towards Bury Park seemed a decent enough outfit. And so it was to prove.

There was a huge police presence on Bury Park Road, so we decided to try and sneak around them by heading into Crawley Road which runs parallel with Dunstable Road – the latter being the route which both sets of supporters would have taken at some point. The walk along Crawley Road (home to some of Luton's prostitutes) was completed in total silence and so efficiently that the OB lost contact with us altogether.

But then – I don't know if it was planned or if they were using spotters, which seems likely – we found our path blocked by a huge firm of Gooners – the Herd were back and wanted revenge. The Londoners began pelting us with missiles and calling us forward to do battle. But we simply collected all our own ammo together with the stuff they had thrown at us and waited until the time was right.

Then, once we all had something to lob, we charged as one making as much noise as possible. The Herd looked like it would stand this time, but at the critical moment we launched everything we had and rushed even faster towards the sea of Arsenal chaps. Once again, they broke off from the battle and split in two, but suddenly stopped and started to regroup on both sides of the crossroads.

We waited at the junction for the expected counter-charge, but it didn't come. The OB had managed to get among the Herd just as their main lads were getting them sorted into something resembling an organised crew. Among them, I spotted Miller seething at the other Gooners – none too happy with their performance so far.

We moved off now, but, seeing our path blocked, we headed towards a shortcut through Moor Park that leads out on to the main route by which Bedfordshire OB escort away fans back to the train station. It was ankle deep in snow and we wouldn't have looked out of place on an Austrian postcard with our bubble jackets and ski hats. It seemed that once again we'd outmanoeuvred everyone and had left the police and the Gooners trying to sort out their differences. However, things weren't quite that simple.

There were nearly 100 of us as we crossed through the park in the snow, but this didn't stop us getting surprised and nearly routed by a small crew of Arsenal, as around 20 lads bowled up behind us. They were easily recognisable: Denton, Miller, Ross and others that had been at the front of the Herd, both in the town centre and outside the ground earlier in the day. They were really fucked off and on a mission now, and without any hesitation they steamed straight into us. Luton panicked and 90 per cent of the lads ran towards the OB appearing at the far entrance to this winter wonderland.

However, along with a few others, I was determined to put up a fight and we managed to get a battle line together to face up to the livid Arsenal top boys. Someone picked out Ross and let everyone know that he was our target. Ross reacted immediately to the name-calling and came bounding towards us through the snow. 'Who wants Ross then? Who wants Ross, you cunts?'

Stupid question! Daryl, a big mixed-race lad and long-time Luton bad boy, stepped forwards and after a short grapple striped Ross across the cheek. He was hurt now and started to panic. At the same time, I was scrapping with another Gooner, known as Brummie. We exchanged handbags and he started to look to his mates for back-up as well, but then he saw the second Cockney stabbed, clutching his stomach and lying bleeding into the snow. Now they knew that we were even more serious than they were.

To the left of me was a path, bordered by a metal link fence, running from one end of the park to the other. I saw Denton clinging to it now, as a pack of Migs tried to pull him down, but he managed to scramble free, clambering over the fence and running back towards the alley he had originally appeared from. A few seconds later and Arsenal had all evacuated the area. Bedfordshire Police were quick to replace them, though, as they came charging into the snow-covered park with truncheons drawn.

We didn't clash with the Gooners again that day and many, including myself, headed home early. The pubs didn't have quite the same appeal when you'd just seen lads cut up in the name of football. Lengthy discussions followed the match and focused on possible repercussions. Many wanted to lie low and keep their heads down and you couldn't blame them, but I knew that I wouldn't be able to keep myself away for long.

As for the trip to Highbury, I reckoned that Arsenal would turn out in force and if we took a mob there it would have to be tight and prepared to go the distance – whatever the odds. But you could tell within days that we would struggle to get a crew together for the match and so it turned out.

Small pockets of Luton lads made the journey to North London for the replay, but there was no cohesion at all. By half-time, we'd gathered around 30 who would be making the journey back to St Pancras and didn't fancy it coming on top. Let's just say the locals had been a bit hostile outside beforehand.

The match itself went into extra-time, but Arsenal still couldn't break down a stubborn Luton defence, led by the superb Steve Foster and his partner in crime Mal Donaghy. Afterwards, we made it back to Luton without any major incident, although a group did get chased around St Pancras by a big old mob of Gooners for a while, but the Metropolitan Police came to our rescue just in time.

Because neither of the ties had produced a winner, it would have to go to a second replay. Luton won the toss and so it was back to Kenilworth Road, two days later on 5 March.

This second replay had to be decided on the night and would go to penalties if need be. There would be no fourth game and so this would be the time to settle things once and for all – both on and off the pitch. It would be a real test of the resolve of both the Mig Crew and the Gooners, and it was inevitable that the violence would be severe with casualties on both sides. I didn't know it, but one of my good mates would come close to losing his life in the battles that raged before and after the match.

I went to work as usual, but spent most of the day wondering who would emerge victorious on the night. The first game had been a bit of a walkover for us and I know Arsenal felt the same. Demus and I were sat in a bar in Lloret de Mar a year later and Miller walked in, recognising us immediately. It was only because we were with Chemist and Winston – both well known to the Gooners – that it didn't turn ugly. Instead, we talked about the battles that night and everyone agreed that we had turned them over. But there was a reason for it – Arsenal's mob that day may have been big, but it wasn't actually that solid.

After work, I rushed home, jumped in the tub and within the hour I was kitted out in my favourite CP jacket and Ciao scarf and ready for action. I took a cab ride to Breakers but only found a small gathering of the lads there. I'd hoped that everyone would have been as eager as me to get down the pub, but as it turned out maybe I was just a little too keen for my own good.

I chose to sit in the top bar with the Jew and another Luton character, Boogie. This guy was never really a football thug, but was a Luton fan through and through and kept us entertained with his wild stories and

Jamaican banter. By about six o'clock, the pub was nearly full in the bottom bar, although upstairs there was still only a scattering of Migs and locals. It was then that Arsenal made their first move.

As we sat drinking and chatting in the corner, the doors burst open without warning and a dozen lads stormed in on the attack. They threw glasses and pub furniture at anyone within range, while another noisy mob of nearly 40 stood outside trying to smash the windows. At first, they caused the desired confusion and we all ran for the door into the corridor leading down to the other bar. But, once the momentum of the initial attack had burned out, we regrouped in the doorway and started to fight back.

One of the Gooners had a Burberry scarf wrapped around his face, but it rose up, obscuring his vision, and, as he stopped to adjust it, a bottle bounced off his head knocking him over. He scrambled to his feet in confusion and fled back out of the double doors. Bottles and ashtrays were hurled and gradually we managed to inch the Gooners back into the street outside. Then, as more reinforcements arrived from the bar downstairs, we surged forward and chased them up the road to the dual carriageway.

It was there that I noticed Ross among the Gooners. His face was covered up and he was a different character from the one that had bounced so confidently through the snow only a few days before. He didn't want to get caught again. As the two gangs fought on the dual carriageway, we had the advantage. Not only because of our superior numbers, but also because we were now armed with pool cues and bits of broken pub furniture.

Unfortunately for us, the Arsenal lads were quality this time round and the tools didn't faze them at all. They stood their ground, held it together against the odds and didn't break as some might have done. With the police station situated only a few hundred yards further down, the OB soon arrived to break things up. No one had really gained a result, but the Gooners had proved their point by bringing the battle to our boozer with what, by Arsenal's standards, was only a small crew.

There wasn't any more action for an hour or so, but, as kick-off approached, we readied ourselves for the journey to the ground and another possible clash with the Herd. The mob we had that night was probably one of the best I had witnessed up to that point at Luton. It had the numbers and had the right mix of old and young too. The Migs contingent was dwarfed by the ranks of black and white lads ready to face the

North Londoners tonight. But it didn't matter, as many of these chaps had been going to football years before we'd even formed our crew.

The pub soon emptied and we headed off together to avoid the risk of splitting into the many factions that were present on this cold night. As the huge convoy passed along Dunstable Road and neared Bury Park close to the football ground, we got our first view of Arsenal's full mob. It wasn't as huge as the crew that we'd come up against before the first leg, but it was different in another important aspect – the quality.

This version of the infamous Gooner Herd was about 200-strong, a mix of races and mature in age, to say the least. I was most impressed as I watched it move across Dunstable Road in the darkness and even more so when it turned, stopped and formed a battle line across the main road. I thought that this lot would have given up by now, especially given the fact that we outnumbered them by over two to one. I really believed that they would lose their bottle and fuck off back to London. But they didn't – this time they meant it.

During the next few minutes, too much happened for me to be able to give a blow-by-blow account of all the clashes in the darkness, but eventually we forced the Gooners to back off into Kenilworth Road itself. Things could have got really nasty for them, but they didn't run or panic – they simply backed up tidily. We didn't have things all our own way either and, as the groups separated, somebody was left sitting on the pavement clutching their ribs. It was one of ours – a black guy known as Henry had been stabbed and was struggling to breathe with a punctured lung.

Angry now, we marched at speed through Bury Park and straight up Oak Road. We wanted blood in return and soon we were going to get it. Halfway up, you come across the entrance to a series of alleys, one of which runs the full length of the ground and links the Kenilworth Road End to the Oak Road. It is a dingy pathway full of dog shit and graffiti and has been the scene of some serious violence at Luton over the years.

Back in the November prior to the Arsenal games, two Birmingham Zulus had found themselves running from a battle with the Migs at the top of Hazelbury Crescent. Their mates had all fled up towards the ground or back down Kenilworth Road, but these unfortunates took the wrong route, were caught in the narrow passage and sliced up pretty badly. I saw the wounds inflicted on one of them and it sickened me.

However, as we approached the mouth of the dreaded alley tonight, a group of lads could already be seen exiting it on to Oak Road. They didn't look familiar and, once they started to wave their arms about in the air, beckoning their associates still in the alley to follow them, it was clear that the Herd had come for more action. They must have run up Kenilworth Road and then been led down the passage to cut off our path by the Luton contingent among them.

I hurried towards the mouth of the alley. If we were able to keep them penned in and cause a bottleneck, we could pick them off as they came out. I wasn't the only one who saw this opportunity. About half a dozen of us steamed into the Gooners' frontline, which now included Aubrey, forced them back and positioned ourselves in a crescent shape at the mouth of the tight corridor. The Arsenal mob was massive in numbers, but, because it was squeezed into such a tight space, they couldn't manoeuvre at all and soon the lads at the back of their firm were pushing the guys at the front out on to the open ground.

Some of the Luton lads broke up garden walls, raining bricks down on the vulnerable Gooners. Others slashed at them with Stanley knives, while the majority of us punched and kicked at them as they popped out. In a few minutes of fighting in the mouth of that alleyway, I saw six or seven Arsenal boys seriously hurt, but it could have been worse and I hate to think what would have happened if the OB hadn't made heavy use of their batons to break us up.

Most of us entered the ground to watch Luton put on a sparkling display of passing football. Super Steve Foster opened the scoring with an unbelievable half-volley and David O'Leary helped us on our way by putting into his own net in the 52nd minute. We had already agreed that this was probably the best performance by the Town in years, when old faithful Brian Stein tapped in from close range to seal a famous FA Cup victory. When the final whistle blew, we stayed behind for a few minutes to clap the players off. I clambered on to a pillar to get a better view of all the supporters singing in unison, hands raised in the air. It made the hairs on the back of my neck stand to attention and a shiver pass down my spine. Then it was back to business.

I was still bursting with pride as I hurried to the gathering point on the corner of Maple Road, where the lads waited patiently until the ground emptied. We knew we needed to keep as many troops together as possible if we were to keep on matching the Gooners for numbers.

Soon we were on the march. However, instead of heading towards Dunstable Road, I managed to convince everyone that we could catch the

Herding the Herd (Another Bloody Replay)

Arsenal lads off guard by taking Dallow Road. We'd never done this before, but the thinking behind it was that Aubrey was now in control of the Herd. I guessed that he would have managed to get a good mob – maybe the best Arsenal could offer – together by now and was probably heading on to Dunstable Road to cut us off, as we moved towards the town centre to meet the rest of the Luton crew. Aubrey was well aware of our usual routes and would want to take us on as soon as possible after we left the ground. He knew that many of our lads wouldn't have bothered with the match and would have been sat in Breakers waiting until it was over.

I didn't think we needed to run the risk of giving Arsenal a chance at backing us off, as we were already miles ahead on points at this stage. But I thought it would be a nice touch to turn up from a totally unexpected direction in the hope that the Herd would have dropped their guard, thinking that we'd bottled it. Aubrey loved his mind games, but this would give us the psychological advantage when we met. And, if luck was on our side, we could link with the boys from Breakers at the same time and then we'd have the numbers too.

With the mob on the move and the plan in place to appear behind the Gooners as they waited on Bury Park for the expected charge of Luton along Dunstable Road, I ran ahead along Dallow Road. It is a fair old trod and it took me a while to jog from one end to the other. As I reached the park at the far end, I saw an OB van hurtling along in the direction of the ground and wondered if Arsenal were near.

As you head along Dunstable Road towards the police station, you come to a roundabout with a series of walkways perched above it. These all converge above the traffic island itself and allow the user to head in many different directions. I headed out of Dallow Road and on to the edge of one of these walkways. From here, I could check five different streets simultaneously and hopefully spot the Herd heading up towards town. As luck would have it, I was right.

Below me, I saw about 100 Gooners bowling across the dual carriageway, heading towards the train station and possibly town. I felt a wave of pride sweep over me – I'd outsmarted Aubrey, my teacher and the original tactician himself. Now I was a step ahead of him and had his firm in my grasp. All I had to do was stay in contact with the rest of the Migs and follow the Gooners until they were at their weakest. Then we would attack.

'There's no need to count them, Tommy – there's about 200 down there!' A feeling of dread passed through me as I heard that familiar softly spoken voice, whispering behind me. 'I thought I told you it was about doing things people don't expect you to do...' I turned to see Aubrey and GM, together with a handful of unknown faces and there was hate in air.

Somehow, Aubrey had read me like a book and I could be in serious trouble now, but, managing to keep cool, I turned and continued viewing the Gooners shuffling along the dual carriageway. Then I responded as confidently as was possible, considering that I had six enemy troops and their general with them. 'You call that a firm? There's only a oner there, Aubs. We'll rain on that, mate!'

My nemesis looked me up and down, but kept smiling. 'That lot's untouchable – there's no divs in the Herd, Tom.' He grinned even more broadly now and asked, 'Where's it going to be then?'

I could sense that he was desperate for a chance to turn us over before heading back to North London with his Cockney mates. He needed a result.

'I've got close to 300 coming down Dallow Road. You know yourself that we don't fuck about. You're on the wrong side today, Aubs. Maybe you should switch back while you've still got a chance, mate.' I was showing confidence now and checked his reaction. But he didn't bat an eyelid and kept grinning like Top Cat.

'Liverpool Road it is then.' He chose the spot, and we shook hands and parted.

A few minutes later, Luton's mob made its appearance on to Dunstable Road. It was an impressive sight and looked almost untouchable. But the sheer size was becoming a liability now, as, although there was no doubting the quality at the core of the crew, there were a lot of younger and less committed thugs mingled in too.

Once everyone was assembled on the dual carriageway, I made a stupid mistake – I decided to split the firm in two. It wouldn't have been such a bad idea, if I'd done it properly. But, instead, I quietly tried to get as many of the Migs as possible to stay back and let the main body carry on towards the train station.

I managed to get about 50 of us together and, instead of following the main route, turned right towards our appointment with Aubrey's hand-picked crew. We chose to head down Inkerman Street and then cut through a small car park. The thought was that Arsenal would have had to turn around by the bottom of Crawley Road roundabout and then head up a narrow footpath to get back to Liverpool Road. I wanted to be at the top of the path when they arrived, so we could employ the same tactics as earlier and pick them off as they came out.

But, as we turned into the car park, I knew something was wrong. I could see lads ahead of us in Liverpool Road collecting bricks and lumps of wood from the skips stationed on the far side of the poorly lit parking lot. 'The Gooners are already here!'

I barely had time to think before they stormed straight at us, catching us off guard. As the bricks began to land, we started to back off in shock. A half brick hit PB and sent him crashing to the ground with blood pouring from a massive head wound. Then they showed their full force and steamed into us with lumps of wood and bits of masonry.

It was a nightmare and we were soon reversing down the route we had taken to Liverpool Road only seconds earlier. We tried to rally as we retreated around the corner and the cries of 'Stand' nearly worked for a change, but another volley of bricks soon had us scampering for the safety of Dunstable Road. Arsenal didn't follow and instead headed back in the direction of the train station, content with the result of their well-timed ambush. So, after all our victories, it was the Herd that had the last word.

I was gutted and knew it was my fault. We should have stuck with the main mob heading towards town. I should have known better than to split up the lads when faced with the quality of the Herd. And, more than anything, I should have remembered that the words 'Aubrey' and 'ambush' always went together. He was the man who schooled us in the ways of the modern football thug in the first place. Obviously, I still had a few things to learn.

But I hadn't been injured, unlike PB who needed to get to hospital quick. We flagged down a taxi and away he shot for some urgently needed treatment. The Migs were going to turn into a St John's Ambulance crew at this rate and we'd seen enough walking wounded for one day. So the remaining pack slowly dragged itself to Breakers to have a beer and meet up with the rest of the boys in the hope that they'd earned a better result than we had.

However, as we entered Breakers, there was another shock in store. Lying sprawled across the pool hall's green, imitation-leather sofa was a very pale Big Cliff. Tefal and Max were trying to pull his clothes off. They'd managed to remove his pale-blue Luhta ski-coat and blood stained the inside.

'He bumped into their whole fucking mob on his own… one of the fucking Luton switchers pointed him out, Tom!'

The result was two stab wounds to his back – one of which had punctured his lung – a slash to his hand and numerous bruises on his face and body. Well practised by now, Tefal and the lads had the wounded Mig into a waiting vehicle in no time and raced him up to the Luton and Dunstable Hospital where he ended up in a bed next to Henry, who'd been stabbed himself before the game. Big Cliff's lung collapsed en route to A&E and he passed in and out of consciousness. They had nearly killed him.

Once I got home, I fell into a deep sleep – it had all been too much and I was knackered. I'm sure that most of the lads involved in the relentless violence over those three games were relieved that it was finally over and that we wouldn't have to face each other for a while.

Now everyone waited with sweaty hands as the draw for the next round was made on BBC's *Match of the Day*. And we got a good one – Everton at home. The blue half of Merseyside had been enjoying success in recent times and reached the Cup Final the previous season only to lose to a curling shot from Norman Whiteside.

On their way to Wembley that year, they disposed of Luton in a close-fought semi-final at Villa Park. A superb effort from our hero Ricky Hill gave us a much-deserved lead, only for Everton to grab a late equaliser that sent the Scousers into a frenzy. Then, as Luton legs tired in extra-time, Derek Mountfield popped up with the winner, which was the signal for us to leave the stadium en masse and storm the Scouse lads. Unfortunately, it never happened, as West Midlands mounted officers chased us all over the big grassy hill adjacent to Villa Park and soon had us shoved back on our Dinsey Coaches heading for Bedfordshire.

So, as we prepared for the visit of Everton, we didn't really have any idea of what to expect from them. In previous league games, they hadn't brought anything spectacular and we had only bothered to visit Goodison in the year we were promoted. No real firm made its way up to the North West even then either, although there was a small clash on the side terrace as a handful of the old Castle Bar boys turned up in the wrong section minutes into the game. The Cup match would be played only three days after the Arsenal trilogy, so the players would be tired, and to be honest I was tired myself. You had to be fit to be a hooligan!

On the morning of the quarter-final tie, I strolled down to the ground with my old mate B who now lived in Ramsgate and had travelled up the night before. He wanted to go to the game, so we headed up to the ticket office and by chance spotted the gates of the ground open. He hadn't seen the place for a few years, so we strolled in to have a little peek.

The first thing we saw was one of the new additions – a brick police observation tower built on the edge of the old Triangle/Maple Road End. It looked out of place. The door was wide open and no one was about, so we stuck our fat heads inside for a look. It was just a few monitors and a couple of chairs but, as we nosed about, I spotted a bunch of keys hanging on the back of the door. I called my mate over and, within seconds, the keys were being used to lock up the watchtower. After establishing that there was more than one key that could do the job, I realised that we had the spares as well.

I don't know exactly what happened to those keys next, but somehow they disappeared. I was always getting a hard time at home for losing keys and here I was on the day of an FA Cup quarter-final losing the keys to the police control room – criminal!

By midday, I was in Breakers and playing pool against Ostrich, so-called because of his hairy neck. He was being his normal nuisance and moving the balls about, when the call went up: 'The Scousers are here. They've brought a firm!'

Some of the black lads from Breakers had been walking past the train station and seen a fair crew of Evertonians emerge and swagger off towards Bury Park and the football stadium. This meant that we would probably get some action today, so the mood grew more serious as we discussed how we should get hold of the intruders and send them packing.

'Watch out for the Scouse cunts, though… they'll be tooled up' was repeated over and over again during the next hour.

It had been announced in the press and on the local radio that Luton OB had now added CCTV to their war on hooliganism at Luton. The Mig Crew were all too well aware of this new threat to their liberty, but we'd decided to send out a message to the authorities that it would take more than a couple of cameras to stop us. Once the chaps were informed of the misplaced control-room keys, spirits rose further and soon everyone was champing at the bit to get out on to the streets of Luton and give Bedfordshire Police the runaround.

It wasn't until half an hour before kick-off that we made our presence felt in Bury Park. The Migs came from Crawley Road, while the rest of the Luton hooligan contingent used the usual Dunstable Road route. As we reached the bottom of Kenilworth Road, Horrible suddenly appeared, jumping around with excitement. He'd seen the Scousers at the top of Kenilworth Road and they seemed game enough.

The boys covered up their faces, as we knew that the cameras might still be rolling in spite of our earlier efforts, and we sprinted up the street until we caught sight of around 50 lads all dressed smartly in their designer gear. They looked startled and surprised to see us charging in their direction. But then it was our turn to be surprised, as one of the Mickeys reached into his coat pocket and sent a flare shooting over our heads. A loud 'CRACK' followed and we all ducked in shock.

The Everton lads fled in the direction of the ground and we gave chase only for a few of the larger Scousers to stop and make a stand. I headed for one of these gamer chaps and leaped at him, but the likely lad was quicker and I felt his fist bounce off of my chin, sending me sprawling on the floor. Around me, though, the lads closed on the enemy and fighting spread until the Scousers beat a hasty retreat, following the same route as their less confident mates before them.

We soon had the company of the OB to deal with and they convinced us that it might be best if we headed back down the hill towards the main Dunstable Road. We did as we were told. But, as we reached the junction, I noticed two things: first, that the stick I was receiving for getting dropped was easing and, second, that there was a small crew of Evertonians standing outside the kebab shop across the road. They froze at the sight of us – we had numbers and they only had a dozen at the most. We'd just been brawling and they were tucking into bags of chips. Now we were going to smash them and they knew it.

The next few minutes were out of order. We chased the frightened Scousers all over the place and the pack soon started to savage them. They knew that they had to escape or it would mean a visit to the Luton and Dunstable Hospital. I chased one into a front garden and wasn't shocked when he started to beg for mercy, as he knew he had nowhere to go now. But, as I hesitated, he picked up an old mop and smashed me in the face with it, cutting my cheek and sending me straight back out of the overgrown garden.

As I held my bruised face, I looked along Crawley Road and saw Luton boys openly sporting knives and lumps of wood now. The poor old Everton lads were taking a severe beating. My Scally mate tried to run past me in the commotion, but I clipped his heel and he dropped with a crash. A couple of the others leaped on him.

Herding the Herd (Another Bloody Replay)

We left the visitors in the road and headed to the game, joining a crowd of 15,500 expectant fans. Initially, things went exactly as I had hoped, with Luton storming to a 2–0 lead, but then tiredness set in and Everton clawed their way back into the match, escaping with a draw. Another bloody replay!

The next day, stories began to circulate concerning the fighting in Crawley Road. They weren't good stories. It seemed that a number of the Scousers had been stabbed or cut and one had a piece of wood driven into his body like a stake. It was worrying news and the OB were now trying to find the culprits, including the would-be vampire slayer. The next week, though, we got a taste of our own medicine.

We travelled to Goodison for the replay on the Wednesday. As was usual at the time, not many fancied the midweek trip up north, so we stuffed a box van with 18 lads and after stopping at an off-licence travelled for four hours, until we reached a certain Stanley Park. Strangely, as we entered the nearby car park, we were handed a leaflet by an attendant.

'Luton Fans: You are warned not to leave the car park without a police escort – your safety cannot be guaranteed tonight, due to the stabbings of innocent Everton fans at Kenilworth Road.'

We were stunned into silence, and it only got worse.

As we climbed out of the van, the two car-park attendants made a comment that no one quite heard properly, but we got the gist – it was 'we hope you get cut, you Cockney bastards' or something similar.

It got a response as Boogie rose to the bait: 'Bwoy! If me wan' kill yah, me nah have fe use a weapon. And I ain't a fuckin' Cockney either, blood.'

Dragging an irate Boogie away, we headed out of the car park and away from the Merseyside OB who had created a holding area next to a burger van, to gather up the more concerned Luton supporters and escort them to the ground. As we wandered off, though, they didn't try to stop us at all and just pointed, laughing out loud at our small band. This was getting unnerving now.

It was only about five seconds after we entered Stanley Park that we heard the Scousers in the darkness. I can't say how many of them there was out there, but it sounded a lot more than the 18 of us bowling along the pathway. Almost immediately, one of the lads shouted in pain. It was PH. A rock had come flying out of the night air and whacked him in the head. As the horde of Scousers emerged from the shadows, we dragged him as quickly as humanly possible out of the nearest park exit and into the well-lit road where the coaches were lined up.

It had been a rather short walk in the park and outside we bumped straight into some more Merseyside plod. However, they didn't take any interest in our little band at all, until they saw PH's head. But they just shrugged their shoulders and suggested that we stay behind the coaches until an escort came along. Then they walked off and left us to it. I looked at the rest of the lads and saw that they were looking a bit worried now. I zipped up my jacket and started across the road.

'Where the fuck are you going?' enquired a dubious Boogie.

'Across the fucking road... I ain't staying over here, stood out like a sore thumb. Let's mingle in with the Scousers and blag our way to the ground.'

He looked even more worried now. 'Wha'? How are we going to mingle, man?'

The lads seemed to like the idea, though, and swiftly joined me among the fans decked out in blue. We weaved our way through the massed crowds of football supporters making steady progress towards the visitors' section of the ground and sanctuary.

But, as we got closer, I became aware of the lads bunching up – something was wrong. Ahead of us, I saw a large group of chaps walking against the tide of the crowd – it was Everton's firm. I looked the opposite way and checked the scene behind us. There was a smaller group of lads coming from that direction too.

There was no way we were going to be able to stroll through this lot, as they were scanning the street looking for Luton boys. The game was up. I felt the need to show a bit of character to the lads and Flower thought likewise, so we marched straight up to the lads closing from behind and simply kicked it off. I smacked some skinny mixed-race lad and watched as he fell backwards against the heavy stone wall. I tried to stamp on him, but he grabbed my legs and soon I was on the floor myself as the two groups weighed into each other.

Once I'd pulled myself up from the street, I turned just in time to avoid being hit by some of the lads coming in the opposite direction. I ran into the middle of the road and turned to face the aggressors. For once, I was happy to see OB close by – he had jumped from his motorcycle and was trying to tear a group of lads apart over by the coaches.

Then I was hit again and turned to see a lump of a lad standing in front of me. He screamed in my face, 'Who wants it with Luton, then?'

Herding the Herd (Another Bloody Replay)

I was taken aback.

'We *are* fucking Luton… we're the fucking Migs!' I bellowed back even louder.

A quick handshake and we were singing from the same hymn sheet.

By now, Demus was keeping a few of the Scouse cunts back with his metal comb. He had seen them producing knives as the fighting escalated and had whipped the comb out and, as long as he kept it flashing about, he would be OK.

Within the next few hectic moments, we established that the guys who had now joined our side were part of a coach party from Houghton Regis, which is just outside Luton. They drank in the Harvest Home, which had a certain reputation a while back. We were happy for their assistance, particularly as they had one giant black geezer among them who was bound to put many of the Evertonians on the back foot – and a certain RB who was handy to have at your side on these occasions too.

So now the battle turned and soon we had backed the Everton lads off. With 40 of us together now, we felt more confident and marched down the middle of the road towards Goodison Park. But there was more action ahead of us near the ground and I have to admit that it got quite hairy. Flower was unlucky and ended up with a swollen eye, but not as unfortunate as RB who nearly ended up blinded in one of his, as a Scouser slashed him just above the eyelid.

Everton won and, although he later missed a penalty, Gary Lineker proved to be the difference between two good footballing sides. Somewhere among the 44,264 crowd was whoever had tried to slash my chest during the rucking outside. He'd cut a six-inch hole in my leather jacket which I hadn't even noticed until I took my seat in the upper tier of the away end.

That night, plenty of Scallies had been carrying craft knives and were keen to use them on us. But the reason so many football lads were carrying them at Goodison Park and, of course, at the home game in Luton was because it was too easy to get away with. As a result, it had been stabbing season all season! The blood had been flowing for a while now and was cited as another important reason why more widespread CCTV had to be made available to the OB to enable them to police football properly.

As I sat next to Big Cliff in the Crown Court, watching CCTV footage of Little Jimmy throwing punches at those Watford idiots, I stopped cursing the fact we were on film for a moment and thought about the state the big guy had been in after the Gooners had got hold of him. At least with CCTV and the other measures now in place, maybe I would never have to see one of my mates stabbed up like a teabag over football again.

10 They Bit His Ear Off

I sat in silence, showing no emotion. On the one hand, I didn't want to look too concerned as many Migs were sat in the gallery to my left, but I didn't want to appear arrogant in front of Judge Cripps either. He continued glaring over his glasses at us in the dock. If he thought for one moment that we didn't fear the law, he'd be sure to hand out harsher punishments to let us know exactly how badly society viewed our crimes.

Earlier in the week, most of the other lads paid no regard at all to how they presented themselves in court or how the judge read their body language. They sat chatting and giggling throughout their hearings and didn't watch their manners at all. Bad language could be heard constantly from Scottish Brian – that's if you understood his broad Jock accent of course.

Most of the lads had decided against wearing suits and instead sat behind the glass barrier dressed as if they were going to an away game at QPR – Stone Island and Paul & Shark with a bit of Aquascutum thrown in was the order of the day. I couldn't understand this myself, because, if I were doing the sentencing for the CPS, I would surely have recognised the uniform immediately. And I'd be well pissed off if those accused of belonging to a hooligan gang sat proudly in my court dressed like thugs.

Personally, I'd decided to make the effort to look nothing like the guy in the police surveillance tape. He had a skinhead; I had now grown my hair. He had a black Stone Island jumper and white trainers on; I now wore a grey suit. He looked like a football hooligan, but today I looked like a stiff! The boys flanking me had also made the effort to look like regular folks as well. There was simply no comparison between those of us sat in front of

Mr Cripps today and the rabble that had appeared earlier in the week. Surely, this had to go in our favour.

In the public gallery, the Luton Town football intelligence officer looked happy enough sat among his fellow officers, but I wondered if he really wanted to see so many faces he'd got to know over the years sent to prison today. Surely, by now, he must have known that we weren't the type of people who deserved to be separated from their families just for a punch-up outside a pub.

Sitting next to him was the CID officer who'd returned my mobile after an earlier committal hearing at Hemel Hempstead Magistrates' Court. When we were first arrested, they confiscated all of our mobile phones to check for any information that proved that we organised violence. The only thing was that, when the OB raided my address to lift me, the only mobile they found had been my girlfriend's. I bet that was really useful for the investigation!

The prosecution had covered most of the details by now and all the videos had been played for the benefit of the judge. During the screenings, he had nodded repeatedly at certain comments passed by the CPS and shaken his head dramatically at other points. Then, as the case for the prosecution was coming to a close, a final piece of evidence was introduced that seriously stank of prejudice. The prosecutor held up a bright-yellow 'high-visibility' waistcoat worn by police on duty at football matches. It had 'POLICE' printed across it – nothing unusual there – but this one also had scuff marks, which he now claimed were footprints!

I couldn't believe the judge allowed this evidence to be admitted, as at no time had it been suggested that we assaulted the OB on the scene during our attack on the Moon Under Water pub. I was also pretty pissed off that none of the defence barristers bothered to object. The prosecutor didn't actually *say* that we'd assaulted the coppers, but the implication was clear. For fuck's sake! If we had wanted to bash them, we could easily have done so, but that's not our thing at all.

After all these years I've actually grown to respect the OB and it hurt when the prosecutor decided to get out the dirty tricks. I can remember seeing the police getting attacked properly at football many moons ago, and it wasn't a pretty sight. It was during another FA Cup run for us, at what has become the most legendary football battle in England...

Everybody in the country, if not Europe, knows Millwall's fearsome reputation. This small club from Southeast London survives on gates not

They Bit His Ear Off

unlike good old Luton Town, and back in the 80s rarely had crowds of more than 5,000 or 6,000 – yet their fans are probably the most violent in the history of English football. Contrary to those who always talk about hooliganism being a minority sport, a huge percentage of Millwall's followers have been involved in violence over the years and saw their off-pitch infamy as being as important as winning trophies on the field.

In March 1985, Luton had just seen off Watford after two replays in the FA Cup. It had taken the only good thing Wayne Turner did in his whole career to separate the teams, as he scored in front of 15,586 fans at Kenilworth Road on his 24th birthday. Off the pitch, Watford were as big a joke as ever, but in sharp contrast Millwall and its legendary hooligans were heading up to our place for the quarter-final.

In the days preceding the tie, there were varying estimates of how many Millwall supporters would make the short trip north to Bedfordshire. It seemed the Lions weren't selling too many tickets and we could only expect 3,000–4,000 on the night. As a result, the police and the club couldn't decide whether to make it all-ticket. Why? Luton had become one of football's favourite battlegrounds, Millwall had a rep as the worst firm in the country and hooliganism was at an all-time high. On the night of the 13th, they would be travelling just 30 miles for an FA Cup quarter-final, and yet nobody in authority saw the threat. What were these idiots thinking?

Maybe the authorities couldn't see what was going to happen, but one person more tuned in was DP, a West Indian man-mountain. He must have weighed about 18 stone when fighting fit and was not someone to be taken lightly in any walk of life. He'd already put the word out in Breakers that everyone should get tickets for the Maple Road seats, so we could muster as much firepower in one place. He also wanted everybody to assemble as soon as they had finished work, so that Millwall wouldn't be able to take the place over before we'd even arrived.

I was still a 17-year-old apprentice decorator at the time and made sure I was working as near to Luton as possible on the day of the game. All morning, I nagged my boss, Frank, about what time we would be calling it a day. He seemed to understand just how important a date I had that night and gave me a much-needed boost when he suggested that we should knock off early to pick up materials from our supplier.

At around three-thirty, I was stood in Gibbs and Dandy with fingers and feet tapping, listening to old Frank chatting to the paint salesman in his

Geordie accent. I wasn't that interested – I'd already heard all the talk about his 'new' Ford Capri 2.8 Ghia and the grab-a-granny night at the Polish Club a million times over. And I had other things on my mind today.

My ears pricked up when the radio behind the counter reported on disturbances in the build up to the football. The expression on my face must have said it all.

Frank stared at me with his beady eyes and chuckled. 'Fookin' 'ell, Tommy, you're not one of these bloody hooligans… are yoos?'

I kept quiet but, before Frank could pry any deeper, the salesman picked up on the report. 'I saw fuckin' loads of 'em up and down Hightown Road during me lunch break.'

Hightown was my manor and my girlfriend worked at a hairdresser's right in the middle of all the pubs on Hightown Road, so I nipped out to the nearest payphone to find out more. I didn't like what I heard.

She confirmed that Millwall were everywhere and that the local pubs were absolutely heaving with pissed-up lads. Some of them had even been into her workplace and tried to chat up all the girls – including her. Apparently, it happened more than once. They had to threaten to call the police at one stage as a group of 10 Millwall lads refused to leave the shop until they got a kiss from each of the girls.

'You fucking better not have kissed some Millwall cunt…'

She cut me off in mid-sentence. 'No I never,' she said, laughing at my insecurity.

I thought she was lying, and I still do today.

This was all I needed to get me fired up for the night ahead and, as I sat in Frank's Sherpa van heading towards Hightown, I was already looking for an opportunity to jump out and slap some Londoners. He dropped me off at home and reminded me that I had work in the morning, but I don't think I answered him because I was in such a hurry to get in and put my garms on.

As I changed, I couldn't stop thinking about those Millwall lads sitting in my girlfriend's salon. I really wanted to get stuck into the cunts tonight. I hoped to get the opportunity to have a 'pop' and exact my own personal revenge. My dad came through the door at the same time as I was heading out. He looked tired and tried to stop me for a chat, but I just barged straight past him in my rush. 'Going to the football, Dad… I'll have my dinner when I get in.' Then I was gone.

I speed-walked down Hightown Road, passing The Gardeners, The Freeholders and The Painters Arms. Although there was no sign of Millwall's hooligan army, there were certainly lots of 'shirts' on display and they were all pretty well pissed, or getting there. I passed my girl's hairdresser's and waved in at her, busy sweeping up. She waved back and smiled.

Then, as I made my way across the old eyesore of a bridge linking Hightown to the train station and the town centre, I peered down to see hundreds of Millwall pouring out of the exits, heading down towards Mill Street. They were laughing and jumping around like it was a carnival procession. I nipped through the Arndale and across George Street, before hiking up King Street and into good old Breakers. The atmosphere here felt more secure. At least a dozen of the lads had positioned themselves around the doorway, as if on sentry duty, which gave the impression the pub was packed when in fact it was only half full. I greeted as many people as I could and headed through the door leading upstairs to the top bar.

This was never really a focal point for the boys to gather and tonight didn't seem any different, except for an unmistakable black presence in the corner closest to the entrance, as if they were guarding it. I returned downstairs and soon racked up a game of pool with Boogie.

For the next hour, the door of the boozer stayed open as a continuous stream of local lads joined the gathering. DP arrived fairly late on, but immediately got to work firing everyone up for the night ahead. Paddy W did much the same, although with his trademark smile rather than a snarl. The Migs sat in our usual spot along the back wall of Breakers and, by the time DP ordered everyone out into the street, we numbered over 50. We happily melted into the huge mob gathering outside and, after a quick pep talk, joined the march towards the ground and a meeting with England's most notorious thugs.

As we reached the junction with George Street, I stepped back from the mass of bodies to take it all in. This firm was huge by Luton's standards – maybe 500-strong – and, as was often the case when we headed out from Breakers, the white boys were in the minority. It wasn't all football lads, though, and contained plenty who probably had no interest in the game at all, but the hooligan grapevine had brought them to Breakers in search of violence. Others were faces from the past, who I remembered fighting alongside against teams in the old Second Division. One thing was for sure – we had more than enough to hold our own.

As we herded past the Town Hall on George Street, though, we lost our focus. With a firm this size, it was inevitable really, especially as it contained so many different elements. Some of us started to move to a position at the edge of the sizeable escort in an attempt to keep everyone in one group. It was proving difficult, though, as everybody had their own idea of where we should be heading to find the Millwall mob.

By the time we passed the green outside the town library, we were already having difficulties controlling the firm as it spread out and people started to play up. It was horrible to watch, especially as by now I was used to seeing our mobs move as one and in almost complete silence. Long gone, or so I thought, were the days of Luton's firms acting like cattle charging about aimlessly before getting split up by the OB into small ineffective groups. But it was starting to happen again – just as I'd seen as a schoolboy.

Then we really blew it. At the corner of the old Co-Op stood a group of five Millwall fans wearing large, square white stickers with a picture of the MFC lion stuck on their jumpers. Maybe they were a form of protection from their own boys – 'don't hit us, we're Millwall too' – because, at the sight of our army passing by, they raised their chubby arms above their heads and started their chant of 'MMMMIIIIIIIIIIIIIIIIIIIIIIIIIILLLLL-WWWWWWAAAAALLLLL!'

The reaction from many of my fellow Luton folk was predictable, but stupid. Around 30 or 40 of our boys charged straight across the road and kicked the shit out of the surprised Cockneys. It wasn't just a few slaps either, as lad after lad stuck the boot into the overweight Millwall lads curled up and confused on the pavement.

I was well fucked off now because the OB had a reason to get among us, which they did within minutes of us picking up the route towards the train station. The local police were on a mission now and noticeably pumped up, either by events earlier in the day or by their bosses at Buxton Road. They steamed into us and started to chase small groups of the lads up the side streets. More damaging than this, though, was the wedge that they drove through the firm, causing us to split in half.

Many of the lads started to mix it with the OB, but this only made them even more determined to divide us into more manageable groups, so the batons came out and soon tempers were fraying. Arrests were inevitable now and all because of a lack of discipline among our lads. The group I was with contained 100 chaps, while the other was roughly double that. We

They Bit His Ear Off   203

were forced towards Alma Street and on towards the Town Hall so Paddy ordered us to cut our losses and move towards the ground while we still could, following the same route as Millwall's police escort would probably take.

As we closed on Mill Street, our numbers swelled by half again as some of the lads managed to escape the clutches of the law and catch us up. We soon came into contact with Millwall lads. Initially, they didn't seem keen to have it with us, but charged forwards once it was clear that they had enough to have a proper go. We met them head on and, with only two or three punches thrown, sent them packing back towards the train station. The OB responded quickly and stopped us chasing them down. Instead, we turned round and headed silently back to the top of Mill Street and on to the ground.

We'd just had our first taste of Millwall's lads and it was a relief to find them just as human as ourselves. It's amazing how a reputation can make some people seem almost superhuman, but we were finding that it might not have been fully deserved.

As you head from Luton Town centre towards Bury Park and the football ground, you come to an area that's a bit confusing to say the least – a classic example of ad hoc town planning. It's a busy roundabout with a train bridge crossing it on one side. Through the arches of this bridge lies Moor Park (scene of the stabbings against Arsenal's Gooners), while at some point or other most visitors to Luton find themselves passing Domino's Pizza on the opposite side. One road leading to the junction in front of the Pizzeria is a busy dual carriageway with traffic heading either into town or out towards Dunstable. This is the only obvious route to Kenilworth Road, so the pedestrian is left with three choices. One is to navigate the busy traffic, after climbing numerous barriers constructed to stop you doing so. Another is to walk to your left along the side of the road until you come to a pedestrian flyover and cross there. The third is a shorter route, through an ugly tunnel passing directly under the dual carriageway. This would all be confusing enough, but, when you also take into account the lack of any signs, you get a rough idea of the problems faced by the Millwall fans pouring towards the ground.

We chose the least obvious of the three routes across the dual carriageway, strolling through the traffic before leaping across the metal railings. Once safely on the other side, we all lined up in the dingy alleyway leading to the back of the West Side Centre. We waited there for around five minutes, over 100-strong and with the OB now unaware of our position. We knew Millwall would be coming this way at any time and were starting to feel confident now. Paddy watched from the mouth of the alley and kept us updated with a running commentary on how many were passing by, if they were proper lads and what the plod were up to.

Then, just as we were getting restless, it was time to come out of hiding. Millwall were across the busy road in numbers, so we charged out and across the four lanes of traffic. The Southeast Londoners stood to face the challenge, and no sooner had we left our hiding place than we were engaged in heavy brawling. I spotted a youngish Cockney with a beer in his hand struggling to get over the crash barriers. Before he could regain his balance, I grabbed him by the jacket and dragged him across, letting him land on his face. Then I started to work him over, holding him down with my left hand and thumping him with my right. Around me, the same scene was repeated, but Millwall's lads continued to scale the central reservation of the dual carriageway and we picked them off one by one.

Somebody nearby shouted, 'They're all pissed!' And he was right, too.

After soundly beating the young lad, I dropped back and surveyed the Millwall legions still trying to cross the busy road. Many of them were so drunk they could hardly stand up, let alone climb over obstacles. But alcohol plays tricks with the mind and also clouds your judgement when it comes to assessing danger – this Millwall mob was getting bashed and didn't even realise it.

Paddy came charging across from the left with Nigel P and Shit Hair. They'd got hold of an eight-foot-long bright-yellow section of heavy gas piping. They stood close to the metal crash barriers and proceeded to bounce it off the heads of the drunken Southeast Londoners. It was comical. Eventually, the Millwall mob lost heart and backed off towards the police bringing another trainload of fans along the road. This lot were mainly shirts and happy just to sing 'Millwall, Millwall', while gesticulating in our direction. Pleased with our performance, we turned and headed on towards the ground.

Everywhere you looked, there was Millwall. Most of the lads we passed were either already shit-faced or carrying tins of beer and in the process of getting shit-faced. We didn't see any real firms until we reached Dunstable Road, though, but here the atmosphere changed immediately. There was a real threat hanging in the air. Minibuses bulging with Cockney chaps passed us, with lads hanging out of the windows and open doors. They looked like they meant business and for the first time that evening I started to feel a bit uneasy.

Once we'd reached the bottom of Kenilworth Road, we stopped as we had a potential problem. Both our entrance and the gates that the Millwall horde would be using were at the top of Kenilworth Road. Would our 100 lads be able to make it through the thousands of pissed-up Cockneys at the top of the road? Or should we make our way around to Maple Road and take the safer route into the stadium?

Paddy surprisingly, or maybe not so surprisingly, pushed for us to take the safer route. The Migs among us now came to the fore and demanded that we shouldn't change our course just because it meant heading into a battle that we might lose. As the bickering grew hotter, 20 of us decided to head on up Kenilworth Road towards the huge Millwall support gathering outside the turnstiles.

It was dark and a cold chill hung in the air. All around us were sights that we weren't accustomed to on our home patch. There were badge-sellers with temporary stalls set up on street corners, flags being waved about and dodgy-looking characters coming from everywhere offering match tickets. It felt like an away game!

As we neared the top of the road, it quickly became apparent that we were going to have problems. There were groups of lads everywhere – and I mean everywhere – and they weren't mugs either. The police, meanwhile, were almost non-existent. By now, Paddy and the rest had caught up with us, but we still knew that we wouldn't have enough to break through.

Opposite the top of Kenilworth Road and Hazelbury Crescent, there was a solid wall of Millwall – all pushing and shoving each other towards the football ground. We decided to launch our attack there, charging at the massed ranks in an attempt to force a way through. But it was a futile effort and, 30 seconds later, we were all trying to regain our breath after being chased halfway back down the road.

We started to head back up the road in the direction of the turnstiles and spotted a skip full of builders' rubbish – in the blink of an eye, it was empty and we were ready for another go. As we reached the top of the road again, we launched what we had at the heaving horde and managed to stand briefly before the dam burst. We might have made a proper go of it, but another mob of the cunts appeared from our left and this time we had to run all the way down to the Dunstable Road.

I was exhausted and, as I watched the lads sucking in lungfuls of air, I clearly wasn't the only one. I'd been kicked in the shin and it fucking hurt, but apart from that I was fine. Should we have another go? Before we could make our minds up, another opportunity for action presented itself. Standing on the junction of Kenilworth Road and Dunstable Road was a group of 30 lads, mostly wearing black leather jackets. Our numbers had melted a bit by now, but we still outnumbered this shady group.

'Who wants it with Arsenal then?'

Arsenal? What the fuck were they doing here?

As I stood hesitating, Shit Hair walked straight over and kicked it off like some cock on heat. The response from the North Londoners was immediate. I can't explain why, but initially I didn't have the stomach for another brawl right then and just wanted to walk away and get to the game. I was tired and a bit bewildered by the night so far. It had been non-stop and we hadn't even reached the ground yet. How many more rucks would we face? How many more times were we going to have to risk our health against London slime? I was getting properly nervous.

The Gooners started to force us along Dunstable Road with repeated charges at our rear. We didn't run in any fashion, but instead just kept on at a steady walking pace whenever they got too close for comfort. Shit Hair was still jumping and wanted us to stop and put up a fight, as did Sinbad – one of our Asian boys. So, as we approached Ivy Road, around 10 of the remaining lads steamed into the Arsenal pack and sent them running back along Dunstable Road in some disarray, but it didn't last.

A giant of a geezer wearing a hooded black leather jacket rallied them. The rest of us should have backed our mates up and maybe together we could have done the Gooners, but we failed to do our duty. Instead, we just stood there and watched as the Arsenal lads, led by the hooded lump, steamed into our boys.

At this precise moment, a shopkeeper came bounding out of one of the many Asian shops lining Dunstable Road and distracted me. He was wielding a massive Alsatian and threatened to set it on us. At the same time, a gap opened in the crowd and I spotted Shit Hair on the ground with the Gooners all round him. He was in danger of getting a tanking, but the rest of the Luton lads were backing off at speed. I had to do something.

On the pavement, close to the snarling Lassie look-alike was a quarter of a brick. Without really thinking what I was doing, I reached down and grabbed it. Then, I ran as close as possible to the giant Gooner looming over Shit Hair and, from point-blank range, threw the brick into his face.

At the same time, I offered myself as a climbing frame to help Shit Hair on to his feet. As we ran away, holding each other's arms, I looked back to see the giant Arsenal lad smiling after us, apparently unhurt.

We ran towards the relative safety of Oak Road, passing thousands of Luton supporters patiently queuing up to get into the ground. They were in a party mood and the noise level was a sure sign of their confidence that we would gain the right result on the pitch and progress to the semi-finals.

Off the pitch, though, things weren't going so well – sure, we had held our own earlier on, but now we were all split up and had no real plan of action. However, we knew that, once we got inside the ground, we'd be able to join up with the rest of the firm in the Maple.

Shit Hair and I joined the queue outside the Maple Road terrace and soon found ourselves caught up in a bit of a crush. Luton supporters were arriving in their droves and the two turnstiles that were open just couldn't cope with the weight of fans. Normally, most fans used the Kenilworth Road entrances, but they were currently swamped by a sea of Millwall.

As more people joined the crush, tales of the violence still raging in the streets around the stadium began to emerge and they weren't exactly encouraging. Apparently, some Millwall thugs had leaped out of their van and attacked a local woman. Grabbing her by her Luton Town scarf, they'd dragged her to the ground and abused her as she curled up sobbing on the floor. She'd been taken to the Luton and Dunstable Hospital still shaking from her ordeal. As this story was broadcast to the tightly packed crowd and the words drifted through the night air, they had a worrying effect – everybody pushed towards the gates to get off Luton's violent streets and into the ground as quickly as possible.

The tales of terror were coming thick and fast now.

'This animal pushed his way to the front of the taxi queue and when a lad tried to stop him they grabbed him by the head and… and bit his ear off!'

Fucking hell! I didn't like the sound of that and nor did the rest of the crowd. There was a communal groan and again everyone pushed so hard to get in that people began crying out in pain and fear.

As I reached the turnstile, I found myself at the sharp end of this mass of bodies. It was getting crazy now and I could hardly move my arms. As I struggled to pull out my ticket, I found myself being crushed against the doorframe to the turnstile with my hands stuck in my pockets. My arm became tangled behind me and I had to push in panic to gain some leverage to free myself. The poor chap working the turnstile, meanwhile, was facing a torrent of abuse as people screamed at him to open the other entrances.

When I finally managed to get through, I spotted some of Luton's better-known faces heading along the front of the Maple Road enclosure, so I tagged along. As I came out of the underside of our ageing Main Stand, I stopped to take in the scene. To my left, the Oak Road terrace was in good voice and contained the bulk of Luton's lads, although it wasn't as packed as I'd seen it on many occasions before. Opposite, stood the Bobbers Stand, which was full. All seemed normal until the section where it joined the Kenilworth Road terrace. Here, gaps could be seen and above the seated supporters was something that I'd never witnessed at Luton before – Millwall fans had clambered on to the roof of the stand and were jumping around with glee.

Then I saw the Kenilworth Road terrace and one of the most powerful sights I've seen in all my years of watching football. The 'Kenny' was full and, when I say full, I mean properly packed – like a sea of swaying sardines. In fact, it was so stuffed that many supporters had climbed on to the crowd-control cages, which divided the three sections and were now seated or stood all over them. Other parts of the fencing and walls that enclosed the large terrace weren't even visible, lost under a sea of Millwall boys.

To the rear of the open terrace was the old 'Wallspan Bedrooms' scoreboard – an eyesore that added to the atmosphere tonight by giving off an orange glow, which in turn reflected on the bald heads among Millwall's 10,000 supporters. It's an image I will never forget. I don't think I've seen anything like it before or since and now we were putting ourselves up against them. It occurred to me that we could really come unstuck tonight.

I made my way along the ground until I spotted Abes, a six-foot-three mixed-race lad who sometimes also ran with Leeds' crew. We shook hands and quickly exchanged views on tonight's invasion. He was his usual deep-thinking self, pointing out that we weren't in fact being overrun by Millwall, but rather by every thug in London and probably half of South East England as well. I could see his point, but it didn't make me feel any better. We pushed our way over to the Triangle, and spotted Paddy, Boogie, Demus and some of the other lads gathering at the back. Things felt a little more relaxed now that DP was visible among the gathering troops as well.

Just as we closed on the Luton gathering, though, the OB stopped many of us from proceeding any further down the terrace. The police were also trying to force others back away from where they'd already taken their seats and, once things calmed down, their intention became clear. At the point where the Triangle narrowed and met the Kenilworth Road terrace, they were keeping a section of seats clear of any fans.

Looking at the heaving mass of Millwall packed together on the open terracing next to us, it looked a sensible idea to keep a sterile area between the two sets of fans. But Captain Sensible had obviously left the building, because then something incredible happened – the police now started to take Millwall headcases out of the Kenilworth, walk them along the edge of the pitch and put them in the fucking Triangle with us!

In other words, to ease crowd problems, the police chose to take the most aggressive visiting fans and put them in the ring with those Luton fans still game enough to come in the ground and have it. It wasn't a clever plan at all and, as more and more of the Cockneys poured on to the pitch to be relocated in the Maple, it was only too obvious what was going to happen next.

I watched with dread while the Millwall who couldn't fit into the Triangle started to walk along the touchline towards the Oak Road End of the ground. As the Londoners made their menacing march along the pitch, they were scanning the stands, checking for potential pockets of possible resistance, and they were about to find some.

One particular character, wearing a Donald Duck T-shirt, made his presence felt in the Maple, as he prowled around the area closest to our small group shouting his wide-boy mouth off. When he realised this section of the ground was not yet completely under Millwall's control, he quickly pointed it out to his pals and a few of them stood up to check us out.

They outnumbered us now and were aware of our position, but we weren't going to be intimidated by a few hard stares and gestures. Donald Duck knew he had to do something to back up his fat mouth and bowled over to the seats immediately in front of us to take a closer look. After DP had exchanged views with him on his ability to back up his big talk, he quickly fucked off back to where he had come from. 'Bottler,' I thought, but he wasn't finished yet.

People started to shove each other about as they vied for a vantage point from which to watch the game. Abes turned and started arguing with a Londoner behind him, but I didn't pay much attention as our friend

Donald Duck could now be seen strutting along the pitch behind the goalmouth towards the furthest of the three Millwall sections. After a brief chat with the lads there, he turned around and brought another bunch of nutters on to the pitch. They were heading straight for the Triangle. This was it.

All the lads must have known that it was going to go off now, as they started to huddle towards the back of the enclosure. There were close to 50 boys in one part and more where we were. There was no doubt we had enough in that stand to put up a good fight. The trouble was that so many people had been displaced by the OB when they put Millwall in our end that we couldn't all get together in one position.

Donald Duck climbed the steps between the seats and his burly mob followed suit, making their way through the crowd until they stood face to face with DP and half the Luton boys. I never heard exactly what he said, but it had the desired effect, as he soon found himself flying backwards into the seats below him. DP had struck the first blow in the Maple and it was a corker! Then everything went mental. I saw the lads closest to DP charge as one into the Millwall loons, forcing them backwards, while a group of lads immediately to our left started to move towards the fight. Abes cut off their path and soon we were all knocked over by a surge from behind.

The rest was a blur of confusion. I scrambled to get upright again before I was crushed under the falling bodies. As I did so, I was smacked once on the top of the head, and saw a familiar face standing over me – it was Paddy. I looked to see if he realised that he'd just hit me, but his eyes were closed as he wind-milled his way through the packed crowd in panic.

Once upright again, I checked to see where Abes had got to. He was close to the pitch and, as the fighting subsided, I headed towards him. We scrambled on to the small wall at the front of the Maple to see what the state of play was back where the fight had kicked off. It seemed that the lads had been backed off from the original point of conflict and now found themselves at the top of the metal stairs leading to the Main Stand. Boogie was grappling with one of the invaders, but his usual smile had long since left his face.

Abes and I jumped on to the pitch and made our way towards the Oak Road in the hope of rallying more troops to the cause. We noticed that the Bobbers Stand was also a hive of activity and it surprised me to see Luton fans chasing Millwall out of areas all along it. For most of my early days watching the Town, the Bobbers had been the stand for old men and divvies. But the fighting there was probably more violent than most other places that night and it was one of the few parts of the ground holding its own against uncountable numbers.

Once I reached the Oak Road, I climbed on to the fencing and started to call out to some of the lads standing below in the section closest to the Main Stand. They quickly congregated around the gate leading from the terrace to the pitch.

But, just as I was getting somewhere with them, a policewoman grabbed me from behind and started to give me a lecture. She'd realised what I was trying to do and attempted to reason with me. 'Please don't do it, you'll lose, you'll lose. Don't do it... please.'

I couldn't believe a copper was pleading with me not to fight, instead of just manhandling me off of the pitch. It was as if she was unsure of her authority on this horrible evening. I noticed her hands shaking and tears welling in her eyes and realised that she was petrified. I shook her off and, a minute later, we had managed to get a small gathering together on the pitch.

We were stood in a semi-circle by the corner flag closest to the Main Stand and the Oak Road. Abes was still with me and we were joined by around 30 others, including CK and Chop. We didn't have much of a plan, but started to pick fights with the Millwall strays still walking along the pitch. Without making it obvious to the massed ranks of Millwall at the far end of the stadium what was going on, we managed to chase the small bands of visitors back to near the halfway line.

Then we made a serious mistake, when, instead of keeping the attacks small scale, we allowed things to escalate. Our numbers were growing steadily as people spotted us on the pitch and suddenly realised that we could fight back. CK had the idea of taking the battle to the Millwall boys who'd got into the Maple Road enclosure at the tunnel end. It seemed achievable, as the numbers were in our favour, so, like a load of sailors jumping ship, we leaped over the low wall into the invaders and got stuck in. Soon, we had the area cleared of Millwall and turned to acknowledge the applause from the Oak Road. What next?

More Millwall supporters were up in the seats designated for visitors in the Wing Stand so we started to exchange verbals with them. The verbals turned into missiles and then we feigned an assault, although we knew we could never really get sufficient numbers to do much damage.

Just as I was trying to pull myself up the wooden wall, Chop hurriedly pulled me back down. 'Look, Tom, they're coming!'

He was right. All this commotion in the far corner of the stadium had caught the attention of the Millwall hordes and now hundreds more loony Southeast Londoners were coming to join in. What to do?

'Stand, Luton!' Those famous and fatal last words!

Two seconds later, I was scrambling over my allies, and forcing my panicky frame over the fencing that separated the Maple from the Oak Road. I breathed a sigh of relief once I was stood safely down on the terrace among the massed ranks of Lutonians.

I watched the game along with only 17,500 other 'paying' customers. Thousands of others managed to gain access to the ground by other means, though, and there must have been almost 10,000 on the Kenilworth terrace and its cages alone. It's well known that the gates to this end of the ground were broken open, so no one was actually controlling the movements of fans to and from the terrace at all.

Meanwhile, Brian Stein broke the deadlock after half an hour and Luton went on to win, reaching their first FA Cup semi-final since 1959, but the air was full of hate instead of celebration.

The final whistle was the signal for the scenes of violence that shocked the nation, as hundreds of Millwall fans scaled the perimeter fence and attacked the poorly led Bedfordshire Police, chasing them from one end of the pitch to the other with a constant barrage of orange plastic seats. The OB had to back off under threat of serious injury and it was certainly the only time I ever saw police dogs running in terror. Eventually, the OB regained control in the ground and even managed to make some arrests, although the rioting in the town continued long into the night.

We got our revenge the following week, when those arrested travelled to Luton Magistrates' Court to answer charges resulting from the evening's carnage. We waited for them outside the court building. When they tried to leave the court and saw the reception party waiting for them outside, they immediately lost their bottle. It was incredible that these lads, so game when they had the whole of London's football hooligan society behind them, now didn't fancy a decent row with the same guys they couldn't get enough of a few nights before. Instead, they ran to the police for protection, something we hadn't done at any point during the evening of the game.

The OB now escorted them to the train station while we pretended to break up and move off. It was a calculated move designed to get the coppers to drop their guard, and it worked. Seconds after the police had left the platform having put the Millwall lads on the London-bound train, we appeared. We stormed the carriages and soon the 30 Southeast Londoners were chased all over the streets of Luton, being robbed of their garms and their jewellery. It was a sweet revenge on the cunts who'd wrecked Kenilworth Road and intimidated so many normal fans on the night of the quarter-final.

At the height of the vicious clash between Millwall and the police on the pitch, a small cluster of people gathered around a motionless body. It was a policeman and without intervention from a brave fellow officer – who was himself attacked while giving mouth to mouth – it's almost certain that we would have witnessed a death on the turf at Kenilworth Road that night.

As I sat perched on the edge of my seat in the Crown Court, watching some podgy barrister wave a high-visibility jacket under the judge's nose, banging on about the bravery of the two bobbies outside the pub in Watford, I couldn't help but feel that all this was an example of the modern police 'making a mountain out of a mole hill'. Those two coppers on duty that day were doing the work they'd signed up to do and at no point were they in any real danger, as they well know. They did a good job and all credit to them for it, but the way this feature of the case was presented was ridiculous. The violence outside the Watford boozer was nothing on the scale of what had happened against Millwall back in 1985 – it was just two groups of lads squaring up and fighting fist to fist. The numbers were small and there were no knives, no coshes and no gas. It was not played out on national TV, no one was really hurt and it was over in a matter of minutes.

Unfortunately for us, at the same time as we were fighting our battle outside the pub on the High Street, a mixture of Migs and MI2s had invaded the pitch at Vicarage Road, attacking Watford supporters and causing scenes of chaos. Maybe the reason for the pitch invasion was that the man in charge of policing made the wrong decision, as they didn't have the correct resources or manpower available on the night and certainly didn't put what was available in the right place. In any event, Hertfordshire Police were embarrassed because they'd fucked it up. With the pitch invasion broadcast repeatedly on national TV, they needed a scapegoat and we were lined up for the job.

Apparently, we were nasty and calculated hooligans who organised the two simultaneous fights with such precision that the OB had no way of containing the trouble. It was a load of bollocks, of course, and I hoped that Judge Cripps would see through it. After all, it wasn't that serious a fight… I mean, no one had their ear bitten off, did they?

 **Old Enough to Know Better**

When I first got hold of a copy of my police surveillance video, I couldn't stop watching it. I happily showed it to my mates, cheering along at the violent scenes, which the OB had kindly dramatised with some clever cutting. After a while, though, my mood towards the images changed and I no longer sat through them with pride. Instead, I started to feel embarrassed about the whole thing. I even began telling people that I'd already lent the video out.

Now, I was being forced to watch the same footage of 12 or so of our lads battling with 30-plus Watford boys in the doorway of a pub on their High Street, over and over again. I tried not to look at the TV screen, but couldn't help glancing up every now and then, as the prosecution added sporadic commentary relating to individuals and their actions at the scene. My feelings of embarrassment returned.

Once the prosecution had presented the case for the Crown, Mr Cripps adjourned for lunch and the courtroom emptied.

As I left the court building, I was feeling a little jaded and in need of a drink. Windy was waiting outside with an old mate – Mad Marcus, the Chelsea lad who'd made me laugh so much with his unhygienic drinking habits in Scotland. I shook his hand and thanked him for making the effort to come down in support.

Marcus looked well and, as always, wore a big smile on his battle-scarred face. 'Fancy a beer, Tom?'

He must have read my mind and in no time we found ourselves sat just round the corner in The Brewery Tap.

Marcus asked how it looked and I told him straight that I didn't think I would be going home that evening. He looked pissed off and we started to try to justify my position in terms of the bigger picture. The conversation did nothing to lift my spirits, though. Instead, I thought about my girlfriend and how much I would miss her; about my kids and how I would cope without them in my life for months on end. It hurt me to think like this and the only comfort I could find was thinking back to the times I had spent at sea in the Navy, and especially one 'jolly' to the Arabian Gulf when I had been away from home for nine months.

And who would comfort them? They hadn't done anything to deserve this and now had to face the upheaval of someone they loved and depended on being imprisoned. Not only would they have to face the loss, but also the embarrassment and all the questions and tongue-wagging that would inevitably follow. I just couldn't justify my actions any more.

Marcus lifted his bulky frame and headed over to the bar, as Windy was busy chatting to Monty. I felt an urge to be alone for a second and made for the toilets to spend a penny. As I stood washing my hands, I took a good long look at myself in the mirror. What I saw looking back at me didn't make me feel any better either.

I looked at the scars on my face and remembered the time Shit Hair glassed me when we were youngsters. My misshapen nose had been broken twice: once in a pub brawl and then again playing football. My hair didn't look like it belonged to me as I'd shaved it to the bone for as long as I cared to remember, but had now let it sprout in an attempt to hide the ugly wounds on my head as well. My blue eyes just looked tired and sad.

I wanted to shout out for help, but was aware that there was nothing to be done and also that I had to stay strong for everyone else's sake. I knew some of the lads felt sorry for me, but wanted them to think I was invincible and couldn't be touched by any emotions unsuitable for a lifelong Mig. I smiled at my reflection in the mirror – 'That's better,' I told myself. One last stare at my ugly mug followed by a deep sigh, then I opened the toilet door and headed back to my mates.

We shared a couple more drinks and chatted like nothing was happening at all. The clock turned slowly until it was time to drink up and make the short walk back to court – I felt better now. Twenty minutes later, I was shaking everyone's hands again and saying my last goodbyes. Daggers was laughing and taking the piss, which helped lighten the mood somewhat.

After what seemed like a lifetime listening to the prosecution and watching the police footage, it was now our legal representatives' turn to earn their money. One by one, they stood and made a show of remorse to the court, pleading for mercy in as many roundabout ways as possible. I was pretty impressed with Big Cliff's brief, who was certainly the pick of the bunch.

Mine, on the other hand, immediately upset Mr Cripps when she stated her belief that I actually had a case for self-defence. The judge looked a bit taken aback: 'Really!?'

But then she made it worse by adding a petulant 'indeed' and suggesting that a jury might well have accepted my argument. Judge Cripps just shook his head, explaining impatiently that he was here to deliver sentences and that there was no jury involved today. He gave me one hard stare at this point.

My brief took the hint and went on to highlight my good record in the Navy. She also presented various letters elaborating on my service in Sierra Leone and the fact that I had 'done something with my life'. After this, she switched tack to cover my violent upbringing and dysfunctional family background, in an effort to show that I had actually achieved a certain amount of success in my life, despite a poor upbringing. Finally, she glossed over my previous convictions, although perhaps without making enough of the fact that I hadn't been convicted of anything for nearly 14 years.

I hated the fact that the court had to hear about offences that I'd committed as a kid. These were things that had happened when I was still at school and I had already paid the price for – here I was over 20 years later having them held against me again. The real problem, of course, was that I had many previous convictions for football violence from the 80s and, rather wisely, she didn't make any attempt to explain or justify my actions. All in all, her attempt at mitigation had achieved very little apart from annoying the judge and, unlike most of the other legal bods, she hadn't even managed to convey any remorse for my actions. How I wished my old brief was here now.

Armchair Alan was next up and his barrister presented a serious package of mitigating circumstances. He explained that Armchair had no previous convictions of any kind and provided a huge bundle of character references – all suggesting that this sort of behaviour was completely out of character for him. The brief even stated that the Luton football liaison officer had seen Armchair stop an attack on other Watford supporters earlier in the same day. For the final touch, a family friend was sworn in and explained how Alan's sick mother had not been able to make her way up to bed at night in her final months. He told how his mum had asked for Armchair, and him alone, to carry her up the stairs in his arms at night. I thought Mr Cripps was going to cry. The rest of us nearly did.

After all the defence lawyers had done their jobs, Judge Cripps retired briefly from the courtroom. We spoke among ourselves and tried to remain upbeat, with fake smiles held on our faces for the friends and family watching from the public gallery. The low hubbub, as everyone discussed the possible outcomes, was brought to an abrupt end as Judge Seldon Cripps returned to pass sentence.

He started by covering the background to the Littlewoods Cup tie at Watford, making it clear that it should have been a day of fun and excitement for all those who attended, whichever team they supported. His voice then deepened as he started to cover our actions on the day and, by the time he reached the 'sustained attack by Luton fans on Watford supporters drinking in the Moon Under Water public house', he looked properly fucked off.

The judge had decided that the only way he could hand out suitable sentences to each individual was by using a pre-determined 'tariff'. This would be set at 12 months and he would then add a month for any punches or kicks thrown during the fighting. Further months would also be added for previous convictions for violence and yet another for any football-related violence. Now we all knew for sure that we were going down. However, there was a positive in all this, as he suggested that we would receive full credit for our early 'Guilty' pleas, which meant that he was obliged to significantly reduce our sentences.

He passed slowly along the six of us standing in the dock and handed out his punishments: Big Cliff – 11 months; Andy P – 11 months; Dave G – 13 months; Little Jimmy – 11 months; Armchair Alan – eight months, and finally myself – 14 months.

The judge made individual comments as he passed sentence to each of us. When he reached me, he frowned, suggesting that he had 'no doubt at all that I organised football violence'. And I guess that's why I received the heaviest slap – even though I hadn't actually been accused of leading anything whatsoever during this trial.

In summing up, Judge Cripps said that he saw a group of successful men stood in front of him and that we were, in his own words, 'old enough to know better'. And you know what? He was right.

I felt surprisingly relieved when he'd finished. I had actually received a fair sentence in the grand scheme of things and felt no bitterness towards the judge at all. However, his final act in this drama was to pass banning orders against us, barring us from any FA-regulated football match and setting out exclusion zones in Luton town centre that we could not enter on match days.

We waved goodbye to the lads in the public gallery and passed through the heavy wooden door to the court cells, where we awaited our transport to prison. Our group of late-thirties lads suddenly felt a great weight removed from its shoulders, and we were smiling and slapping each other's backs as if we'd gained a result. In some ways, of course, we had, because when we were originally arrested our solicitors had been suggesting that we might get sentences of two or three years. Now it was over, we had all received sentences of under 18 months and, if we were accepted for early release on the 'Home Detention Curfew Scheme', would hopefully only serve about a quarter of that. So, after all the waiting and worrying and all the endless chat, we could actually start the process of putting everything that occurred on that fateful day in Watford behind us. Maybe the worst aspect of our punishment had been putting our lives on hold as we awaited sentencing.

I had tried to get things moving again some time earlier in September when the Town entertained QPR. We mobbed up and, although already banned from the town centre, had chosen to drink right on the edge of the excluded area. It was a calculated statement to the OB – we're still here.

We gathered in The Railway Tavern at the bottom of Hightown Road, just across from the station, but Bedfordshire OB immediately surrounded the place and started to stop and search anyone in the area. Then, at around two o'clock, we received reports that QPR had arrived in a mob of about 60 and were being escorted towards The Nine Bar in town.

Many of the Migs drinking in the Tavern with us now left and made their way down town, to reinforce the sizeable crew already gathering at The White House. Our small band of outcasts, meanwhile, knowing that we couldn't cross into the 'forbidden zone', instead walked along its border until we reached the Hightown Recreation Centre. Here we plotted up and chatted about the chances of teasing a few QPR lads up Villa Road for a chat.

Unfortunately, we were spotted by a vanload of local OB and soon found ourselves being rounded up and handcuffed. They'd recognised us as 'known faces' and, apparently unsure if we had broken our bail conditions, decided to hold us while their superiors looked into the facts of the matter. Nice approach, OB! Meanwhile, I saw it as a perfect opportunity to be remanded and get on with serving any sentence the courts might eventually throw at us for Watford. So I decided to play up.

I started to give it the large and act like a complete prat – I gave the coppers some serious abuse, telling them I didn't give a fuck about their bail conditions and their exclusion zones. I really thought they might lock me up right there and then. But it wasn't to be and they just left me to shout myself to a standstill.

Baby B, though, had almost started crying while I was mouthing off, and begged me to tell the OB that we hadn't broken the court rules and should be released. Dibble, who had not been placed in cuffs, was trying to calm the youngster, but I couldn't have cared less. Eventually, our friends from Bedfordshire OB got the call to release us and B began to calm down.

We were traipsing back in the direction of The Railway Tavern when a police car came shooting down from the top of the road. We all bent our heads to see what the panic was, as you do, and staring back at us was a familiar face – Scottish Brian. Although banned like us, the mad cunt had been spotted by the OB with a mob of our lads looking for Rangers boys in the vicinity of the station. Now he was on his way to the cop shop.

When I'd sobered up that evening, I felt relieved that the OB hadn't locked me up because maybe, just maybe, I wouldn't end up being sent to jail. Or so I hoped at the time. Now I found myself sat in the holding cells under Luton Crown Court, hoping that prison wouldn't be so bad after all and consoling myself with the fact that I'd be home in four months.

The lads were all processed and then put aboard the Group 4 transport. Each one of us was given a packet of crisps or a bar of chocolate by the cheerful security staff, who told us they'd carted the rest of the Luton lads off to Bedford Prison earlier in the week. Apparently, they had all been pissed up and sung about being Migs for the whole journey, rocking the big white van from side to side, as they trundled northwards to prison.

'They did yer proud,' cackled the old bag driving us.

As I sat in my little box and watched the outside world rattling by, I no longer felt that the regular Joes going about their daily business were the mugs. It was us, the Migs, that were actually the mugs – stuck inside a Group 4 van trading jokes with security guards. The punishment process had kicked in now.

The conversation in the vehicle had initially been quite jovial and Armchair Alan had us all in stitches with his talk of us being 'real heroes now'. However, this gradually died down as we sank into our own thoughts and soon the only voice to be heard was that of an armed robber travelling with us to Bedford. After a while, he was told to shut his Cockney mouth as well, because he was pissing us all off with the racket.

An hour or so later, the guards informed us that we were 'home' and to prepare to be handed over to the prison staff, which was actually a relief as I was starting to feel claustrophobic caged up in the modified box van.

One by one, we were taken out and our ID checked. Next, we were led up a short staircase into an office manned by three members of the prison staff.

A large overweight screw scoffed at me, 'Another Mig looking for a room, is it?'

I ignored the comment. We didn't know it at the time, but the whole prison had watched our story on the evening news and was expecting us – we were famous now! Any thoughts that our newfound celebrity status might be of use was quickly extinguished, though, as a bitter-looking female screw snapped, 'Get your hands out of your pockets, prisoner!'

It was like being back on board HMS *Illustrious* and having the 'Buffer' breathing down my neck for making his ship look untidy, as I strolled around the deck with my fists stuffed inside my 'fives' trousers. I did exactly the same now as I did then – pulled my hands out, while holding my gaze on the person giving the orders. The bitch didn't like my manners and let me know by matching my stare.

The fat screw quickly broke up the staring contest by dragging me away for my strip search – which just about summed up the day I was having. After I'd allowed my balls to drop out of my hand, the staff confessed that they didn't actually have enough prison-issue clothes to kit us all out that night, so I could wear my Armani suit until the next day.

Armchair and myself were now separated from the others and taken through a narrow corridor and out on to the prison landing. I'd seen all this before, but poor old Armchair looked a bit daunted at the sight of the cages and multi-level landings. The sounds of prison are something that have to be experienced to be fully understood and I don't think Alan was enjoying the ambience that HMP Bedford had to offer. He stood motionless clutching his bed pack, his jaw hanging by his feet, as he stared up at the vast ceiling space. 'That's it, we're in prison,' he sighed, as if it was going to surprise me.

Our group made its way across the exercise yard and entered a building that almost looked out of place here, because it was actually quite modern. Most of Bedford Prison was built in Victorian times and looked as you might expect. The wing we now found ourselves on, though, looked nothing like the rest of the place from the outside and I hoped it would be modern inside as well.

I was not to be disappointed and, in fact, the whole layout of the place was better than I could have hoped. It smelled a lot better too! I was led to a small, but clean, cell with toilet facilities inside. It was a good start to my prison term.

When you first walk into a prison cell, you are basically heading into an unknown environment. The lad already installed could have been there for many months; he may be a sound person or he could be a nutter. The cell might be clean, or it might be dirty. It could be that the lad already in there really likes his space and doesn't want to share with anyone else. So your arrival might cause some serious upset and provoke resentment towards you. It really is a lottery. I had already considered what I wouldn't accept in a cellmate – I didn't want to share with a smelly dirtbag or a basket case. But, most importantly of all, I definitely didn't want to share with a junkie and had made this clear to the guards from the moment I arrived.

My first cellmate was actually sound – although perhaps not so sound of mind. He was from Cambridge, in his mid-twenties, didn't do drugs and by the look of things kept the pad pretty clean.

We shook hands and soon I was unpacked with my bed made and my grey Armani suit hanging in the regulation locker. I asked him what he was inside for and he told me he was banged up for car-jacking. He'd stolen a cab from a taxi rank, so he could get back from a party late one night. He had been in for four months so far, but hadn't been sentenced yet and fully expected to get two or three years when he did.

It seemed so stupid to end up wasting two or more years of a young life for the sake of a stolen taxi ride home. What did his parents think?

'I've never met my dad – and my mum was the one who helped me rob the taxi in the first place.'

I could have choked on the apple that I'd just sponged off him!

I found myself watching the lad's shadow on the wall as he rocked back and forth sketching scenes of heaven and hell on a large paper pad resting on his bed. As I watched it swaying to and fro against the lime-green cell wall, I found myself getting heavy-eyed. It had been a long day and, after waiting over a year, I could finally start to put the violent events of the Watford v Luton Cup match behind me.

As I cuddled up to my pillow, I thought of two things: how were my girlfriend and kids? And where exactly did Mathew Spring dig up that wonder strike from? He was 30 yards out and struck the ball so sweetly that no keeper on earth would have stopped it.

'Fuck Watford!' That night I slept like a log.

If you haven't been to prison, then you can never know the mixture of feelings that your mind churns out as time slowly passes. In my opinion, two of the worst moments you can encounter are when you walk on to your wing for the first time and that first morning when you wake up caged in there. After a night's deep sleep, I now faced the realisation that I really was in jail… it was horrible.

I didn't go down for breakfast and instead grabbed my towel, found the filthy showers and tried to wash the smell of HMP Bedford from my skin. I could feel myself becoming low already, but knew I just had to get on with it and stay strong for the lads. I knew that they would look to me to help them through these dark days.

Later on that morning, I was taken from my cell to join Armchair Alan, Beaky – whose flagpole attack on Watford supporters was beamed out across all the TV channels – and Alfie, who received the shortest sentence and should never have been sent down at all. Then we were led across the exercise yard to rejoin the rest of the lads in the 'new entry' area of the prison. It was like a reunion.

As we entered the large open-plan seated area one by one, we shook hands and hugged. The spirit among the lads lifted us all out of the depression that had just started to bite. Somehow, laughter and great big smiles broke out all round and all was well. Scottish Brian, in particular, looked happy with his new surroundings. Brian's home life wasn't as it should be and he had been moving from place to place for some time – now for a few months at least, he had a place he could call home.

Bedford Prison is quite small, with the majority of its lodgers coming from the Luton area. It's also a bit old now and in need of some urgent upgrading. I discovered that most drugs were available, at the right price, to anyone foolish enough to use them. It's classed as a Category B prison – in essence, simply a holding jail while a place is found for you at a larger establishment.

So, just as Scottish Brian thought he'd finally found himself a permanent address, he was asked to go and sit with the allocation officer. He returned seconds later, having been told he would be going to Wellingborough Prison when a place became available. We followed one by one and after an hour we all knew our allocated prisons up and down the country.

From the moment we were told of our placements, I saw a change in everyone as little groups started to become even tighter. Those heading for 'The Mount' talked together, as did those going to Wellingborough, Spring Hill, North Sea Camp and Woodhill. The rest of the day was spent seeing the many sights Bedford Prison has to offer its visitors, including the fine library. Here, we were most surprised to find that 'True Crime' was by far the biggest section of books.

A while later, we were led to a classroom for a written test so the prison education team could assess our academic skills. Although the rest of the group wanted to take the exam, Big Cliff stubbornly refused, as he wasn't stimulated by the level of courses on offer. Instead, he requested a newspaper from the tutor and, after turning down the *Daily Mirror*, eventually found himself studying how his shares were faring in the *Guardian*!

It was all a bit surreal sitting in a classroom in Bedford Prison watching Big Cliff browsing his broadsheet with his legs crossed, while in the opposite corner two tattooed villains sat on the floor scratching their names into the side of a bookcase – their pencils discarded on the floor, like some kid's unwanted Christmas present. We all scraped through the exam and some even managed to complete the task before Big Cliff had finished reading his left-wing rag.

That night I chatted some more with my cellmate and began to feel even sorrier for him. He really needed some help from somewhere or he wasn't going to make it. As we passed on our respective life stories, I started to drop a few hints as to how he might get on better once released. But, just as it seemed he was taking some of it on board, there was a bang on our cell door.

The spy hole opened and a beady eye peered in. It squinted as the owner's voice asked for my pad mate by name, before passing a folded piece of paper through the tiny gap at the bottom of the cell door. My sorry-looking mate scrambled to open it before smiling and proudly announcing: 'That geezer is going to marry my mum… in prison!'

I gave up on trying to help him out at this point.

After a poor night's sleep, I climbed out of my pit and made my bed. My mate was still slumbering, so I kept the TV volume down. I'd just poured myself a cup of tea when the cell door opened and in stepped a smartly dressed screw.

'Robinson, get your gear and follow me.'

I threw my stuff together as quickly as I could and didn't even get a chance to say goodbye to my snoring cellmate.

'Come on, come on. Meet you at the bottom of the stairs.'

Once I'd gathered all my worldly possessions together, I legged it down the stairs and joined another inmate there. He had obviously just been turfed out of his luxury surroundings as well. 'Where are we going now?'

'It's good news. We're off to E Wing, mate.'

E Wing was well known for having the best living conditions in Bedford Prison. However, it also had a name for housing grasses and arse lickers. It has to be said, of course, that the lads spreading this around were the ones with no chance of gaining a place on this model wing anyway. In any event, I didn't kick up a fuss.

Upon arrival at our new accommodation, we were met by a certain Mr H and his sidekick, Mr R. The latter was a smart-looking chap who reminded me of an old chief petty officer of mine. He was well over six feet tall with a friendly manner about him and made us feel welcome from the start. Soon, he became a rare source of humour and entertainment amid all the nastiness and bitterness that you find in every prison.

Mr H took us on a tour of E Wing and I liked what I heard and saw – the cells had TV/videos and were only locked at night. There was Sky TV in the rest room, PlayStation 2 was available to those who wanted it and we could use the gym three times a week as well.

After D Wing and the 23-hour bang-up, this was heaven. I started to look at it like being locked up in my bedroom when I misbehaved as a kid. Things were getting better. There was a catch to all this, of course – every morning we had to be up before eight o'clock and ready for our soul-destroying 'work'. This involved sticking labels on tins of kitty mush or – my personal favourite – unwinding those plastic headphones you get issued on aircraft when flying to your favourite holiday destinations. Now you know how they do it!

Once Mr H had finished the tour, I was allowed to mingle with the other lads on the wing and was pleasantly surprised to find Big Cliff and Andy P already housed here. We were soon to be joined by Little Jimmy, Dave G and Dean E as well.

Over the following weeks, we tried to make the most of our surroundings and managed to keep our heads up, even finding ourselves actually enjoying some of our time in the slammer. I met some real characters, including an Irishman serving 99 years for killing Catholics and an armed robber who seemed completely at ease with the life sentence he got after holding his sawn-off shotgun to the head of an argumentative shop owner.

My favourites, though, had to be the Triads. This crowd were the only group bigger in numbers than the Migs in the whole place and saw prison as a career hazard. Most of them had served many sentences before and they really had things sewn up on E Wing. They controlled the food, the spare-clothing store, the tobacco and even had the only qualified hairdresser, who did a blinding fade for two Mars bars! They belonged to the Wah Sing Wah clan, which was obviously a serious money-making machine.

Individually, they weren't anything spectacular or threatening, but as a group you could feel their solidarity and loyalty to each other – not that they didn't have the occasional altercation with each other, usually ending with a swift fist to the throat. They trained together religiously as a group in the gym and spent all their social hours together chatting in Mandarin or some other Chinese tongue. They had been arrested on deception charges – the result of running an illegal cigarette factory and supplying moody fags to half the country. I don't know how much money they had made while they were in business, but their main player was expected to find £750,000 to stop extra charges being filed by the Home Office.

It was funny as fuck listening as they laughed at our crew for getting ourselves locked up for no better reason than having the crack at football. 'You go jail, but you make no money!' Followed by riotous cackling and pointing of fingers.

The only thing we could throw back at them was: 'Yeah, but we're getting out this year – unlike you cunts! Why don't you let us go and spend it for you?'

The poor old Chinese crew just couldn't understand that our only motivation was the buzz of being in the thick of the action in a good old row. To them, life was just about getting paid. This wasn't the first time I'd heard this aimed at us.

Many years previously, I listened to an old Scouser called Kirby, who'd just moved to Luton, complaining that he couldn't grasp what the Migs were all about. During his short stay in town, he'd witnessed two clashes between our crew and the local chapter of Hells Angels.

He had taken over the Blockers pub in Hightown some months earlier and tried to change its appearance and clientele. Many of the Mig Crew came from the Hightown area and had grown up knowing that the bikers frequented the Blockers. They were always quite civil and never really threatening, despite a fearsome reputation. Sure, there had been fights and violent scenes at the Blockers, but to our knowledge most of this was 'in house' disputes.

However, the status quo was disturbed when a few of our lads entered the music scene as DJs and started to put some sets together in the Blockers on a Sunday evening. During one of these sessions, the bikers took exception to the style of music being played – something I still laugh at when I remember some of the head-banging crap they listened to.

As the hairy fellows were entertaining a special guest from Germany, they decided enough was enough and started to perform. Instead of discussing the flavour of the music with the chaps, they simply trashed the decks and handed out slaps to all the lads gathered around that night. The result was a couple of the Migs and their associates pretty badly beaten and requiring hospital food.

Our response was immediate. Calls were made and we discovered that the bikers would be found celebrating the arrival of their guest from the Rhine country at The George later that week. On the night in question, a pitched battle was fought outside the pub, with a mixture of local lads and football hooligans gaining the upper hand and forcing the bikers to break and flee the scene on foot. The police arrived shortly afterwards to discover the German guest of honour with a serious head injury and needing English hospital treatment.

It just so happens that Kirby himself had been stabbed in the ribs in a separate fight with some of our lads and had two of his other pubs wrecked in the weeks leading up to the battle with the biker gang. Luton Police now decided enough was enough – arrests followed and, one by one, members of our group were charged with a variety of offences.

Some of us were remanded, while others, including myself, were charged with Conspiracy to Cause Affray and bailed to reappear at a later date. This particular charge was plain ridiculous, because there had been no conspiracy and the Crown actually relented and all charges were dropped.

Shortly afterwards, I saw Kirby again and we exchanged views.

'Fucking hell, Tommy, if you lads had any sense you'd be running every door in Bedfordshire and cleaning up big time. You could be making serious money, but you're just stupid cunts!'

He couldn't see it. We weren't after any financial gain and had no particular aspirations to join the criminal underworld either – the Mig Crew were just mates sticking together and watching each other's backs. 'That's where you went wrong though, mate. You had to hire your back-up – ours comes for free.'

He didn't reply, but put his pet Alsatian back on its lead and walked off shaking his head.

Not long after this chance meeting, Kirby sold up and fucked off – never to be seen in Luton again.

We did come across the bikers again, though. At one of the court appearances resulting from the clash at The George, a heavy-set middle-aged chap was seen noting down the lads' addresses as they were read out in court. We knew instantly what the score was and waited with baited breath for reprisals during the following months, especially when the police warned us that we should expect some sort of revenge attack.

I heard reports that a sum of cash was handed over to the local chapter of the Hells Angels as a peace offering, but this is not the case. There were also stories that some of the local bikers who had caused the unnecessary violence at the Blockers in the first place were subsequently punished by more senior members of their organisation. I reckon the latter of the two stories is the more likely. There was certainly nothing to gain for the bikers in fighting with local football lads. In any event, honours were even now and neither gang really wanted to carry on a pointless clash of cultures that would only lead to unwanted police attention for both sides.

So as Mr Wong and his Triad mates laughed at the lack of earnings resulting from our criminal activities, I just thanked my lucky stars that I wasn't going to be spending as many years as them in prison.

After a couple of months, some of the lads were moved on, as they were downgraded from Category B to C, and eventually to D. The move to Cat D was especially important, as it allowed you to be relocated by the authorities and usually to a semi-open prison. Big Cliff and Little Jimmy took full advantage of this and were soon packing their bags for HMP Springhill near Bicester.

Andy P was also offered the chance to move there, but had recently received some bad news. His father had died. Poor old Andy was gutted and the pain was clear to see, as he tried to deal with the realisation that he would never see his old man again. At least they'd told him that he would be taken to the funeral service to say his goodbyes.

On the day of the funeral, he was 'stood down' from work and allowed some time to get dressed appropriately. His transportation was arranged and we all offered our condolences as the time for his departure approached.

Time passed slowly that morning and I found myself feeling pity for a mate with whom I'd recently had a few differences. He stayed calm and kept a brave face until the time for his pick-up to arrive came and passed with no sign of him being picked up at all. Then he started to get agitated and kept asking the screws what was going on. They in turn became concerned and uncomfortable, but a potential scene was averted when the wing access door opened and a burly chap came and called for Andy. Soon he was gone and we all relaxed.

Later that day, though, Andy returned to E Wing and he wasn't happy. This was to be expected, of course, as he had just been to a funeral. Or so we thought. In fact, the main reason he was upset was that the unthinkable had happened – he had missed his own father's funeral. We were fuming for him. The screws on E Wing took a lot of flack, but they were genuinely embarrassed by their bosses' failure to get a son to his father's funeral.

There was a silver lining on that cloudy day, though. As Andy stepped out of his late transport, he was greeted by his girlfriend and their newly born son. While eating his porridge, he'd become a father and now he was meeting his boy for the first time. That night back in HMP Bedford, he was the proudest dad inside and wasted no time in showing us all his collection of photographs of his pride and joy. It made a pleasant change from browsing through polaroids of his bulldog George, dressed in matching Burberry coat and socks!

The rest of my days in prison passed pretty smoothly. Our only real concern was whether we would get our early release on Home Detention Curfew. The subject began to dominate our conversations and we all clung to any positive information about similar cases to our own. We'd heard that a group of a similar size to our own had passed through HMP Bedford not long before us, after being convicted of Violent Disorder following a pre-season friendly between Peterborough United and Nottingham Forest. It seemed that, although they were the lesser known of the two rival firms, Peterborough definitely took the battle to the Forest lads. The only problem was that the bulk of the action was caught on CCTV and arrests soon followed, resulting in even heavier sentences than those we had received. These lads all got early release and so I couldn't see any reason why we wouldn't as well.

As the time for my release approached, I found myself getting as nervous about going back into society as I'd felt waiting to be sentenced. I remembered that I had bills to pay, work to sort out, urgent repairs on my home to complete and relationship issues to resolve as well. All of a sudden, the outside world didn't seem quite so enticing.

On my last day, I had to leave Dean E behind in Bedford. We'd been sharing a cell for some weeks now and had bonded well. He was nearly 15 years younger than me and was struggling to come to terms with prison life. I was worried about leaving him alone there, as he was a fiery character and had already had some fall-outs with other inmates. I tried to lecture him about keeping his head down and reassured him that he would definitely get his 'tag' and an early release like the rest of us. We shook hands, then I turned and walked towards the prison gates and freedom.

As I stepped out of HMP Bedford, and back into society, I was greeted by two of my old chums, Monty and Sick Nick, who'd driven over from Luton to pick me up. 'You look well, Tom. What diet are you on, mate?'

Pulling away from the prison gates, I resisted the urge to look back – I just wanted to forget all about the shithole. Monty was up for heading straight to the boozer, but I'd been ordered to report immediately to my allocated probation officer. I did so and then shot straight home to have the electronic tag fitted to my ankle. Even though I was out of prison, I realised that it would be some time yet before I was really free.

In fact, my punishment continued for many weeks afterwards, as I had to repair the damage I had caused to my family and friends. Work also had to be sorted and that transition didn't pass without its stresses either. Eventually, though, all returned pretty much to normal and my rehabilitation was complete. I worked hard for the rest of the year and spent two weeks in Mauritius just before Christmas as a way of letting myself know that it was all behind me now.

Over the following months, I mulled over the whole Watford affair. I was gutted that I had wasted my time in prison, when I should have been watching my children grow and being a good partner to my girlfriend. Many of the former Migs, who had retired from football violence long ago, passed comment about me packing it all in and growing up. The constant nagging struck a chord and soon I'd promised myself never to risk my liberty in the name of football violence again. It felt as though the years were starting to catch up with me, and the MI2s were now strong enough to stand on their own two feet – even though some of their dress sense left a lot to be desired and the spiky hairstyles weren't exactly 'the football look'.

The desire, which had grown from the need to be part of something exciting and special, was dying now. So, after 20 exciting and eventful years, I finally decided to join the growing ranks of ex-Mig Crew members myself – although, of course, I knew it was going be tough to make the break and leave the buzz behind me for good.

12 When in Rome

When I was approached by the Area Health Authorities following a trial with the Luton Schools football selectors as a 12-year-old, I initially felt excitement. Like any 'wannabe' footballer, I thought I'd cracked it when the elderly-looking gentleman with a bundle of paperwork under his arm smiled and came over to introduce himself. My father was with him and had watched me play for the very first time. All looked so hopeful.

The kind-mannered gentleman exchanged idle chat with me. Being of a young age and already not trusting adults as a rule, I didn't pay much attention to his verbal exchanges with my dad. Football was mentioned eventually, though, and it was at this point that I became interested in the conversation.

Staring at my legs, he enquired, 'Did he get those bruises playing football?'

My dad looked worried now and repeated the question to me.

Immediately, I knew that I had to lie to protect my mother. 'Yes, Dad' was all I would say on the matter.

The gentleman turned away and strolled off with my father in tow. I looked down at my legs and could see the long grey bruises along my thighs and the red lumps on my calf muscles. I quickly pulled my socks up and hid them from the world. I can't explain why, but up until this moment I never really knew that I was the victim of a violent parent. As I'd been chased around at home while attempting to evade the blows from the green plastic baseball bat, I'd thought it was my bad behaviour that had earned all the violence from my mother. I'd believed it was normal to take a beating.

That day at the football trials, I watched my dad struggle to fully comprehend what was happening in his home. He worked hard, paid the bills, provided two holidays a year and was a real gentleman. He loved my mum, so he wasn't prepared for the news that his son was the victim of regular beatings from her. How could he be? That was when I realised my life would never be normal, and so it has proved over the years.

After the court case and the prison term, after two decades of following Luton Town Football Club and 25 years of violence and hurt, sometime in November 2004 I found myself chatting on the phone to one of the lads – The Chief. He was returning from Milton Keynes where Steve Howard had just bagged a hat-trick in a 4–1 victory at the newly formed Milton Keynes Dons and wondered if I was interested in making a trip down to the West Country just before Christmas to celebrate my old school chum and original Mig Crew member Demus's birthday. By coincidence, Luton were playing at Bristol City on the same day as his birthday and, taking into account my banning order, The Chief proposed we have a night out in the nearby historic city of Bath.

Immediately, I felt a surge of excitement at the prospect of joining up with my old mates and jumping on the train down to the West Country to spend a night catching up with some senior Mig Crew members, many of whom had stopped going to football many years before.

After the initial surprise, I paused to consider exactly what might happen during the trip to Bath. How would the OB view it if I was found on a train heading from Paddington Station to Bath on a Saturday, with Luton playing only a few miles away in Bristol? Would they have grounds to arrest me? What if I ended up in a fight with some Bristol chaps taking the same train? I knew the risks were too great, so, after a brief chat with Maz, we decided to drive down instead of getting an Inter-City.

Maz booked us into the Travel Lodge and not long afterwards I received my official invite to Demus's get-together. Over the next few days, I thought of nothing but the trip and meeting up with the lads. I'd even decided to watch the rugby union match due to be played on the same day at Bath's Recreation Ground.

As Demus's birthday approached, more of the lads decided to travel to Bath with the prospect of a good pre-Christmas piss-up in a beautiful city. At the same time, news began to circulate that the MI2s were travelling to Bristol to confront the locals on their own patch. This gave me some cause for concern, as no doubt the football intelligence teams from Luton and

Bristol would be asking for extra resources to combat any risk of violence. I would have to be extra careful not to get caught up in any 'activities' on the day of the match, or else I'd be for the high jump.

On the Saturday, Maz picked me up at just after eight in the morning. We were determined to get to Bath early, so we could take in some of the sights and start the day off on the right note. I kissed my son and girlfriend goodbye – holding her for an extra second to savour her warmth – and then I leaped into Maz's company diesel van and we were away.

As we headed down the M1 and on towards the West of England, we discussed the lads who would be making the journey from Bedfordshire. Fashion's name was thrown into the ring. He and Maz had become close mates in the past few months and he recounted the story of their clash with Sheffield Wednesday lads on the train station bridge the previous season. When the fighting was over, the Sheffield boys had either got on their toes or been knocked out and were lying on the deck. Maz, Black K and good old Fashion had been in the thick of the action.

As Maz was laughing out loud and recounting blow-by-blow details of the scrap on the bridge, my mobile started to pump out its annoying little tune. Looking at the small display screen, I saw the word 'Tuse' displayed in luminous blue. I pressed the answer key on my mobile and heard his well-spoken voice on the other end of the line.

Tuse had long since departed the hoolie scene. He spent time as an entertainment lawyer before enjoying some success in management on the black-music scene. The Casual thing never leaves you, though, and he would reappear through the 90s with records with Aquascutum sleeves and press clippings of his rappers dressed up like football chaps.

More recently, he'd travelled with the Ultras and made a film about football in Portugal, which he'd managed to get on TV. So now he'd turned his attentions back to English football boys and was working on a documentary about hoolie books. Naturally, Tuse planned to include something about the Migs in the film and was hoping to meet up today to discuss it. He was on the train down to Bristol and wanted to know if I could tell him anything about the movements of the MI2s.

I knew nothing, of course, but told him the location of Demus's birthday gathering that afternoon and explained that, if all else failed, he could come along and have a chat with the many retired football lads that would be assembled there. He agreed and asked that I keep him informed of my movements through the day.

Maz and I arrived in Bristol – by mistake – at around 10 and stopped for a piss before heading along the scenic route to Bath. As we approached the outskirts of the Roman outpost, my blower sounded off again – it was Baby J who was already well drunk and baying for war. He wanted to know if I would be bringing any of the original and older Mig Crew members into Bristol during the day. I informed him that some of the lads had match tickets and only around 15 of us would be staying in Bath for the all-day session. I added that I'd be going to watch the rugby.

He didn't sound impressed: 'You what?'

We booked into our hotel and, after changing, moved on into Bath city centre. I felt pretty well turned out, as I'd purchased a new CP jacket in dark green with goggles built into the hood. When it was zipped up, I looked like an extra from some sci-fi movie. I topped my uniform off with a white CP skullcap and a smart new pair of Timberland boots. Maz stuck to his classic black Stone Island jacket, but ruined the look by dropping some spray-on jeans from Next, which drew attention to his fat arse. 'No way is he pulling tonight,' I chuckled to myself.

We strolled into town like two old gunslingers with our hands resting on our side pockets. We might have imagined that we looked like old sharp shooters, but in reality we were just two tired travellers looking for somewhere to get a bite to eat. Even though I knew we weren't there for trouble, I still felt that old stirring in the pit of my stomach – something that only football lads arriving in a foreign town on a match day can recognise. It was wonderful to feel it again – it made me come alive. I walked taller and with my old confident swagger.

Bath is a beautiful city – its buildings are a mixture of Roman, Medieval and Georgian designs with distinctive sandstone brickwork. When you've been brought up in a tired-looking town like Luton, you really appreciate idyllic places like Aqua Sulis – the name given to Bath by the Romans in AD43.

As we wandered through the streets, we passed the rugby ground, set alongside the River Avon in a wonderful position with just a footpath separating it from the free-flowing water. Maz and I popped into the ticket office and I purchased a few tickets for the game, which, somewhat ironically, would be starting around the same time as Luton kicked off against Bristol City 10 miles down the road.

After grabbing a quick bite to eat, we headed towards the train station and found a grubby hotel bar overlooking the entrance to the platforms where we waited for the others to arrive. The lads were all gathering in Bristol for a beer, as there were tickets to be distributed and Demus's party invites, with the attached map, to be handed out.

Maz grew impatient and wanted to move on into Bristol itself as well. I didn't fancy the idea, as I knew the OB could arrest me on 'Prevention' grounds and then hold me in the cells for as long as they pleased. The debate ended when Maz answered his mobile and spoke to Melv and Daggers who were en route but running late and planned to join up with us all later in Bristol. The news enabled Maz to convince me to jump on the next train, so by midday I was handing in my ticket to the guard at Bristol Station and heading down a side route to a pub containing the bulk of the Luton lads – The Knights Templar.

As we marched closer to the pub, my phone rang – it was Little Jimmy. He was sat inside The Knights Templar and warned us that the OB had just discovered their gathering. It was then that I spotted the MI2s moving towards us. They were about 60-strong and looked menacing all decked out in black. To a man, they had caps or scarves wrapped around their heads and most stepped with the football hooligan's confident swagger.

Now they spotted Maz and me standing by the bridge closest to the station. Initially, they spread out while adjusting their individual choice of headgear or collar and I had a brief insight as to how this mob would look going into battle. Then, when they'd recognised us, their postures returned to the normal confident strut that I had seen only seconds before.

As the group closed, I spotted many of the better-known MI2 members: Yax – a natural leader; Baby J – fast becoming a legend; Baby B – original MI2; Lord G – Wellington Street urchin; Fashion – nutcase; and Black K – Bermondsey loon. They were followed by Sappy, Kev Mac, Maurice and Elvis – the list just went on and on.

Standing tall above everyone was a lad now becoming a familiar face at Luton and especially at away games – Cambridge Lee. He's a giant, but has the face of a 10-year-old child topped off with shit hair and he was walking alongside Will – an 80s throwback.

I would like to say that Will is a confused young man but I can't, because he's actually a confused old man. Most lads run with just one firm in a lifetime, but Will is a bit different and has gone with Reading, Chelsea, QPR, Tottenham, Blackpool and even Milton Keynes Dons in his time on the terraces. In truth, he just loves the day out and is a proper source of entertainment when on the piss – someone I would welcome at Luton any time.

As the lads streamed past me, they were followed by scores of panicking OB, shaking their heads and trying to get answers on what to do via their walkie-talkies. The coppers were all from the Bristol area and didn't look like they had a clue what they were doing. I had to giggle.

After the police had passed me – hiding in a phone booth – I made my way back into Temple Meads Station to get the shuttle service back to Bath. I took one last look at the lads, now splitting up to confuse the OB and chuckled again as the plod hesitated, trying to decide which group to tail.

Soon I was rattling back towards lovely Bath alongside Little Jimmy, Cambridge Lee, Will 'the confused', Baby B and, of course, the slowly balding Maz. I became irritated by Baby B's gum chewing – the MI2s had been 'ploughing the snow' for most of the morning and now some of them were showing signs of chemical poisoning of the lower jaw. Baby B was worse than most and it amazed me how much punishment his teeth could take without cracking or falling out. The cunt looked like he was auditioning for a gurning contest.

Once safely back in Bath, our tight band of midgets, giants with small heads, ginger gurners, bald fat Italians and confused ex-Milton Keynes thugs headed back to the hotel bar. We stayed put for a couple of hours consuming as much alcohol as possible. As we chatted, a story emerged – Bristol OB had already arrested Windy and Sappy and accused them of handling counterfeit £20 notes. I wondered how they'd ended up being collared for this, as it seemed unlike either of them to do such a thing. In any event, the Inter-City train the lads had been travelling on was swamped with fake twenties. The buffet bartender had a pot full of them and to make things worse half the cab drivers in Bristol were now moaning about Luton lads passing them moody cash as well.

Next, stories started to creep through that the MI2s and the rest were getting the runaround from Bristol City's lads. Every meet that had been called on was attended only by the Luton lads and there was no sign of Bristol's infamous City Service Crew anywhere. To us, though, all this didn't really matter because we were having a good time and our ranks were growing steadily. By the time I left to watch the rugby at The Recreation Ground, there was close to 20 Migs gathered in the dingy hotel bar. Spirits were high as the lads prepared for the night out ahead and Tuse arrived to capture the scene with his video camera.

We left with Baby B and followed the footpath along the River Avon to the rugby ground. We entered the tight little stadium and watched as

18-stone men smashed into each other, exchanging menacing glances while they queued to get to the bar! Anyone who thinks football fans are rowdy should try mixing with the rugger buggers. On the field of play, the two teams lined up and the crowd let out a roar to lift their chosen heroes, while Baby B and I, having both done time because of CCTV, instinctively hid from Tuse and his lens.

An hour and a half later, after a few pints and a competitive game of rugby – which I really enjoyed – we found ourselves back in the hotel bar opposite the station. The happy crowd of both older Migs and younger MI2 members had now grown beyond 30 and it was an impressive mix of characters. Daggers was shouting insults in his Cockney accent at anyone who strayed into his line of fire; Scouse was smiling, as always; Jimmy was doing an interview with Tuse; and then another old face who had made the long trip down from Luton caught my eye – Chemist was here as well.

When I think back to the very early days of the Casual scene and the formation of the original Migs, Chemist was always there. He was a main face in the crew back then. Some years previously, though, he had moved to the California coast where he'd fallen foul of the law on a couple of occasions, with his first offence being the theft of a frozen chicken! However, Chemist's crimes grew more serious and one fine morning he was arrested for handling hard drugs. He had been under observation by the LA Police and a full investigation was implemented. As a result, he was sent to the State Penitentiary and spent three years behind bars in the desert.

Now he was back in England after being deported. He was also back at football for the first time in years, dressed head to toe in the best designer garms – apart from the horrible Prada hat!

Black K was strolling around with the very annoying Fashion following in his wake. K is a nutter and, to be honest, I was surprised that he chose to run with our mob instead of Millwall's because he grew up around Bermondsey in London. I remember being down at Millwall one night when he was offering it on a plate to some of their youth crew at South Bermondsey Station. The worried-looking South-east Londoners replied, 'Fuck off, K – you only live two doors away from me. We know you!'

Black K tried to brush this aside. 'My name's not fucking K – you don't know me!'

It was hilarious watching the confused faces of these Millwall boys as our K kept up the bullshit – they just didn't know what to say.

It was even funnier when our liaison officer stepped in. 'Move away, K, or I'll nick you, son!'

Black K now shared a flat with Fashion and they'd become good pals, so now Fash wandered behind him, getting involved in any conversation he could find an annoying point of view on. He was pissed and soon became so irritating that he was threatened with being thrown through the pub window, unless he got a grip. Even the usually passive Melv took time from discussing his theory on the death of Lady Diana to threaten Fashion with a violent end after he'd unwisely insulted Melv's Royal Navy-style dress sense.

As the afternoon wore on, more of the MI2s found our happy banning-order crew. Then Baby J arrived and suddenly the mood changed completely. He'd been in conversation with some of the Bristol lads and they had agreed to bring a mob over to Bath for a toe-to-toe outside the station. It never happened, but we did receive a visit from one of the Bristol contingent, who shot off as fast as his feet could carry him when some of the chaps tried to stop him for a chat.

As day turned into night and the game in Bristol finished, many of the lads drifted into Bath for Demus's birthday bash. This was my cue to head back to the hotel and change out of the football clobber into some nightwear. Before I made my exit, however, I was approached by Lord G, who informed me that Baby J was taking a small team back into Bristol. It seemed they had finally got some of their lads together and were ready for some action. Most of our lads couldn't be bothered, though, as they'd been on a promise from the West Country boys all day and let down every time so far.

Undaunted, Baby J left with a group of no more than 10 MI2s and headed into the train station. I watched them go and felt an urge to join this small band of half-cut lads hunting the elusive Bristol City Service Crew. It had surprised me just how little we had heard from them during the day, because they're a big city club with a reasonable reputation. So, although we hadn't made the trip to this part of the world in some years, we still expected a reception of some kind.

I had experienced the full force of Bristol lads many years previously, when Luton had drawn City's neighbours Rovers in the FA Cup back in 1986. On that memorable occasion, the Gas Hit Squad had marched into our town centre with over 100 game lads. The resulting action had been pretty even until we met up for about the fourth time outside the ground. This time they backed us off outside the turnstiles as we tried to enter their section of the Kenilworth Road terrace. I guess we should have known that, with Bristol's history, they wouldn't have been intimidated by a multi-cultural crew bouncing down the road and making monkey noises at them. Maybe we'd got used to calling the bluff of some of the trendy First Division crews, but this lot were proper lower-league brawlers and they weren't here to pose about.

As we had retreated into the ground, they even had the cheek to follow us into the back of the Main Stand where the two substantial mobs clashed full on. This time, with DP leading the line alongside Sinbad and Mickey D also throwing his considerable weight into the contest, we forced them into the corner of the Main Stand.

As the OB were weighing in to break it up, we spotted Nick Owen, the TV presenter, dragging his children out of the stand and down the stairs to safety. We stood back and Tony Baloney politely assisted him in getting his family out of harm's way, which, when accomplished, was the signal to charge towards the Bristol Rovers lads and kick things off again. The Gas lads didn't back off this time and, as the police held the majority of the two sets of hooligan gangs in their respective corners, I spotted a burly chap with a pink sweater and a pirate's eye-patch chatting to some of the Hockwell lads.

Apparently, they were parked at the back of the Post Office building on Dunstable Road and would meet us there after the game. We turned up still charged from the earlier battles, but unfortunately the fighting here was all too brief because the Rovers lads were so outnumbered. Two of them were set about and looked none too healthy lying in the road after taking a serious beating when their mates drove off in panic and left them to it. They had made their mark in Luton that day, though, and almost turned us over on our own patch. Clearly, those old Bristol Rovers lads were a bit more aware of our ability to have a go than the modern City lads were, or so it seemed.

After changing and grabbing a quick sandwich on the sly, we rejoined the lads in the centre of Bath for the expected party. Demus looked surprised at the secret get-together and I think he enjoyed the attention, although he didn't seem so grateful for the endless drinks that were passed his way. Nevertheless, he had a laugh and managed to drink most of the strange concoctions. The lads were in party mood now and mingled with the locals, including a group of ladies on a hen night.

As the sky darkened and the weather turned wet and bitter outside, a call came in from Toys – one of the MI2s. He reported that it had just kicked off in Bristol on an estate near St Paul's and that they'd finally been in a decent battle with the Bristol City Service Crew. He said they'd been seriously bashed, but stood for as long as possible, although well outnumbered. Apparently, they backed the City mob off at first, but couldn't keep it going after an extremely pissed Fashion had been felled by a bottle and then battered.

Lord G had also taken a bottle to the head and was bleeding badly while Baby J had a deep wound to his cheek. Things sounded pretty bad. The reaction of the boys in the pub in Bath was to storm straight out of the doors and head towards the train station. We were going to head back to Bristol and find the lads responsible for giving the small pack of MI2s such a hiding.

Now the heavens opened and a cold wind bit into us as we marched through the darkened Roman streets. In an instant, the warm and pleasant city had turned into a place of hatred. The sight of 40-plus lads, heads down and hoods up, stepping through the freezing rain in the darkness is an image I will never forget. We were a team again and I was along for the ride – it wasn't football now, this was vengeance.

We gathered at the station, shaking the rain from our expensive jackets and let those trailing behind catch up before we set off for Bristol. Then, as the first lad was handing over his cash at the ticket booth, another call from Toys stopped us in our tracks. Apparently, there was no point heading back into Bristol now as all the lads were either on the train heading to London or in taxis making their way back to the party.

I felt mixed feelings at this news. I was relieved because I knew the lads were OK, but also disappointed as I was well up for having it with the City Service lads. This was the danger, though – I'd decided to knock football on the head forever only months before, but here I was soaked through in an unknown town and ready to get stuck in for the Migs yet again. It had to stop. But how?

That night, while the lads who travelled down for the weekend partied on, I returned to my hotel and watched *Match of the Day*. I picked up my mobile, noticing a missed call from my girlfriend, and promised myself I would not get into this position again. I looked across at the CP jacket hanging on the chair by the TV – it was a fucking waste of money. I could have taken my partner and my son to Greece for a week with the same amount as I'd spent on it. I'd probably only wear it once or twice more before I had to buy another anyway. Everything suddenly became clear. It was time to change my whole life, not just stop going to football. It was time to grow up.

Since that day, I've changed in many ways. I don't spend half my life talking about all the football scraps I've been involved in and I don't dream about taking a mob to some nutty town in the eternal quest for a hooligan confrontation. My shopping habits continue, but not as expensive as in times gone by and, unlike Maz or Windy, I won't spend good money on rubbish.

To help wash the addiction to footy violence out of my system, I always volunteer to do the Saturday shift at work and because of the location of our factory I often see the OB doing match-day checks in the nearby pubs. From my desk, I can spot coppers taking the visiting liaison teams on a tour of the watering holes frequented by the remaining Migs and growing number of MI2s.

These MI2s are a pretty serious mob now. When all turned out, they have about 60 or 70 lads and a quality frontline. I don't know how many more they will recruit over the coming seasons, but, with Luton Town now back in a division worthy of their footballing style, the club's higher profile will surely attract new faces. Of course, the police are well up to speed now and will try to counteract this new wave of Luton hooligans with banning orders and high-visibility policing. But, in my opinion, the sheer numbers of new faces could make it harder for the OB to stop disorders in Luton town centre.

One of those new faces first came to my attention in Bath when, as I stood with Demus and The Chief, stuffing a handful of chips in my big gob, a young chap was introduced to me. He stood about five foot ten and looked as innocent a lad as I had seen at football, but his clothes were dark and I could see in his eyes that youthful and dangerous twinkle which the Yid lying in the lane had spotted in me and Demus almost 25 years earlier.

Now he was seeking my approval in joining the crew and I knew just how to provide it. I asked his name, turned to some of the older Migs and played around with it, using all sorts of fucked-up 'rules', until we arrived at a suitable nickname – from this day onwards, he would be known as 'Carling'. The newly christened Carling looked happy enough with his new name and even more so with his acceptance into the fold. He was now a Mig, or at least a probationary one.

Only time can prove Carling's worth to the group. He would be expected to travel with the likes of Baby J and Yax into some pretty precarious situations – just like the one on the estate in Bristol, which resulted in so many injuries to the youngsters. He could certainly expect plenty more of that in the years to come.

During the previous season, Baby J had led the MI2 charge against QPR at Ravenscourt Road. On that occasion, the young Migs had travelled into West London to clash with older and more experienced Rangers lads. The Cockneys had the numbers in their favour and were tooled up with coshes, but Yax and Baby J simply snatched the weapons from the West Londoners and turned them on their carriers.

If Carling thought that things would always go in the MI2s' favour, though, he would be mistaken. Back in 2002, Luton had travelled to Northampton for a match which some saw as a derby fixture because of the proximity of the two clubs, although to most of our supporters – especially the older lads in the firm – it was never that way. So, when we heard that the MI2s would be travelling north, we were surprised and doubted they'd find any action. We were to be proved very wrong.

Their visit started badly as the dozen or so who travelled fought to keep a pub full of Northampton inside, but failed and found themselves scattered. They regrouped at The Britannia further into town and, led by Yid, RC and his mate Berlin B, they called it on again. This time, they managed to hold the pub doorway and inflict some serious injuries on their rivals, but the cost was high, as RC took a battering and most of the MI2s, including Baby B, ended up sitting in the cells with head wounds.

In total, 28 Luton and Northampton lads were nicked and GT was eventually convicted of Violent Disorder at Northampton Crown Court. He was sentenced to 22 months at Her Majesty's pleasure, while Sol, Yax, Russell, Dirty Den and various others were acquitted or had their charges dropped.

So Carling was now starting off more or less where I had over two decades previously.

In my opinion, football violence will never really cease. The OB will keep on coming up with new technological advances to assist them in their fight to keep a lid on the football hooligan gangs, but at the same time the lads will keep on evolving and changing tactics.

It's possible, of course, that many of the OB in charge of policing football don't really want to win the war against the thugs anyway. If they did, they might well be putting themselves out of what is surely one of the more interesting and enjoyable jobs in the police force. So, with this in mind, and knowing only too well the determination of some of the football lads out there, I don't expect to see an end to football hooliganism in England in my lifetime.

If there was a single defining moment in my time on the terraces that says everything about football violence, it would have to be when I travelled to Rome in 1997 to watch England take on Italy in a World Cup qualifier. I flew to Nice and then joined the lads in a motor travelling down through Italy and on to Rome. We had a good bunch including Flower, Sick Nick, The Chief and Sheridan. After arriving in the city centre in the early hours, we parked up and got on the sauce for the day.

I have an interest in ancient history and often travel to see sights left behind from the Old World, so a visit to the Roman Coliseum was high on my list during this trip. After posing like a good tourist for photos with the Roman Centurions gathered outside the famous landmark, I made my way into the remains of the once glorious stadium.

After passing through the darkened underground chambers used by brave men about to fight to the death in the name of entertainment, I climbed the steep stairwells and emerged on to the upper tier of the arena to a truly wonderful spectacle. It wasn't the architecture or the sheer scale of the Coliseum that pleased me – it was the scores of England flags now hanging from the once sought-after balconies, where ancient Romans would watch groups of men dressed in helmets and body armour, wielding large shields and swords in a fight to the death. West Ham, Chelsea, Plymouth and many more club names were fluttering in the breeze swirling around the ancient stone building. I wondered for a moment what Caesar might have thought if, all those years ago, one of his advisers had told him that people from the Roman Province of Britannia would one day hang their battle standards in his beloved Coliseum.

That afternoon, the English travelling support drank the city dry as over 15,000 of us took part in the invasion of Rome. I joined Big Cliff and Andy P as we mixed with locals and England fans alike in the backstreet bars. It was a fantastic day and there was very little trouble. The beer was good and the women even better. We sang our hearts out as the booze took control and I even ended up naked when Flower thought it would be funny to lock my clothes inside our hire car.

When in Rome

Later that evening, I was stood on the sky-blue plastic seats in the Olympic Stadium, home to both Lazio and Roma. In front of me was a line of men in helmets and body armour wielding large shields and batons – Italian riot police now preparing to charge into our massed ranks. Like myself, over 200 English lads had managed to obtain tickets for the Italian section of one of the ends. Tension filled the air as they prepared to find out firsthand what the English football lad was all about. Some looked keen and formidable, but others trembled. As more of them lined up, so our firm grew in size as well. This was going to be a historic battle.

As we readied ourselves for the onslaught, I thought back to the scene inside the Coliseum earlier in the day and the images in my head of armoured gladiators lining up to do battle. All around me, English lads were making the decision whether to fight or flee. I wasn't too sure myself either, until a lad from Sunderland standing close by stepped to the front like an army general and delivered some famous and decisive words, which helped me make my choice in an instant. 'Remember the old saying, lads… When in Rome!'

As he stepped towards the riot police, I turned to Big Cliff and Sick Nick: 'I ain't running – no way!'

Seconds later, I was on my back – along with many other English lads – and taking a pasting from an Italian copper with a shiny blue helmet on. As he struck me repeatedly with his heavy truncheon, I looked in his eyes and saw he was terrified. In fact, he was so scared that he just kept on hitting me and anyone else who tried to get up. The blows continued, until eventually one of his colleagues pulled him back. I climbed to my feet and started to laugh. My arm and back hurt like fuck, but I couldn't stop. 'Fucking brilliant,' I thought. And that's the point – no matter how hard they hit us, we'll just keep on coming back.

13 Mig Down, Over And Out

The new football season had just begun. Luton Town had been promoted to the First Division and, on the opening day of the 2005/2006 season, we faced Crystal Palace away at Selhurst Park. Expectations were high, as they always are when your team has just enjoyed a successful season. Thousands of Lutonians were travelling to cheer on the mighty Hatters as they triumphantly returned to their rightful division. I decided to head into London to soak up a bit of the atmosphere and mingle with the lads making the trip south of the Thames.

Sure, I knew the risks with being banned and all that, but I thought I'd proved to myself that football violence was out of my system at Bristol City the previous season. I had no intention of breaching my banning order and I was sure there was no way I'd get caught up in any possible clashes that day. The last thing on my mind was trouble and, to be honest, if I'd known how things would turn out, I would have stayed in bed.

Twelve hours later and I was sitting alone in a cold cell with the walls closing in on me. I realised that I was on a hiding to nothing from now on. It didn't really matter that I had acted in self-defence and it didn't really matter that my intentions that day were entirely innocent and non-violent. Because of my previous convictions, especially the one for Watford and the Moon Under Water incident, I could get hammered by the courts again and end up in prison. Again. After all my big talk, I'd done it all over again.

It's all very well having good intentions, but, when you're an addict, your mind is controlling you and your body doesn't even realise it. Without getting all Tony Adams about it, you can tell yourself whatever you like, you can make yourself a million promises, but an addiction is an addiction. A cocaine addict can tell himself and everyone around him that he's given up, but still finds himself round at his dealer's, thinking, 'How the fuck did I get here?'

Football hooliganism might not be cocaine, but you can still build up quite a habit over more than 20 years and I could see it was going to take more than a patch or some chewing gum to stop it messing with my life. It was becoming like a hooligan's version of *Groundhog Day*, so now I had to do something more radical than just talking about giving up.

I made a decision. Over the previous weeks, I had repeatedly been offered the chance to move jobs and relocate. I'd been working for some time in a supervisory role within the car-manufacturing industry in Luton and earning pretty good dough. I was settled and had a good career path ahead of me, but I was bored and frustrated as well. I had learned a lot from my prison sentence and, although I was determined to stick to my guns, football just carries on all round you.

At the same time, I was having relationship trouble because my long-time girlfriend was still suffering the knock-on effects from my previous jail term and the understandable damage that the sentence had done to her family's opinion of me. As a result, we were living apart while trying to resolve our differences as best we could.

I was unsettled and already feeling low when a guy, known simply as The Mexican, had offered me the chance to look after his and his partners' investments on the Costa del Sol. I had put him off for weeks, but now I knew for sure that it was an offer I couldn't refuse.

In the end, the only way I could be sure of not getting myself into the same kind of trouble was to put thousands of miles in between myself and the Migs. That way there'd be no possibility of just nipping along for a few beers, or to see some old faces, and ending up in the same old jail cell.

Given my addiction to all things football and Luton Town, including the Casual culture, it seemed that, after many years of trying to remove football violence from my life, the answer actually lay in removing me and my life from the scene by moving abroad. This way, I could never put myself in harm's way or in the face of the OB and eventually the justice system. Maybe they could never take the Luton hooligan out of me, so now it was time to take myself out of Luton and for this old Mig to take a retirement flight to Spain.

Mig Down. Over and out.

I passed through the turnstile and up into the stand. All around me, the baying crowd waved their clenched fists, spittle flying from their mouths, as they screamed for their champion. They all had one thing in common in my eyes – they were aliens. I didn't recognise a single one of their faces. The packed stadium itself was also a new sight for my squinting eyes. I was on foreign soil for sure.

I surveyed the scene. To my left, a fat hairy twat punched the air repeatedly, pulling his sweat-stained shirt away from his overstuffed waistline and the cheap-looking belt struggling to keep his ample girth in check. He sickened me. To my right, two youngish lads wrapped their arms around each other as they performed a victory dance, bouncing up and down over and over again. Their faces were a picture of happiness.

I found myself wishing I had a few of the MI2s with me. They would surely have dished out some heavy slaps to these wankers. I'd have loved to see Baby J launch an assault on them. Maybe I should just do it myself. The rage was starting again. I could feel the hairs on my sunburned neck standing on end as the adrenaline rushed to my brain. My anger was starting to get the better of me. It wouldn't be long before I was pinging anyone who got in my way.

I stood and turned to face the crowd behind me to assess any threat in case it went off. I stared into their eyes and looked for any signs of fighting prowess. 'Weak, fucking weak,' I said to myself. As I stood facing the celebrating fans all about me, I started to pick where my punches should land – he'll get one to the throat, him an uppercut to the chin and fat boy a 'Glasgow kiss' on the nose. Next, I needed an escape route. Where's the nearest exit?

Getting out of here once it went off was of paramount importance. I didn't fancy the odds, but more importantly I really didn't need another 'pull' right now. As I peered through the cheering aliens, looking for the exit I might need at any moment, a distant part of my brain cut into my thoughts – 'What am I doing going back down this path again? Why am I getting so angry? Hadn't I learned yet again where all this aggression leads to only a couple of months earlier?'

My heartbeat slowed to a normal pace as all the alien bodies around me returned to their seats. The noise inside the stadium dropped off and was replaced by the buzz of adults discussing what they'd just witnessed. My anger was still there, but it was under control, as I didn't really have a cause to kick off for.

After drying the sweat from his forehead, fat boy next to me tucked his dirty shirt back into his jeans and turned to spout some bullshit in my direction. I didn't respond, as I didn't understand him. How could I? I didn't speak Spanish. But I imagined he might be saying: 'Whose side you on, pal?' Or 'You're in the wrong end, mate,' or words to that effect.

He and this whole crowd only cared for one thing and that was their fix of cruelty, watching six or seven Matadors torture a lone bull in the centre of the bullring by prodding it with spears, knives and swords, until it was so confused and exhausted that it gave up the will to fight for its life.

As its tongue hung out in the evening sun, the 'brave' Spaniards sapped the last of its energy, using horses wrapped in padded armour to crush the sorry-looking beast till it could stand no more. The proud bull refused to lie down until it was stabbed repeatedly between the shoulders, at which point he collapsed in a cloud of dust.

Whole families looked on and cheered. I felt alone in the crowd and wanted the poor animal to look up and wink as if to say: 'It's OK… I'll be all right', just like the Yid in the lane had done all those years ago at Tottenham. But, of course, it never happened.

And they call us animals.

Glossary

Babies – Younger hooligans, youth

Baghdad paperboy – Term for someone's face looking of a rough appearance (deriving from the phrase 'He must have had a tough paper round')

Banning order – Court order to prevent disorder by restricting a person's movement to attending regulated football matches

Basket case – Nutter, one who does crazy things, mad person

Bobbies – Police

Booze – Alcohol, to drink

Boozer – Pub

Bottler – Someone who loses their nerve, chickens out, bottles it

BPYP – Bury Park Youth Posse, local Asian firm

Brief – Legal representative, barrister, solicitor, lawyer

BS – Leicester Baby Squad

Buffer – Ship's handyman

Bushwhackers – Millwall's firm

City Service Crew – Bristol City mob

Copper – Police officer

Cop shop – Police station

Dance – Invitation to come and fight, row, ruck

Divs – Idiots, mugs, clueless person

'Doing the Ayatollah' – Fans manically jumping up and down waving their arms and patting their heads

Dough – Money

EBF – Shrewsbury's English Border Firm

Face – Top boy, main man, somebody of note
Fives – Navy trousers
Frontline – Wrexham's firm The Frontline
FYC – Oldham's Fine Young Casuals
Garms – Clothing garments
Gas Hit Squad – Bristol Rovers firm, Gas heads
Gavvers – Underworld term for police
Gear – Clothes, can also refer to drugs
Glasgow kiss – Head-butted
Gooners – Arsenal fans
Gregory – Rhyming slang for neck, Gregory Peck = neck
'Hair of the dog' – Hangover remedy
Hatters – Luton Town FC
Headhunters – Chelsea's main firm
Herd – Arsenal firm calling itself the Herd
ICF – Inter-City Firm, West Ham
Jacks – Swansea lads
Jew – Someone careful with their money, tight, shred, a miserly person
Joe Public, Joes – Ordinary members of the public
Jolly – Outing, trip, day out
Kitty mush – Cat food
Mancs – Manchester lads, both City and United
Matlot – Dutch word for sailor also used to describe RN servicemen
Met – Metropolitan Police force
Melt – Anonymous, to suddenly slip away, become unnoticed
MI2s – Luton Mig Crew Youth, the younger firm or today's player
Mugs – Insulting term to say, you're a fool, you're nothing, a wanker
Necking – Guzzling beer down your throat
Ointment – Bradford City hooligan firm
Old Bill, OB – Police
On the piss – Heavy drinking session
Pissed – Drunk, very drunk
Pissed off – Fed up, angry, unhappy
Plod, Mr Plod – Police
'Ploughing the snow' – Reference to snorting Charlie/cocaine
Pompey – Portsmouth lads, 6.57 Crew
Robocops – Term for riot police (deriving from their sci-fi uniforms)
Rozzers – Police

Glossary

Ruck – Fighting
Scarfers – Regular, non-hooligan, fans, wearing scarves or team colours
Scraps – Rows, fights
Screw – Prison warder
Shady Express – Mansfield Town hooligans
Shit-faced – Very drunk appearance
Shoeing – Giving someone a good kicking or receiving one
Spotter – Police intelligence officer
Taking the piss – Mocking, taking the Mickey, making fun of
TCE – Plymouth's firm, The Central Element
A Tony Adams – Reference to someone being an addict
Twat – Derogatory term for someone being a fool, stupid, silly
Under-Fives – Younger firm to the ICF
Yids, Yiddos – Tottenham fans, a term they use themselves, and reference to their firm, Yid Army
Zulus – Birmingham City firm, Zulu Warriors